I0032961

VIET NAM

SECONDARY EDUCATION
SECTOR ASSESSMENT, STRATEGY,
AND ROAD MAP

FEBRUARY 2020

ADB

ASIAN DEVELOPMENT BANK

Creative Commons Attribution 3.0 IGO license (CC BY 3.0 IGO)

© 2020 Asian Development Bank
6 ADB Avenue, Mandaluyong City, 1550 Metro Manila, Philippines
Tel +63 2 8632 4444; Fax +63 2 8636 2444
www.adb.org

Some rights reserved. Published in 2020.

ISBN 978-92-9262-021-9 (print), 978-92-9262-022-6 (electronic); 978-92-9262-023-3 (ebook)
Publication Stock No. TCS200036-2
DOI: http://dx.doi.org/10.22617/TCS200036-2

The views expressed in this publication are those of the authors and do not necessarily reflect the views and policies of the Asian Development Bank (ADB) or its Board of Governors or the governments they represent.

ADB does not guarantee the accuracy of the data included in this publication and accepts no responsibility for any consequence of their use. The mention of specific companies or products of manufacturers does not imply that they are endorsed or recommended by ADB in preference to others of a similar nature that are not mentioned.

By making any designation of or reference to a particular territory or geographic area, or by using the term "country" in this document, ADB does not intend to make any judgments as to the legal or other status of any territory or area.

This work is available under the Creative Commons Attribution 3.0 IGO license (CC BY 3.0 IGO) https://creativecommons.org/licenses/by/3.0/igo/. By using the content of this publication, you agree to be bound by the terms of this license. For attribution, translations, adaptations, and permissions, please read the provisions and terms of use at https://www.adb.org/terms-use#openaccess.

This CC license does not apply to non-ADB copyright materials in this publication. If the material is attributed to another source, please contact the copyright owner or publisher of that source for permission to reproduce it. ADB cannot be held liable for any claims that arise as a result of your use of the material.

Please contact pubsmarketing@adb.org if you have questions or comments with respect to content, or if you wish to obtain copyright permission for your intended use that does not fall within these terms, or for permission to use the ADB logo.

Corrigenda to ADB publications may be found at http://www.adb.org/publications/corrigenda.

Notes:
In this report, "$" refers to United States dollars, unless otherwise stated.

ADB recognizes "Laos" as the Lao People's Democratic Republic, "China" as the People's Republic of China, "Vietnam" as Viet Nam, and "Hanoi" as Ha Noi.

Cover design by Michael Cortes and photos taken by Sakiko Tanaka.

Contents

Tables and Figures

Tables

Figures

Acknowledgments

This report provides an assessment of the secondary education sector in Viet Nam and documents the strategic investment priorities of the Government of Viet Nam and the Asian Development Bank (ADB) in the secondary education sector, which covers lower secondary education and upper secondary education including secondary technical and vocational education and training (TVET).

Ron Cammaert, lead education consultant, authored this report. Senior Social Sector Specialist Sakiko Tanaka of ADB's Southeast Asia Department (SERD) and Associate Social Sector Officer Vinh Quang Ngo of ADB's Viet Nam Resident Mission provided significant input and guided the completion of the report. Bui Van Thanh, a national education consultant, provided support in collecting data and updating tables. Nguyen Ngoc Thuy, operations assistant at the Viet Nam Resident Mission, and Luvette Balite and Kamela Dua, SERD operations assistants, provided administrative support. Tuesday Soriano copyedited the report, while Michael Cortes typeset it and designed the cover.

Director Ayako Inagaki at SERD's Human and Social Sector Development Division and Country Director Eric Sidgwick at ADB's Viet Nam Resident Mission provided overall guidance and direction. Valuable comments from Principal Social Sector Specialist Karin Shelzig at ADB helped finalize the report.

Many other individuals also contributed to this report. Nguyen Hai Chau, former project director of ADB's Secondary Education Sector Development Program, and Tran Dai Hai at the Department of Planning and Finance of the Ministry of Education and Training, gave significant advice on education policies and strategies.

In addition, experts and representatives from international organizations, such as the United Nations Educational, Scientific and Cultural Organization (UNESCO), the World Bank, and the International Labour Organization, gave important contributions.

This report was produced by ADB under the Regional Policy and Advisory Technical Assistance 8977: Knowledge Support for Southeast Asia.

Abbreviations

ADB	–	Asian Development Bank
ASEAN	–	Association of Southeast Asian Nations
CCT	–	conditional cash transfer
CPD	–	continuing professional development
DOET	–	Department of Education and Training
EDS	–	Education Development Strategy 2011–2020
EMIS	–	Education Management Information System
GIZ	–	Gesellschaft für Internationale Zusammenarbeit
GDP	–	gross domestic product
GDVT	–	General Directorate of Vocational Education and Training
GSO	-	General Statistics Office
HERA	-	Higher Education Reform Agenda
ICT	–	information and communication technology
ILO	-	International Labour Organization
JICA	–	Japan International Cooperation Agency
Lao PDR	-	Lao People's Democratic Republic
LSE	–	lower secondary education
LSS	–	lower secondary school
MDG	–	Millennium Development Goal
MOIT	–	Ministry of Industry and Trade
MOET	–	Ministry of Education and Training
MOLISA	–	Ministry of Labour–Invalids and Social Affairs
MPI	–	Ministry of Planning and Investment
NAM	–	National Achievement Monitoring
NER	–	net enrollment rate
NGO	–	nongovernment organization
NOSS	–	national occupational skills standards
NQF	–	national qualification framework
ODA	–	official development assistance
OECD	–	Organisation for Economic Co-operation and Development
PISA	–	Programme for International Student Assessment
PPP	–	public–private partnership
PPP	-	purchasing power parity
PRC	–	People's Republic of China
PSE	–	professional secondary education
SEDP	–	Socio-Economic Development Plan 2011-2015
SEDS	–	Socio-Economic Development Strategy
STEM	–	science, technology, engineering, and mathematics
SY	–	school year
TVET	–	technical and vocational education and training
UNAIDS	-	Joint United Nations Programme on HIV/AIDS
UNDP	–	United Nations Development Programme
UNESCO	-	United Nations Educational, Scientific and Cultural Organization
UNICEF	–	United Nations Children's Fund
USE	-	upper secondary education
USS	-	upper secondary school
VASS	-	Viet Nam Academy of Social Sciences
VET	–	vocational education and training
VTC	–	vocational training center

Currency Equivalents

(as of 4 December 2019)

Currency Unit		dong (VND)
VND1.00	=	$0.0000431
$1.00	=	VND23,177

NOTES

(i)   The fiscal year (FY) of the Government of Viet Nam and its agencies ends on 31 December.

(ii) The school year (SY) in Viet Nam officially starts in September and ends on 31 May. "SY" before a calendar year denotes the year in which the school year starts, e.g., SY2017/18 ends on 31 May 2018.

Executive Summary

This secondary education sector assessment, strategy, and road map documents the assessment of the Asian Development Bank (ADB) and strategic investment priorities of the Government of Viet Nam and ADB in Viet Nam's secondary education sector, which covers lower secondary education (LSE) and upper secondary education (USE) including secondary technical and vocational education and training (TVET).

Viet Nam can no longer rely on low-skilled jobs. Viet Nam has evolved from one of the world's poorest countries in the 1990s when the government opened the economy, to a lower middle-income country with a per capita income of $2,111 in 2015—more than 20 times larger than that in 1990 ($98.03). To make the most of its middle-income stage of development and to avoid being perpetually trapped there, Viet Nam will need to create productive job opportunities, support intermediate technology, and promote research and development and innovation. At middle-income stage, skills become more important as the need to increase productivity, product innovation, and value addition grows. Relying only on low-skilled jobs is no longer enough. Ranked 77th out of 140 countries on the Global Competitiveness Index 2018, Viet Nam's labor productivity levels are lower than other countries in the region. Productivity is particularly low in agriculture, which has remained the largest economic sector. A shortage of skills and gaps in the labor force are already affecting Viet Nam's ability to absorb new foreign investment and limiting prospects for expanding productive employment (only 21.5% of the employed labor force has qualified skills—24.1% of men and 18.8% of women). The education system needs to be reformed to give students equitable access to relevant skills.

Net enrollment rates have yet to be realized. The general education system consists of preprimary programs catering to 3- to 5-year old students; a 5-year program of primary education for students starting at 6 years of age; LSE covering grades 6–9 and catering to 11- to 14-year old students; and USE for grades 10–12. Viet Nam's birth rate has been declining, which is reflected in the dip in the total number of students in the education system around SY2008/09. Enrollment in preprimary and primary have increased in the last 5 years, but enrollment in LSE and USE are still lower than historic highs. In SY2015/16, about 7.79 million students were enrolled in primary (3.74 million girls), 5.14 million in LSE (2.51 million girls), and 2.43 million in USE (1.30 million girls). In SY2015/16, universal primary education has been achieved in Viet Nam with a net enrollment rate (NER) of 99%. However, the government's targets of achieving a NER for LSE of 95% and 80% for USE have not yet been realized (in SY2015/16 LSE was at 92.3% and USE at 63.0%).

Viet Nam has made impressive achievements in its education sector. The government's high priority on education has resulted in new teacher standards, introduced student-centered teaching, established a new school accreditation agency, and expanded learning opportunities for disadvantaged youth. The 2012 and 2015 results from the Programme for International Student Assessment (PISA) showed that Vietnamese students are internationally competitive. The Socio-

Economic Development Plan 2016–2020 also indicates that the education sector performed well over the period 2011–2015. But several constraints and unmet targets persist.

The quality of secondary education remains weak and not relevant to the labor market. As the economy becomes modernized and industrialized, the challenge for secondary education is to produce graduates and school leavers who are technically skilled and able to critically analyze and solve problems. The government's Education Development Strategy (EDS) 2011–2020 notes that (i) the quality and effectiveness of the education sector are low, and (ii) workers' knowledge and skills do not meet labor market requirements. In a rapidly evolving world, science and technology education is important. Although the results for PISA 2012 and 2015 were at or above the Organisation for Economic Co-operation and Development (OECD) average, the results for mathematics and reading declined from 2012 to 2015, lower than neighboring economic competitors, and Viet Nam had few high-performing students. Having a low percentage of students performing at the top levels signals the absence of a highly educated talent pool for the future. Viet Nam's high performance could also reflect rote learning and proficient test-taking skills, rather than meaningful learning or the ability to use knowledge in new situations. The National Achievement Monitoring (NAM) test results show a decline at the grade 9 level in all subjects and a decrease in mathematics at grade 11. NAM results indicate that only 46.7% of grade 9 students passed the national 2012/2013 mathematics assessment (boys at 46.7% and girls almost equal at 46.6%), while only 52.2% of grade 11 students passed the 2014/2015 mathematics assessment (boys at 48.0% and girls significantly higher at 55.8%), and only 40.4% of grade 11 students passed the English assessment (boys at 38.5% and girls at 45.2%).

Secondary education does not provide students with the skills to succeed in the workplace. The present curriculum was designed to be broader in scope and relevant to labor market needs. New textbooks were developed, and teachers received extensive training on new approaches to learning and teaching. Despite these efforts, a 2010 study by Viet Nam's National Institute of Education Sciences concluded that (i) the curriculum did not equip students with the knowledge and skills needed for future careers, and (ii) the low quality of secondary education constrained the development of a skilled labor force. For secondary education graduates—who enter the labor market immediately after graduation and students who continue post-secondary education—jobs are difficult to find. Secondary education does not provide students with the cognitive, social, and behavioral foundation skills that are critical to succeeding in the workplace. The returns to education for LSE and USE graduates were only 1.2 and 1.5 larger than primary education graduates, while college and university graduates earn 2.4 times more than primary graduates and 1.8 times more than USE graduates. Vocational orientation in secondary schools does not help students acquire sufficient vocational awareness and understanding of available jobs, does not reflect local labor market's needs and features, and is not gender sensitive.

Professional development strategies are needed to change teacher behavior. Recognizing the need for a fundamental and comprehensive renovation of secondary education, the government is designing a new curriculum to better match market needs. However, the professional development model for teachers does not appear to have changed teaching behaviors. The challenge will be to find professional development strategies or new school models that will change teacher behavior in the classroom so that students will, in fact, acquire the desired competencies.

A high percentage of the population is not obtaining secondary education. Because too many young people are not receiving enough education, Viet Nam cannot move forward economically and socially. In SY2015/16, about 430,000 youths (240,250 boys and 189,750 girls) of LSE age were not enrolled in the school system. At the USE level, over 1.4 million young people (821,400 boys and 602,600 girls) were not enrolled. Having such a high percentage of the population not obtaining secondary education represents a significant loss to the economy. Lack of access to and poor quality of secondary education affect the labor force. Despite the government's continued efforts to increase access to education and retain in school students from vulnerable groups, including ethnic minorities, disabled, and girls living in the Northern Midland and Mountainous regions, inequality in educational access and quality persists, especially among boys and girls from different ethnic minority groups and geographic regions.

Education opportunities for ethnic minority and children with disabilities remain restricted. Several projects funded by overseas development assistance and government programs targeted ethnic minority students. In addition to not being able to take advantage of access to education, ethnic minority students who are in school achieve considerably lower than the majority. There have been few targeted interventions for youth with disabilities. According to the 2009 Viet Nam Population and Household Census, around 7.8% (7.1% males and 8.5% females) of the population 5 years old or older live with one or more physical or mental disabilities. However, in SY2013/14, only 13,572 students with a disability attended LSE, which is 0.3% of the student population at this level, and 1,520 or 0.1% of students at USE. While the government has provided financial support programs to the disabled, education opportunities for these children remain restricted leading to fewer opportunities for employment and integration.

Resource management is ineffective and inefficient. The government aims to further decentralize education financing by strengthening the financing capacity of provincial governments and increasing the autonomy for site-based decision-making and thereby improving the effectiveness of resource utilization. In many ways, Viet Nam's education system is already highly decentralized, with 88% of funding for education coming from provincial and local level governments. While the national government is responsible for determining national policies and programs, local autonomy for management decisions has been a long-standing feature in Viet Nam but the planning capacity of Ministry of Education and Training (MOET) staff, provincial staff, and school principals is still generally weak, particularly in decentralized decision-making.

Measurement and monitoring are vital. Viet Nam's ranking on the Worldwide Governance Indicators, compared with all countries, has fallen since 1996. As governments invest significant public resources in education, the public and the policy makers are concerned about the quality of education. The educational system needs an accountability framework involving the annual collection, analysis, planning, and reporting of several elements at the national, provincial, and school levels. The lack or inconsistency of sex-disaggregated data for analysis, planning, monitoring, and reporting remains an issue. For Viet Nam to achieve the Sustainable Development Goals (SDGs), measurement and monitoring will be vital to inform the policies needed by stakeholders working to make a positive impact on the education system. The country has made a significant start in developing outcome measures of student performance at the national level by developing the NAM and participating internationally in PISA.

The government is committed to enhancing education quality. The policy framework for the long-term development of education is defined by (i) the Socio-Economic Development Strategy, 2011–2020; (ii) the Education Development Strategy, 2011–2020; (iii) Resolution No. 29; (iv) Resolution No. 44; and (v) Decision No. 2653. The government is committed to enhance education quality through comprehensive reforms that will foster integration of disadvantaged groups in education and competitiveness in the labor market. Viet Nam is committed to achieving the United Nations' 2030 Agenda for Sustainable Development and the SDGs and to achieve gender equality through the adoption of an Action Plan on Gender Equality of the Education Sector for 2016–2020.

Education reforms are being planned. MOET is planning changes in multiple areas to achieve the desired renovation of the system: (i) simplify and modernize the curriculum to better address labor market requirements; (ii) have teaching and learning methods that encourage the learners' independence, creativity, and application of knowledge; (iii) ensure that textbooks, teaching, and learning materials suit the needs of corresponding learners, remove gender stereotypes, and promote positive attitudes to ethnic minorities or those who are disabled; (iv) establish examinations and classroom assessments that measure the desired student competencies; (v) equip educators by changing the aims, content, methods of training, retraining, and evaluation of teachers and management officials; (vi) ensure that students receive career guidance; (vii) have local education administration agencies participate in decisions on personnel, finance, and administration; (viii) strengthen gender mainstreaming in education; and (ix) assess and disclose the quality of educational institutions throughout the country.

The government is targeting to spend 20% of its total budget on education and training. In 2015, Viet Nam's expenditure on education and training was 15.3% of the total government budget, which is comparable to Viet Nam's middle-income neighbors and to the regional average of East Asia and the Pacific. At 5.5% of gross domestic product, Viet Nam's public expenditure on education compares well with some of East Asia's wealthiest nations. The government is targeting to spend 20% of its total budget on education and training, signifying the importance of education as a strategy for human resources development. The government has also made steady efforts to improve the efficiency of expenditure in the education sector. In 2015, the government approved a revised State Budget Law, which has helped to address critical weaknesses in public financial management systems. This law introduced a 5-year medium-term expenditure framework and public investment plans that will allow for more strategic and disciplined expenditure planning, including for MOET.

Viet Nam must improve the quality of secondary education. Key to improving quality is the introduction of a new curriculum that is better attuned to the needs of economic development as Viet Nam transitions to a middle-income country. MOET is already developing a competency-based curriculum which has the potential to better meet the needs of the workplace and society as a whole. However, MOET has not succeeded in introducing the last new curricula. It will need to introduce professional development models, which go beyond the ineffective cascade model of teacher in-service that merely transfers knowledge, to other models that actually change teacher behavior in the classroom. Other models, such as coaching/mentoring and community of practice, have much larger potential to impact teachers. Teacher assessment should also be part of their continuous professional development. Viet Nam has made excellent progress in developing a teacher assessment system based on national professional standards, but it now needs to unify that system with the professional development of teachers.

Access and relevance of upper secondary education needs to be improved. The NER in primary and lower secondary education in Viet Nam has reached or is close to reaching the respective targets but enrollment in LSE and USE has dropped. Several recommendations suggest to either remove barriers to transition or to encourage students and their parents to enroll in USE. The current elitist system of requiring students to graduate from LSE and pass an entrance examination to enroll in USE is restricting the number of students who can enroll and hindering those who wish to continue to USE.

Some parents and students do not see the relevance of USE to their better future employment and higher education opportunities. Hopefully the new curriculum and efforts to introduce career and vocational orientation will help address this perceived lack of relevance, but other strategies will likely be required such as making TVET more appealing to students and their parents. Programs, such as conditional cash transfers, have been shown to increase enrollments by reducing the lost opportunity cost associated with attending, particularly among students from poor families such as those of ethnic minority. An increase in USE enrollment will require more classroom space. As MOET has had difficulty in allocating funds to capital improvements, it will need to find alternative means such as using public–private partnerships to finance classroom improvements. Also, MOET needs to examine alternative cost-effective methods of delivering education particularly in remote areas.

Management of schools must improve. There is a relationship between curriculum reform, teachers' continuous professional development, and the way schools are managed. In the classic bureaucratic system, teacher-centered and teacher-delivered instruction is consistent with a work organization that takes directions from a central organization. The teacher standing in front of the classroom telling students what to learn is akin to a management model that externally directs and supervises the teacher. However, a system that attempts to deliver a competency-based curriculum in which students master complex ways of thinking, may need (i) a professional development system, (ii) a teacher assessment system, and (iii) a management system that has highly professional teachers working in a collegial manner. If teachers are being directed as to what to do and how to do it, they may find it difficult to understand and model the learning environment required for the acquisition of complex competencies.

The findings from PISA relative to autonomy and accountability indicate that in countries where schools have greater autonomy over what is taught and how students are assessed, students tend to perform better. Further, in countries where schools are held to account for their results and where schools enjoy greater autonomy in resource allocation, students tend to do better than those in schools with less autonomy. Viet Nam has been moving to increase autonomy of its schools and developing an accountability system through participation in PISA and the development of NAM. MOET needs to consider how it can move further to a site-based management system and improve its accountability system.

I. Sector Profile

1. This secondary education sector assessment, strategy, and road map documents the assessment of the Asian Development Bank (ADB) and strategic investment priorities of the Government of Viet Nam and ADB in Viet Nam's secondary education sector, which covers lower secondary education (LSE) and upper secondary education (USE), including secondary technical and vocational education and training (TVET).[1] It highlights sector performance, priority development constraints, government plans and strategy, past ADB support and experience, other development partner support, and future ADB support strategy. This strategy is linked to and informs ADB's country partnership strategy for Viet Nam, with both targeting 2016–2020. This strategy will be updated as strategic developments and program changes are needed and will help to provide background information on education for investment and technical assistance operations.

2. Viet Nam is a development success story. Economic growth has been stable and inclusive while at the same time making impressive progress in alleviating poverty and improving other dimensions of social welfare. However, the inability to improve economic competitiveness and labor productivity, combined with insufficient progress in including marginalized groups in the country's development, calls into question the durability of the current development model. The government sees the improvement of education as a key strategy to helping achieve its goal of becoming a modern industrial nation. Despite large gains in educational attainment the goals are constantly moving, and the country will require increasing levels of achievement to meet its economic and social goals.

A. Economic Development Context

1. Background

3. **Population.** Viet Nam's population grew from about 24.8 million in 1950 to 93.6 million in 2015, which was an average increase of about 1.3% per annum (Figure 1.1). The growth rate is predicted to slow down to an annual growth rate of about 1% until 2020 and then gradually slow to 2060 when the population is expected to start declining.[2] As can be seen in Figure 1.2, there are more females in the population than males, and the gap is expected to widen. Although the population in 2015 was relatively young, with 32.5% of total population below the age of 15 and 25% classified as "young" at 15–34 years of age, the country will face a structural demographic transition toward an aging society starting around 2020.

---

[1]   ADB Viet Nam Technical and Vocational Education and Training Sector Assessment, Manila, 2019.

[2]   Predictions for 2015–2100 are based on medium fertility variant.

Figure 1.1: Total Population of Viet Nam, 1950–2100

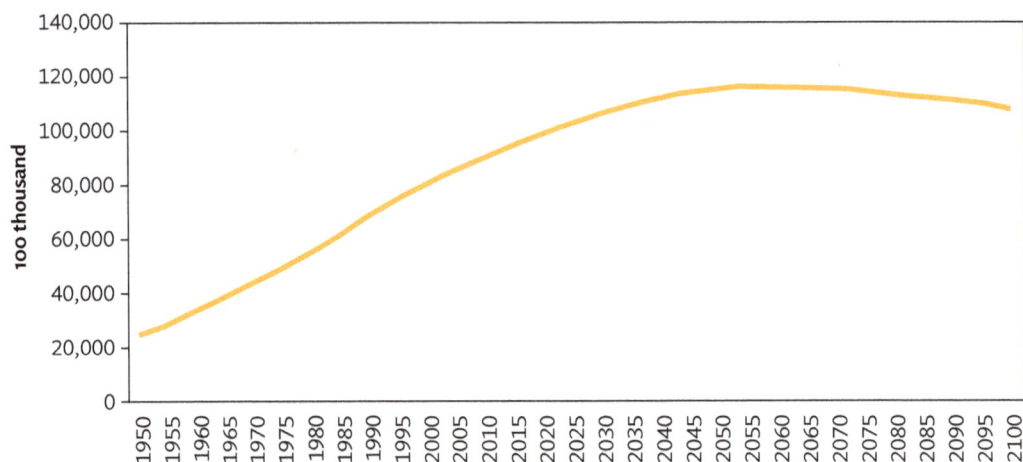

Source: United Nations, Department of Economic and Social Affairs, Population Division. 2017. *World Population Prospects: The 2017 Revision.* New York.

Figure 1.2: Population of Males and Females in Viet Nam, 1950–2100

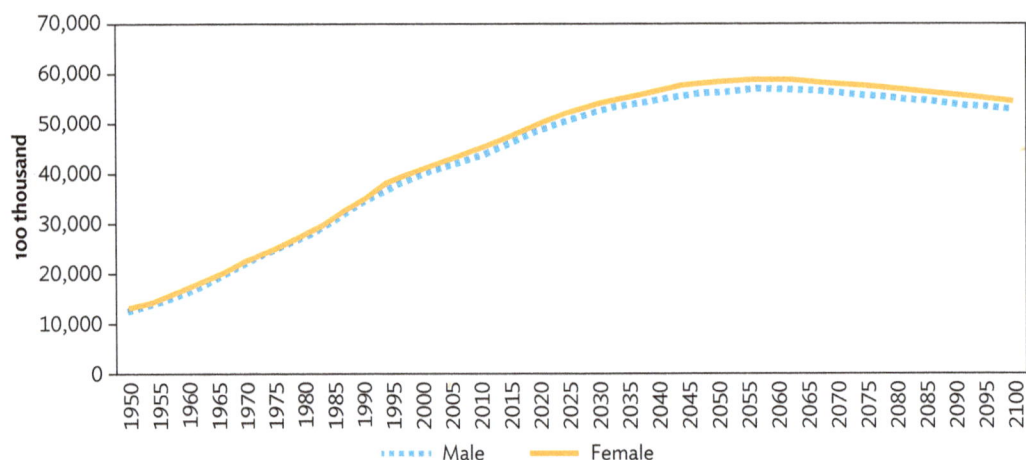

Source: United Nations, Department of Economic and Social Affairs, Population Division. 2017. *World Population Prospects: The 2017 Revision.* New York.

4. **Gross domestic product.** Viet Nam has evolved from one of the world's poorest countries 25 years ago when the government opened the economy, to a lower middle-income country with a per capita income of $1,965 in 2018 (Table 1.1), more than 20 times larger than that in 1990 ($98.03) (World Bank, World Development Indicators). Viet Nam has gradually stabilized its macro economy and controlled inflation. Between 1990 and 2007 Viet Nam had an average growth in its gross domestic product (GDP) of over 7%, and between 2010 and 2018 the rate was around 6.2% although it increased in the last 2 years (Table 1.2). However, there is great disparity across the country, with the southeast region enjoying a GDP per capita of $8,021 and the Northen Midland and Mountainous Region at only $1,939 (UNDP and VASS 2016). A gulf is forming between farm and nonfarm incomes, and income inequality is rising within rural areas (Table 1.3) (World Bank 2016).

Table 1.1: Gross Domestic Product per Capita
(constant 2010 $)

2008	2009	2010	2011	2012	2013	2014	2015	2016	2017	2018
1,198	1,251	1,318	1,3856	1,444	1,506	1,579	1,667	1,753	1,853	1,965

Source: World Bank. World Development Indicators. http://data.worldbank.org/country/vietnam (accessed 10 July 2019).

Table 1.2: Gross Domestic Product at Constant 2010 Prices for Viet Nam, 2010 to 2015

Item	2010	2011	2012	2013	2014	2015	2016	2017	2018
Total Viet Nam GDP (VND billion)	2,157,828	2,292,483	2,412,778	2,543,596	2,695,796	2,875,856	3,054,470	3,262,548	3,493,399
Annual growth rate of GDP (%)	6.4	6.2	5.2	5.4	6.0	6.7	6.2	6.8	7.1

GDP = gross domestic product.
Source: World Bank. World Development Indicators. http://data.worldbank.org/country/vietnam (accessed 10 July 2019).

Table 1.3: Changes in the Urban–Rural Income Gap

	2002	2004	2006	2008	2010	2012
Whole country	356	484	636	995	1,387	1,999
Urban	622	815	1,058	1,605	2,129	2,989
Rural	275	378.1	505.7	762	1,070	1,579
Urban/rural ratio	2.3	2.2	2.1	2.1	2.0	1.9
Urban–rural income gap	347	437	552	843	1,059	1,409

Source: World Bank Group. 2016. *Vietnam Development Report 2016: Transforming Vietnamese Agriculture: Gaining More from Less.* Ha Noi.

5. Viet Nam's economic objective during 2011–2020 is to maintain macroeconomic stability, with GDP growing at 7%–8% per year.[3] Viet Nam's initial heavy reliance on export-led growth (Table 1.4), anchored on early investment in basic education, yielded the necessary skills to take advantage of cheap labor to build the foundation for its transition to prosperity. The growth momentum was sustained through inflows of domestic and foreign investment. Between 1988 and 2010, the number of foreign investment projects in Viet Nam rose from 37 to 1,237. According to data from the General Statistics Office, foreign registered capital reached nearly $20 billion in 2010, up from only $735 million in 1990. Large multinational companies such as Samsung, Intel, and Nokia have established offices in the country. Also, as labor costs are edging up in the People's Republic of China (PRC) the workshop of the world has started shifting its location to neighboring countries such as Cambodia, the Lao People's Democratic Republic (Lao PDR), Myanmar, and Viet Nam (APO 2016).

---

[3] Government of Viet Nam. Vietnam's Socio-Economic Development Strategy for the Period of 2011–2020 Approved by the Eleventh Congress of Viet Nam Communist Party. Ha Noi.

Table 1.4: Exports of Goods and Services as a Percentage of Gross Domestic Product, 2000–2018

Country	2000	2005	2010	2015	2018
PRC	20.9	33.8	26.3	21.4	19.5
Indonesia	41.0	34.1	24.3	21.1	21.0
Malaysia	119.8	112.9	86.9	70.6	69.7
Thailand	64.8	68.4	66.5	68.7	66.8
Viet Nam	**53.9**	**63.7**	**72.0**	**89.8**	**95.4**

GDP = gross domestic product, PRC = People's Republic of China.
Source: World Bank. World Development Indicators. http://data.worldbank.org/country/vietnam (accessed 10 July 2019).

6. **Economic issues.** The government has recognized in its latest socioeconomic development plan that the economic recovery has been slow, growth rates have not met the targets, and the development gap between Viet Nam and others in the region is still large.[4] Further, it acknowledges that national competitiveness has improved little, especially in terms of economy institutions, infrastructure, and technological innovation. The plan notes that improvement of human resources quality has been slow, resulting in a shortage of high-quality workers. It finds that science and technology have yet to drive productivity, increase competitiveness, and promote socioeconomic development. The plan sets the following specific targets to be achieved by 2020: (i) average growth of 6.5% to 7% per year; (ii) GDP per capita to reach $3,200–$3,500; (iii) industry and service sectors account for more than 85% GDP; (iv) productivity increases by 4% to 5% per year; (v) urbanization reaches 38% to 40%; (vi) the agricultural labor force accounts for 35%–40% of total labor; (vii) educated and trained workers account for 65% to 70% of total workforce; (viii) workers with certificates and degrees account for 25% to 26%; and (ix) the poverty rate reduces by 1.3% to 1.5% per year.

2.   Labor Force

7. **Growth in labor force has been significant but slowing down.** Between 2000 and 2015, the country's labor force grew from 39 million to 54 million or about 2.7% each year or about 40% over the 15 years. Between 2000 and 2011 around a million workers were added to the workforce each year, but between 2013 and 2014 only about half a million new workers joined the workforce, and between 2014 and 2015 the number dropped to only a quarter of a million new workers. A majority of workers are still located in rural areas, although this is rapidly changing as a result of urbanization (Table 1.5). Men and women each account for roughly half of the workforce and female participation is relatively high compared with other countries in the region (Table 1.6).

8. While the country has been reaping demographic dividends over the last decade or so, the population is aging as a result of declining fertility rates, decreasing mortality rates, and increasing life expectancies (UNPF 2011). Viet Nam's General Statistics Office (GSO) estimates that by 2049, individuals aged 60 years and above will account for 26% of the total population.

9. **Unemployment has been relatively low and stable.** Viet Nam's unemployment rate is low, averaging only 2.37% between 2008 and 2015, with higher rates in urban areas. During the same period, underemployment averaged 3.37% (Table 1.7), with higher rates in rural areas. However, unemployment among the youth (i.e., individuals aged 15–24 years) at 6.7% in 2015 is higher than

---

[4]   Government of Viet Nam. *National Assembly Resolution No. 142/2016/QH13 Socio-Economic Development Plan 2016–2020.* Ha Noi.

Table 1.5: Composition of Viet Nam's Labor Force
('000)

Year	Total	Sex		Residence		Age		
		Male (%)	Female (%)	Urban (%)	Rural (%)	15–24 (%)	25–49 (%)	50+ (%)
2000	38,545	50.7	49.3	23.1	76.9	21.5	66.1	12.4
2001	39,616	51.0	49.0	23.9	76.1	22.1	66.2	11.7
2002	40,716	50.9	49.1	24.2	75.8	21.6	65.8	12.7
2003	41,847	51.3	48.7	24.1	75.9	22.4	63.3	14.1
2004	43,009	51.0	49.0	24.9	75.1	21.0	63.3	15.6
2005	44,905	52.3	47.7	25.5	74.5	20.4	63.7	16.3
2006	46,239	53.2	46.8	26.5	73.5	21.0	62.3	15.3
2007	47,160	50.8	49.2	26.3	73.7	18.2	62.2	19.5
2008	48,210	51.3	48.7	27.3	72.7	18.1	61.4	19.7
2009	49,322	52.0	48.0	26.9	73.1	18.6	61.4	20.0
2010	50,393	51.4	48.6	28.0	72.0	18.3	61.3	20.3
2011	51,398	51.5	48.5	29.7	70.3	16.5	61.2	22.2
2012	52,348	51.4	48.6	30.3	69.7	15.1	61.2	23.8
2013	53,246	51.4	48.6	30.1	69.9	14.9	59.8	25.2
2014	53,748	51.3	48.7	30.7	69.3	14.1	59.7	26.2
2015	53,984	51.6	48.4	31.3	68.7	14.9	59.2	25.9
2016	54,445	51.6	48.4	32.1	67.9	13.8	59.5	26.7
2017[a]	54,824	51.9	48.1	32.2	67.8	13.8	59.5	26.7

[a] Preliminary.
Source: General Statistics Office of Viet Nam. www.gso.gov.vn/default_en.aspx?tabid=775 (accessed 10 July 2019).

Table 1.6: Female Labor Force Participation, 2019

Country	Percentage of Female Population ages 15+ (modeled ILO estimate)
Cambodia	75.2
India	23.4
Indonesia	52.3
Korea, Rep. of	52.7
Malaysia	51.1
Philippines	45.9
Sri Lanka	34.8
Thailand	59.2
Viet Nam	**72.5**

Source: World Bank. World Development Indicators. https://databank.worldbank.org/source/world-development-indicators (accessed 7 February 2020).

for the entire population.[5] Table 1.8 shows that Viet Nam's unemployment rate is low relative to neighboring countries and its unemployment rate is higher in the 15- to 24-year age group, a common trend in other countries. Breaking down the unemployment rate in the 15- to 24-year age group, Table 1.9 shows that unemployment rate is highest for urban males and lowest for rural females. The labor market also has a high rate of informality: approximately 6 out of every 10 workers, majority of whom are women, are own-account or unpaid family workers (ILO n.d.).

---

[5]　The General Statistics Office of Viet Nam calculated from a labor force aged 15–24 years, 8.102 million of an employed 7.449 million.

Table 1.7: Unemployment and Underemployment Rates, 2008 to 2017, by Residence

	Unemployment Rate			Underemployment Rate		
	Whole Country	Urban	Rural	Whole Country	Urban	Rural
Prel.2017	2.24	3.18	1.78	1.62	0.82	2.03
2016	2.30	3.23	1.84	1.66	0.73	2.12
2015	2.33	3.37	1.82	1.89	0.84	2.39
2014	2.10	3.40	1.49	2.35	1.20	2.90
2013	2.18	3.59	1.54	2.75	1.48	3.31
2012	1.96	3.21	1.39	2.74	1.56	3.27
2011	2.22	3.60	1.60	2.96	1.58	3.56
2010	2.88	4.29	2.30	3.57	1.82	4.26
2009	2.90	4.60	2.25	5.61	3.33	6.51
2008	2.38	4.65	1.53	5.10	2.34	6.10

Source: General Statistics Office of Viet Nam. www.gso.gov.vn/default_en.aspx?tabid=775 (accessed 22 July 2019).

Table 1.8: Unemployment Rate by Age in 2016 for Selected Countries

Country	Age 15+ Years	Age 15–24 Years	Age 25+ Years
Cambodia	0.7	1.1	0.6
India (2015)	3.5	9.8	2.2
Indonesia	4.3	15.8	2.1
Korea, Rep. of	3.7	10.7	3.1
Lao PDR (2015)	1.4	3.6	0.6
Malaysia	3.4	10.5	1.9
Philippines	2.7	7.7	1.6
Sri Lanka	4.2	212.9	2.3
Thailand	0.7	3.7	0.3
Viet Nam	**2.1**	**7.4**	**1.2**

Lao PDR = Lao People's Democratic Republic.
Source: International Labour Organization. ILOSTAT database (accessed 22 July 2019).

Table 1.9: Economic Activity of Youth (Aged 15–24 Years)

	Total	Male	Female
Young population ('000 persons)	12,071.1	6,234.5	5,836.6
Urban	4,247	2,194.2	2,232.9
Rural	7,644.1	4,040.3	3,603.7
Employed youth ('000 persons)	6,712.4	3,652.3	3,060.1
Urban	1,757.6	896.3	861.3
Rural	4,954.7	2,756.0	2,198.8
Unemployed youth ('000 persons)	510.8	255.9	254.9
Urban	211.2	102.2	109.0
Rural	299.5	153.6	145.9
Youth labor force participation rate (%)	59.8	62.7	56.8
Urban	44.5	45.5	43.5
Rural	68.7	72.0	65.1
Youth unemployment rate (%)	7.1	6.5	7.7
Urban	10.7	10.2	11.2
Rural	5.7	5.3	6.2

Source: Ministry of Planning and Investment, General Statistics Office. 2018. *Report on Labor Force Survey (Quarter 1, 2018)*. Ha Noi.

10. **Agriculture is still the primary provider of employment.** Despite structural transformation of the economy from agriculture to industry and service sectors, agriculture provided the largest share at 44.0% of total employment in 2015 (Table 1.10). Employment in industry grew from 18.9% in 2007 to 22.8% in 2015, with most jobs from manufacturing and construction. Employment in services increased from 27.7% to 31.7% during the same period, with a large share of workers in wholesale and retail trade.

Table 1.10: Employed Population, 15 Years Old and Above by Economic Activity, 2007–2017

	2007	2008	2009	2010	2011	2012	2013	2014	2015	2016	2017[a]
TOTAL	**100**	**100**	**100**	**100**	**100**	**100**	**100**	**100**	**100**	**100**	**100**
Agriculture, forestry, and fishing	52.9	52.3	51.5	49.5	48.4	47.4	46.7	46.3	44	41.9	40.2
Industry	18.9	19.3	20.0	20.9	21.3	21.3	21.2	21.4	22.8	24.7	25.7
Mining and quarrying	0.7	0.6	0.6	0.6	0.6	0.6	0.5	0.5	0.5	0.4	0.4
Manufacturing	12.5	12.9	13.5	13.5	13.8	13.8	13.9	14.1	15.3	16.6	17.3
Electricity, gas, steam, AC supply	0.3	0.3	0.3	0.3	0.3	0.3	0.3	0.3	0.3	0.3	0.3
Water supply, sewerage, waste management	0.2	0.2	0.2	0.2	0.2	0.2	0.2	0.2	0.2	0.3	0.2
Construction	5.2	5.3	5.4	6.3	6.4	6.4	6.3	6.3	6.5	7.1	7.5
Services	27.7	28.0	28.1	29.1	30.0	31.1	31.6	32.0	32.8	33.0	33.7
Wholesale and retail trade; repair of motor vehicles and motorcycles	10.9	11.0	10.8	11.3	11.6	12.3	12.6	12.6	12.7	12.6	12.9
Transportation and storage	3.0	3.1	3.0	2.9	2.8	2.9	2.9	2.9	3	3	3.3
Accommodation and food service activities	2.4	2.8	3.3	3.5	4.0	4.2	4.2	4.4	4.6	4.7	4.6
Information and communication	0.4	0.4	0.5	0.5	0.5	0.6	0.6	0.6	0.6	0.6	0.6
Financial, banking, and insurance	0.4	0.4	0.5	0.5	0.6	0.6	0.6	0.7	0.7	0.7	0.7
Real estate activities	0.1	0.1	0.1	0.2	0.2	0.3	0.3	0.3	0.3	0.3	0.4
Professional, scientific, technical	0.4	0.4	0.5	0.4	0.4	0.5	0.5	0.5	0.5	0.5	0.5
Administrative and support	0.3	0.3	0.4	0.4	0.4	0.4	0.5	0.5	0.5	0.5	0.6
Activities of Communist Party, sociopolitical organizations; public administration and defense; compulsory security	3.7	3.6	3.3	3.2	3.1	3.1	3.1	3.2	3.2	3.2	3.2
Education and training	3.3	3.2	3.3	3.4	3.4	3.4	3.5	3.5	3.6	3.6	3.8
Human health/social work	0.9	0.8	0.8	0.9	1.0	0.9	0.9	0.9	1	1.1	1
Arts, entertainment, recreation	0.3	0.4	0.4	0.5	0.5	0.5	0.5	0.5	0.6	0.6	0.5
Other service activities	1.6	1.5	1.2	1.4	1.5	1.4	1.4	1.4	1.5	1.6	1.6

Continued on next page

Table 1.10 continued

Others	0.4	0.4	0.4	0.4	0.4	0.3	0.3	0.3	0.3	0.4	0.4
Activities of households as employers; undifferentiated goods and services producing	0.4	0.4	0.4	0.4	0.4	0.3	0.3	0.3	0.3	0.4	0.4
Activities of extraterritorial organizations and bodies	0.0	0.0	0.0	0.0	0.0	0.0	0.0	0.0	0.01	0	0.01

[a] Preliminary.
Source: General Statistics Office of Viet Nam. www.gso.gov.vn/default_en.aspx?tabid=775 (accessed 22 July 2019).

3.   Moving Forward: Economic Issues and Challenges

11. **Limited competitiveness.** Table 1.11 shows that Viet Nam's Global Competitiveness Index has shown some marginal improvement in 2015 and 2016 but is still around the middle among the rated economies.[6] In 2016, Viet Nam ranked 60th out of 138 economies on this index, with a score of 4.3 out of 7. It ranked lower only in the market size component of the index, at 32nd, but rated higher in all other factors, ranking 96th in business sophistication and 92nd in technology readiness. Over this time frame the PRC, Indonesia, Cambodia, and the Philippines have shown improvements in their competitiveness. The Government of Viet Nam has acknowledged the need to improve the country's competitiveness by improving infrastructure and developing a more highly skilled labor force.

Table 1.11: Global Competitiveness Index, Ranking among Selected Economies, 2007–2018

Economy	2007/ 2008	2008/ 2009	2009/ 2010	2010/ 2011	2011/ 2012	2012/ 2013	2013/ 2014	2014/ 2015	2015/ 2016	2016/ 2017	2017/ 2018
Singapore	7	5	3	3	2	2	2	2	2	2	2
Taipei,China	14	17	12	13	13	13	12	14	15	14	13
Malaysia	21	21	24	26	21	25	24	20	18	25	25
Korea, Rep. of	11	13	19	22	24	19	25	26	26	26	15
PRC	34	30	29	27	26	29	29	28	28	28	28
Thailand	28	34	36	38	39	38	37	31	32	34	38
India	48	50	49	51	56	59	60	71	55	39	58
Indonesia	54	55	54	44	46	50	38	34	37	41	45
Philippines	71	71	87	85	75	65	59	52	47	57	56
Viet Nam	**68**	**70**	**75**	**59**	**65**	**75**	**70**	**68**	**56**	**60**	**77**
Sri Lanka	70	77	79	62	53	68	65	73	68	71	85
Cambodia	110	109	110	109	97	85	59	52	90	89	110
Lao PDR	n/a	n/a	n/a	n/a	n/a	n/a	81	93	83	93	112

Lao PDR = Lao People's Democratic Republic, n/a = not applicable, PRC = People's Republic of China.
Source: World Economic Forum. 2018. *Global Competitiveness Report 2018*. Geneva.

12. **Low labor productivity.** Levels of labor productivity in Viet Nam are low compared with other countries in the region with the exception of Cambodia and the Lao PDR (Figure 1.3 and Figure 1.4: Output per Worker). Viet Nam has progressed rather slowly and has failed to increase labor productivity as substantially as Singapore, Japan, the Republic of Korea, and Malaysia have (OECD and

---

[6]   The World Economic Forum ranks nations according to their competitiveness using a global competitiveness index comprising 12 main variables derived from more than 100 indicators. The variables are legal and administrative framework, transport and communications infrastructure, macroeconomic stability, health and primary education, higher education and training, market efficiency for goods, labor market efficiency, financial market development, technological readiness, market size, business sophistication, and innovation. This listing illustrates the complexity of the task of boosting national competitiveness and shows multiple pathways to greater competitiveness.

World Bank 2014). According to the World Bank and the Ministry of Planning and Investment (MPI) (2016), labor productivity growth in Viet Nam has actually been declining since the end of the 1990s across most industrial subsectors, as well as in mining, finance, and real estate. Between 1994 and 1996, productivity grew at an average of 7.0%, but between 2010 and 2012 it only grew by 3.6% which was lower than the PRC, Indonesia, the Lao PDR, and Cambodia (UNDP and VASS 2016). In addition, World Bank (2016) reports that Viet Nam lags behind regional peers in relation to agricultural land, labor, and water productivity and has seen its once robust growth in total factor productivity decline in recent years. Viet Nam trades mostly in raw commodities, typically sold at prices lower than those of leading competitors due to quality or other differences. On the Global Competitiveness Index, Viet Nam ranks 77th out of 140 countries on labor market efficiency (World Economic Forum 2018). Low labor productivity is in part related to workers' low levels of skills, which is linked in turn to their effective and efficient performance of tasks, competencies which the education sector should be able to impart to students.

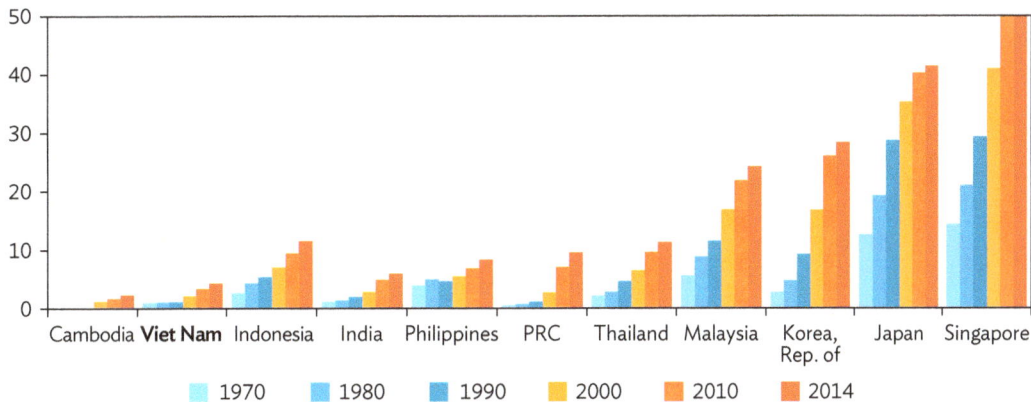

Figure 1.3: Labor Productivity per Hour, 1970, 1980, 1990, 2000, 2010, 2014

PRC = People's Republic of China.
Source: Asian Productivity Organization. 2016. *APO Productivity Databook 2016.* Tokyo: Keio University Press.

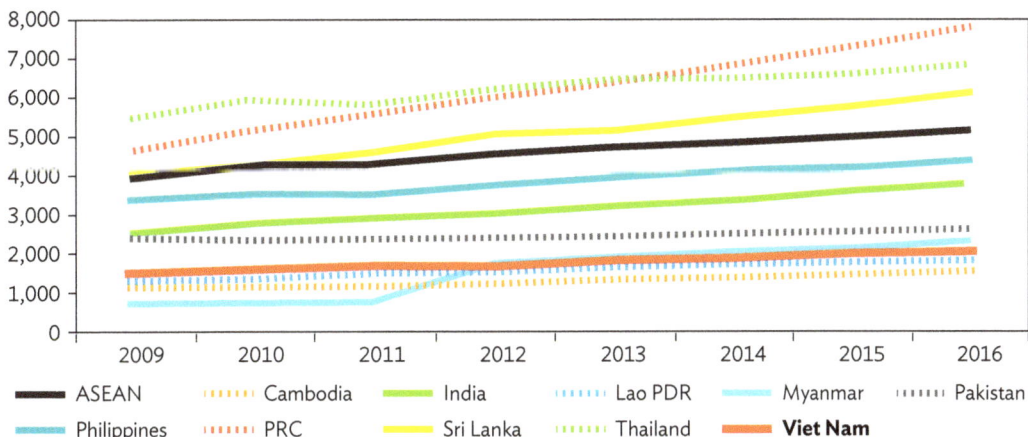

Figure 1.4: Output per Worker
(GDP constant 2005 $)

ASEAN = Association of Southeast Asian Nations, GDP = gross domestic product, Lao PDR = Lao People's Democratic Republic, PRC = People's Republic of China.
Source: International Labour Organization. 2015. *Key Indicators of the Labour Market,* Ninth Edition. Geneva.

13. **Shortage of skilled workers.** The shortage of skilled workers hampers economic competitiveness and impedes the country's capacity to realize the full benefits associated with rapidly growing investments. When Viet Nam's executives were asked for the Global Competitiveness Report about the most problematic factors for doing business in Viet Nam, they mentioned most frequently inadequately educated workforce (Figure 1.5) and poor work ethic as the sixth most significant problem. Employers are looking for directors, managers, supervisors, and experienced team leaders (*Vietnam Briefing* 2014). The rising demand for technical experts, such as engineers and information technology professionals, reflects Viet Nam's "skill-biased occupational transition," which began in the 1990s. Over the last 2 decades, jobs characterized by routine manual tasks have been declining and are being replaced by nonroutine analytical ones (Figure 1.6).

Figure 1.5: Most Problematic Factors for Doing Business according to Executives, 2016

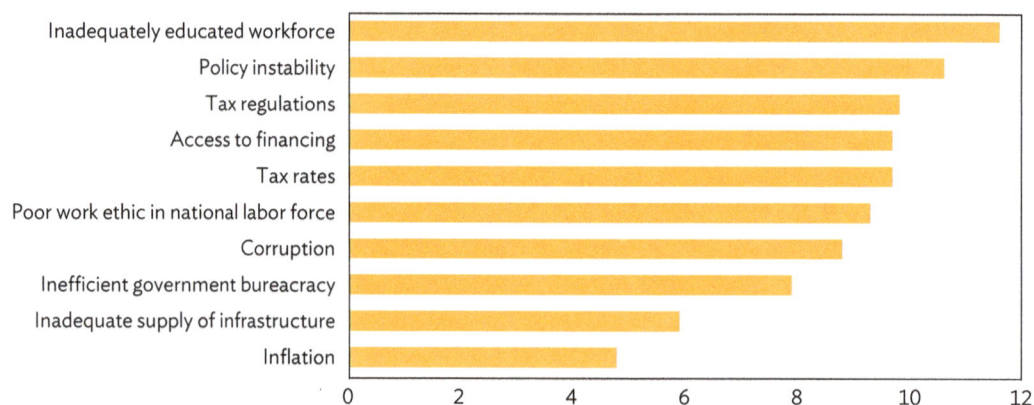

Source: World Economic Forum. 2016. *The Global Competitiveness Report 2016–2017.* Geneva.

Figure 1.6: Viet Nam's Skill-Biased Occupational Transition

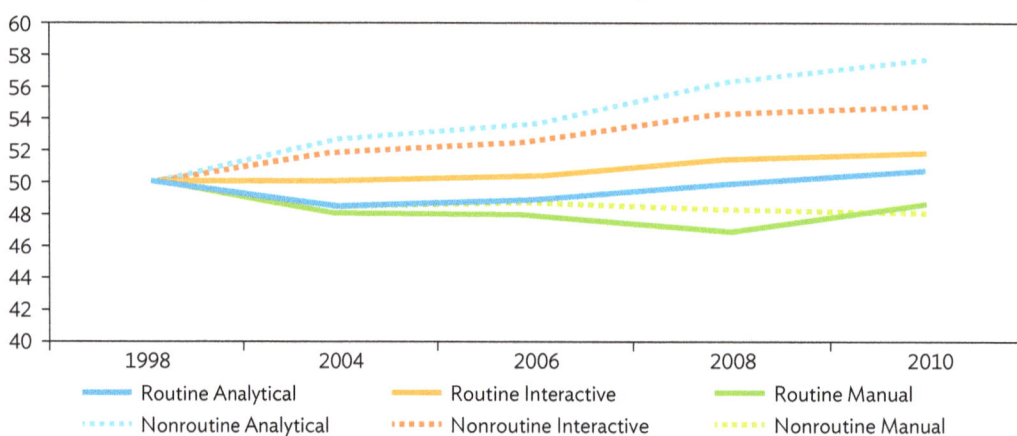

Source: World Bank. 2013. *Vietnam Development Report 2014.* Ha Noi.

14. Table 1.12 shows in the first quarter of 2017 that 78.5% of employees aged over 15 years had no qualifications. Males are slightly more likely to have some qualifications than female workers (24.1% for males and 18.8% for females). However, the gap in qualifications is larger between urban and rural,

with 62.5% of urban workers and 86.3% of rural workers having no qualifications. The Ministry of Labour–Invalids and Social Affairs (MOLISA) and the International Labour Conference Report from September 2014 showed that 22 million people without (formal) qualifications and certifications were employed in positions that require technical workers. Table 1.13 looks at the level of education achieved and shows a similar picture. The government's Socio-Economic Development Strategy (SEDS) 2011–2020 aims to increase by 2015 the percentage of trained workforce over total labor force to 55%.

Table 1.12: Technical and Professional Qualifications of Labor Force Aged 15 Years and Over, First Quarter of 2017

Technical and Professional Qualification	Number ('000 persons)			Percent		
	Total	Male	Female	Total	Male	Female
Entire country	54,505	8,297	26,208	100.0	100.0	100.0
No qualification	42,774	21,482	21,292	78.5	75.9	81.2
Vocational training of more than 3 months	2,933	2,508	425	5.4	8.9	1.6
Professional secondary school	2,132	1,027	1,105	3.9	3.6	4.2
Professional college	1,547	640	907	2.8	2.3	3.5
University and higher	5,118	2,63	2,479	9.4	9.3	9.5

Source: Ministry of Planning and Investment, General Statistics Office. 2017. *Report on Labor Force Survey (Quarter 1, 2017)*. Ha Noi.

Table 1.13: Employment by Educational level for Population Aged 15+ Years

Educational Level	Number (million)	Percent	Employed (Wage or Salary)	Self-Employed in Primary Industry	Self-Employed in Non-Primary Industry
No degree	14.0	21.1	3.4	7.1	2.0
General education	46.5	69.9	15.1	21.3	8.7
Primary	15.1	22.7	5.0	8.7	3.2
Lower secondary	18.6	28.0	5.1	9.8	3.6
Upper secondary	9.3	14.0	2.4	2.5	1.6
Vocational education	6.0	9.0	3.3	1.8	1.3
Short-term technical	2.2	3.3	1.1	0.8	0.7
Long-term technical	1.3	2.0	0.7	0.3	0.2
Professional secondary	2.3	3.5	1.3	0.7	0.4
Vocational college	0.2	0.3	0.2	0.0	0.0
Tertiary general	3.5	5.3	2.7	0.4	0.3
Total	**66.5**	**100.0**	**21.8**	**30.2**	**12.0**

Source: Ministry of Planning and Investment, General Statistics Office. 2014. *Report on Labour Force Survey (Quarter 3, 2014)*. Ha Noi.

15. Countries on the lower rung of the development ladder tend to have a larger agriculture sector as a share of value added. Figure 1.7 shows the industry composition of Asian economies in 2014, indicating a broad, negative correlation between the share of the agriculture sector and relative GDP per capita. Economies in the lowest-income group have the largest agriculture share, and Viet Nam,

where the agriculture sector makes up 20% of the value added, is only in the next highest-income group. Agriculture, mining, and manufacturing in Viet Nam together make up 32% of the value added and tend to be industries that require lower skills.

Figure 1.7: Industry Shares of Value Added, 2014

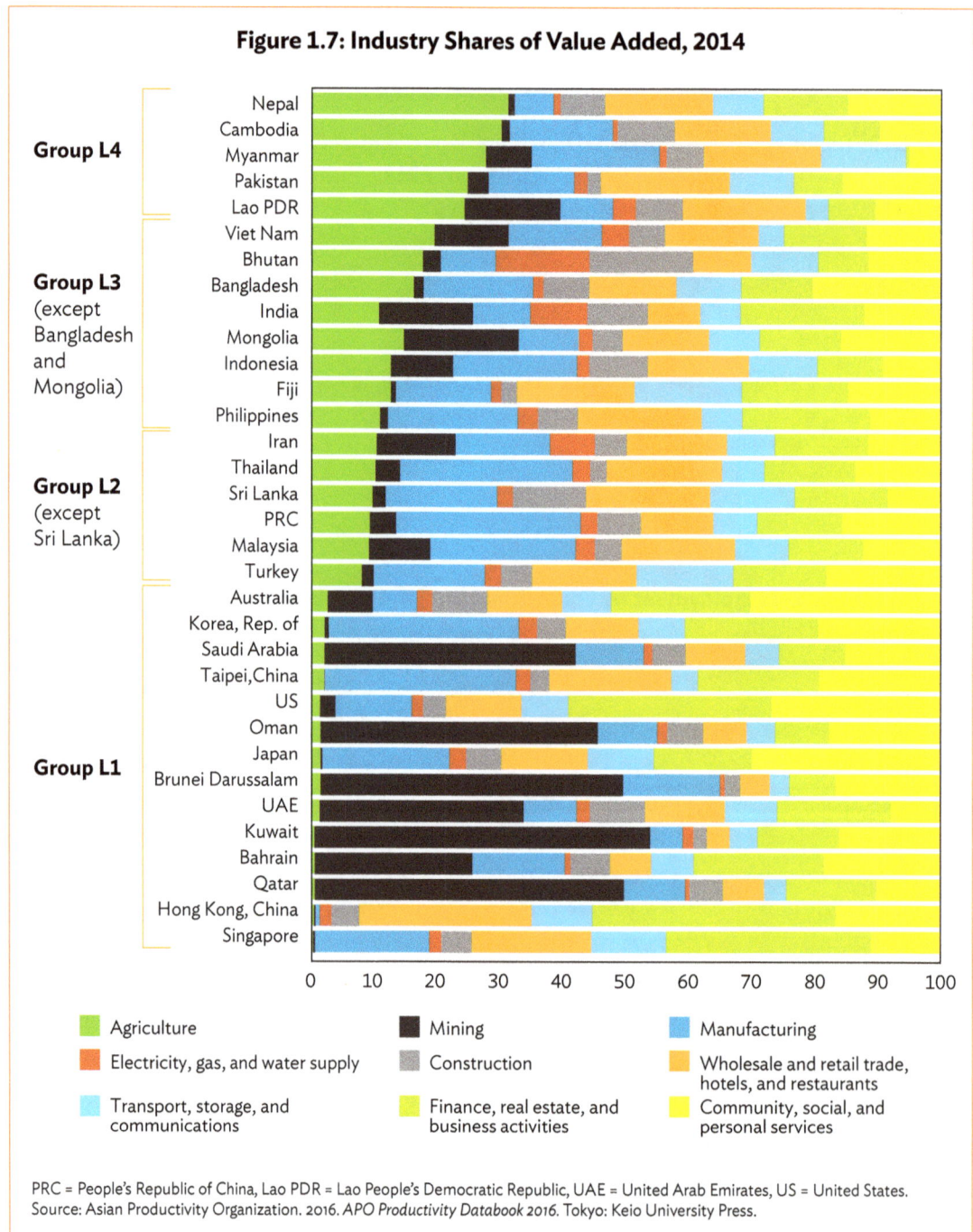

PRC = People's Republic of China, Lao PDR = Lao People's Democratic Republic, UAE = United Arab Emirates, US = United States.
Source: Asian Productivity Organization. 2016. *APO Productivity Databook 2016*. Tokyo: Keio University Press.

16. According to a World Bank (2014) survey of employers in Ha Noi and Ho Chi Minh City, job-specific technical skills are the primary consideration in the hiring of both blue and white collar workers. Nevertheless, strong cognitive and noncognitive skills are also important. Next to technical

skills, employers favor workers who can lead, solve problems, work in teams, and communicate well (Figure 1.8).

Figure 1.8: Skills Required by Viet Nam's Employers

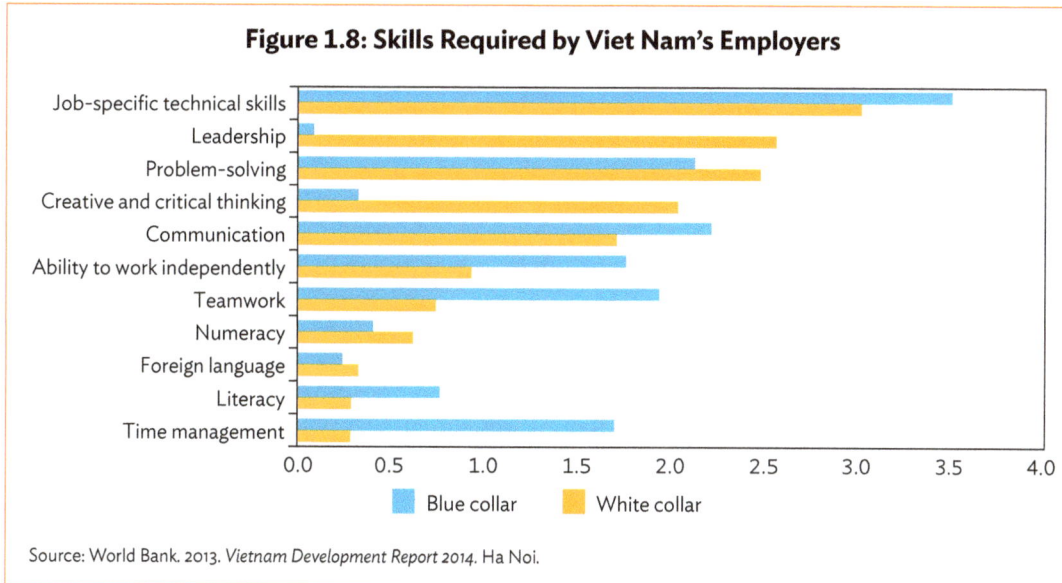

Source: World Bank. 2013. *Vietnam Development Report 2014*. Ha Noi.

17. Cognitive skills, also known as "learning skills," are used to acquire and process information. These include attention, short- and long-term memory, logic and reasoning, and visual and auditory processing. Cognitive skill formation begins at the early stages of life, and is associated with various factors such as genetics, parental investments, education, and the environment. Noncognitive skills, otherwise known as "soft skills," character, or socio-emotional skills, pertain to individual attributes which cannot be measured through intelligence quotient or achievement tests. Psychologists have grouped noncognitive skills into the Big Five—openness to experience, conscientiousness, extraversion, agreeableness, and neuroticism. Noncognitive skills, which are also formed throughout the life cycle, are influenced by many factors; and technical skills, those that are used to accomplish specific tasks, are developed through higher education, as well as on-the-job training.

18. As indicated in Table 1.14 and Table 1.15 the government is forecasting the need for a large increase in the number of trained persons entering the workforce over the coming years. However, the formal training system of public schools and colleges is not able now, nor will it be able in its present form, to meet the country's projected needs for skilled labor. Without a restructured education program, the country's capacity to meet its skills needs will remain restricted.

Table 1.14: Type of Workers Needed, by Training in 2015 and 2020

Workers by Kind of Training	2015 (million people)	2020 (million people)
Total number	55.0	63.0
Trained	30.5	44.0
Receiving vocational training	23.5	34.4
Receiving training through education and training system	7.0	9.4

Note: Figures in 2015 and 2020 are estimates in the Human Resources Development Master Plan.
Source: Government of Viet Nam. 2011. Human Resources Development Master Plan, 2011–2020. Ha Noi.

Table 1.15: Type of Trained Workers Needed, by Vocational Training Level in 2015 and 2020

Training Level	2015 Number (million people)	2015 % of Trained Workers	2020 Number (million people)	2020 % of Trained Workers
Elementary vocational training	18.0	59	24.0	54
Intermediate vocational training	7.0	23	12.0	27
Collegial vocational training	2.0	6	3.0	7
Tertiary training	3.3	11	5.0	11
Postgraduate training	0.2	1	0.3	1
	30.5	100	44.3	100

Source: Government of Viet Nam. 2011. Human Resources Development Master Plan, 2011–2020. Ha Noi.

19. **Youth unemployment.** Young workers aged 15 to 24 years constitute almost half of the country's unemployed population. In 2017, youth unemployment was at 7.4%. Viet Nam faces relatively high unemployment among young graduates with professional and tertiary certificates, particularly in urban areas (Table 1.16). The assumption that skills mismatches are one of the dominant factors contributing to this situation can be substantiated by the responses of Viet Nam's employees—when asked if their current job matches their field of study or occupational training, only 34.3% agreed and 55.7% stated that they were not sufficiently trained (GSO 2017).

Table 1.16: Youth Unemployment Rate, by Level of Education or Training

(%)

Level of Training	Whole Country	Male	Female	Urban	Rural
Total	**11.26**	**10.22**	**12.17**	**11.14**	**11.38**
Short-term VET	2.93	3.57	0.35	2.70	3.10
Mid-term vocational/ professional training	11.59	9.40	13.55	9.19	13.07
Colleges	11.82	9.88	13.20	11.75	11.87
University and higher	13.83	16.81	12.00	13.99	13.60

VET = vocational education and training.
Source: Ministry of Planning and Investment, General Statistics Office. 2019. *Report on Labor Force Survey (Quarter 1, 2018)*. Ha Noi.

20. **Lack of innovation and research and development capacity.** The World Bank's Knowledge Economy Index represents a country's preparedness to compete in the knowledge economy. Table 1.17 shows that Viet Nam ranks 104th out of 144 countries. On the Global Competitiveness Index, Viet Nam ranked 77th out of 140 countries in innovation in 2016 (World Economic Forum 2018). The country's ability to compete in the knowledge economy is dependent on (i) an efficient innovation system comprising firms, research centers, universities, think tanks, consultants, and other organizations that can tap into the growing stock of global knowledge, adapt it to local needs, and create new technological solutions; (ii) an educated and appropriately trained population that is capable of creating, sharing, and using knowledge; and (iii) a modern and accessible information and communication technology infrastructure that serves to facilitate the effective communication,

dissemination, and processing of information. On the 2016 Global Competitiveness Index, Viet Nam ranked 106th of 138 on availability of latest technology and 91st on mobile-broadband subscriptions per 100 people.

Table 1.17: Knowledge Economy Index, 2015

Country or Territory	2015 Rank	2012 Rank	2000 Rank
Sweden	1	1	1
United States	14	12	4
Japan	24	22	17
Singapore	25	23	20
Korea, Rep. of	31	29	24
Malaysia	51	48	45
Thailand	71	66	60
PRC	92	84	91
Philippines	101	92	77
Sri Lanka	109	101	87
Viet Nam	**113**	**104**	**113**
Indonesia	117	108	105
India	119	110	104
Lao PDR	142	131	129
Cambodia	143	132	116

Lao PDR = Lao People's Democratic Republic, PRC = People's Republic of China.
Source: World Bank. 2019. Knowledge Economy Index. Washington, DC.

21. The Organisation for Economic Co-operation and Development (OECD) and the World Bank (2014) found that Viet Nam's science, technology, and innovation capabilities are weak and the national innovation system is in a nascent, fragmented state. In 2016, the Global Competitiveness Index of the World Economic Forum (2016) ranked Viet Nam 98th out of 138 countries in the quality of scientific research institutions. Research and development (R&D) is still a peripheral activity in both the business and the public sectors. Increased competition in globalizing markets makes it more important than ever to invest early in advanced technological capabilities, including R&D. Stronger innovation capabilities are essential for enterprises to position themselves better in global value chains. The 2016 Global Competitiveness Report found that Viet Nam's technological readiness remains low (ranked 92nd) and that businesses are especially slow in adopting the latest technologies (106th), thus forfeiting significant productivity gains through technological transfer (World Economic Forum 2016).

22. Table 1.18 shows that Viet Nam devotes relatively limited resources to R&D; Table 1.19 shows little innovation and less R&D in Viet Nam's business sector; and Table 1.20 shows that Viet Nam has few patent applications. The 2016 Global Competitiveness Report ranked Viet Nam 95th out of 138 countries when comparing the percentage of patent applications per million population (World Economic Forum 2016).

Table 1.18: Research and Development Expenditure as a Percentage of Gross Domestic Product and Researchers per 1 Million Inhabitants, 2011

Country or Territory	Researchers (FTE) per Million Inhabitants	R&D Expenditure as a % of GDP
Singapore	6,505	2.2
Korea, Rep. of	5,804	4.03
Japan	5,137	3.39
Malaysia	1,643	1.07
PRC	963	1.84
Thailand	332	0.25
India	160	0.81
Viet Nam	**113**	**0.19**
Sri Lanka	103	0.16
Indonesia	90	0.08
Philippines	78	0.11
Cambodia	18	0.05
Lao PDR	16	0.04

FTE = full-time equivalent, GDP = gross domestic product, Lao PDR = Lao People's Democratic Republic, PRC = People's Republic of China, R&D = research and development.
Source: UNESCO Institute for Statistics. Gross Domestic Expenditure on R&D (GERD). http://data.uis.unesco.org/index.aspx?queryid=81 (accessed 29 May 2017).

Table 1.19: Full-Time Equivalent Researchers by Employment Sector, 2011
(Per researcher [FTE], constant PPP $)

Country or Territory	Business Sector	Higher Education Sector	Government	Private Nonprofit
Cambodia	15.7	12.5	50.7	21.2
PRC	62.1	18.9	19.0	–
India	38.7	11.5	45.6	4.2
Indonesia	35.7	29.6	34.8	–
Japan	74.8	19.2	4.9	1.1
Korea, Rep. of	77.4	14.1	7.3	1.2
Lao PDR	29.9	34.5	35.6	–
Malaysia	11.5	80.8	7.7	–
Philippines	39.0	31.8	28.4	0.8
Singapore	51.7	42.9	5.4	–
Sri Lanka	31.7	27.1	41.0	0.2
Thailand	29.6	54.5	15.7	0.2
Viet Nam	**10.4**	**32.4**	**56.5**	**0.7**

– = data not available, FTE = full-time equivalent, Lao PDR = Lao People's Democratic Republic, PPP = purchasing power parity, PRC = People's Republic of China.
Source: UNESCO Institute for Statistics. Gross Domestic Expenditure on R&D (GERD). http://data.uis.unesco.org/index.aspx?queryid=81 (accessed 29 May 2017).

Table 1.20: Number of Patent Applications, 2013

	Number of Applications
PRC	825,136
Korea, Rep. of	204,589
India	43,031
Singapore	9,722
Malaysia	7,205
Thailand	7,404
Indonesia	7,450
Viet Nam	**3,995**
Philippines	3,285
Cambodia	75

PRC = People's Republic of China.
Source: World Intellectual Property Organization. 2014. *World Intellectual Property Indicators.* Geneva.

23. The OECD believes that human resources are the key to innovation. A nation's innovation capacity depends crucially on the quality of education and training for scientists, technologists, and a wide range of professionals, and on the inclusiveness of the education system. The OECD contends that increasing the quantity and improving the quality of human resources are necessary, particularly at the tertiary and secondary vocational levels. Funding of tertiary education has been insufficient to cope with the increase in technical and research students. Further, the skills supplied through formal education and training are often out-of-date or too theoretical and do not meet labor market demands.

24. **Conclusion.** To expand productive employment, the United Nations Development Programme and Viet Nam Academy of Social Sciences (UNDP and VASS 2016) summarize what needs to occur in Viet Nam's labor market: continue to maintain macroeconomic stability while increasing economic efficiency and enhancing connectivity and technological readiness as well as nurturing innovation.

B. Social Development Context

1. Background

25. Inclusive economic growth requires not only high sustainable growth but also ensuring that all members of society participate in and benefit from growth and that adequate protection has been provided for the poor and vulnerable. Economic growth in Viet Nam has been coupled with impressive progress in alleviating poverty and improving equity over recent years.

26. The Social Protection Index (SPI) of the Asian Development Bank (ADB) summarizes the extent of social protection in Asia and Pacific countries, providing a comprehensive measure of social protection (Table 1.21). On this index, Viet Nam is 5th behind Malaysia in terms of social protection while its expenditure as a percentage of GDP is robust.

Table 1.21: ADB Social Protection Index for Selected Countries, 2012

	Social Protection Index, Overall	Social Protection Index for Social Insurance	Total Social Protection Expenditure, as % of GDP
Cambodia	1.2	0.3	1.2
India	1.3	0.5	1.6
Indonesia	1.2	0.4	1.2
Japan	11.7	10.6	22.1
Korea, Rep. of	5.1	4.0	7.5
Malaysia	4.2	3.7	3.8
Philippines	2.2	1.8	2.6
PRC	4.3	3.7	6.5
Singapore	6.3	4.4	4.7
Sri Lanka	2.7	2.3	2.6
Thailand	2.9	1.9	4.4
Viet Nam	**4.0**	**3.3**	**5.0**

ADB = Asian Development Bank, GDP = gross domestic product, PRC = People's Republic of China.
Source: ADB. Social Protection Indicator. http://spi.adb.org/spidmz/index.jsp (Online query on 29 June 2017).

27. Figure 1.9 shows Viet Nam's progress on the UNDP's Human Development Index (HDI) compared with several countries in the region. On this index, Viet Nam ranks 115th out of 188 in the medium human development range of countries. Viet Nam made very good progress in terms of HDI before the global financial crisis of 2008 but its relative progress has been weaker, and its rate of improvement has slowed as has been the case for most comparator countries (UNDP and VASS 2016).

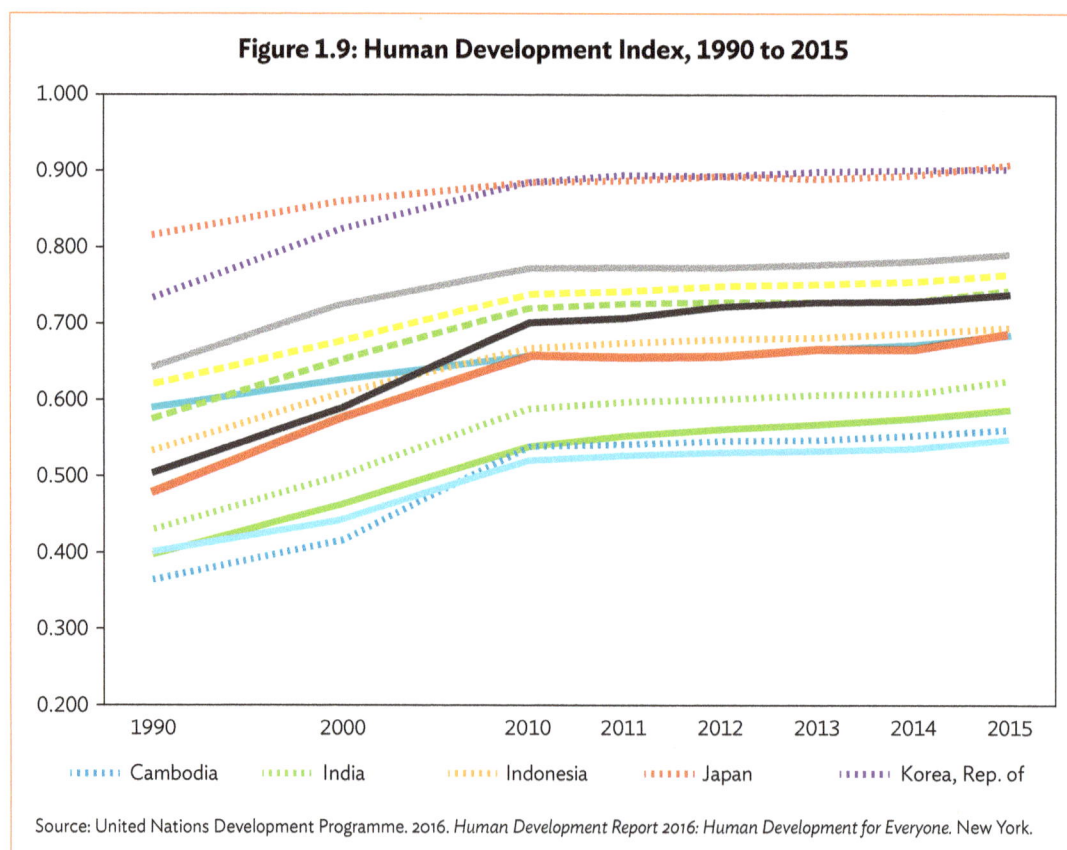

Figure 1.9: Human Development Index, 1990 to 2015

Legend: Cambodia, India, Indonesia, Japan, Korea, Rep. of

Source: United Nations Development Programme. 2016. *Human Development Report 2016: Human Development for Everyone.* New York.

2. Millennium Development Goals

28. Viet Nam has made impressive progress toward achieving the Millennium Development Goals (MDGs)(Table 1.22).[7] It has successfully achieved the MDG targets for (i) eradication of extreme poverty and hunger, (ii) attaining universal primary education, (iii) promotion of gender equality in education, (iv) reduction in child mortality rate, (v) improving maternal health, and (vi) reduction in the HIV/AIDS prevalence rate (UNDP 2015).

Table 1.22: Viet Nam's Progress to Meeting the Millennium Development Goals

Goal	Target	Progress
Goal 1: Eradicate extreme poverty and hunger	• Halve the proportion of people whose income is less than $1.25 a day • Achieve full and productive employment and decent work for all • Halve the proportion of people who suffer from hunger	**Achieved** • Population below $1.25 (PPP) per day (1993 = 63.7% and 2012 = 17.2%) • Employment-to-population ratio (1996 = 74.5% and 2014 = 76.1%) • Population undernourished (1991 = 45.6% and 2013 = 12.9%)
Goal 2: Achieve universal primary education	• All children complete a full course of primary schooling	**Achieved** • In 2013, the completion rate for primary was 97.5% • In SY2014/15, the NER in primary was 99.0%
Goal 3: Promote gender equality and empower women	• Eliminate gender disparity in primary and secondary education	**Achieved** • In SY2012/13, the ratio of girls to boys in primary was 91.3%, in lower secondary it was 94.3%, and in upper secondary it was 113.7% (sex ratio at birth was 93 to 100 in 2000 and 88 to 100 in 2013)
Goal 4: Reduce child mortality	• Reduce by two-thirds the under-five mortality rate	**Nearly Achieved** • Children under-five mortality rate per 1,000 live births (1990 = 50.6 and 2014 = 22.4) (reduced by 53%)
Goal 5: Improve maternal health	• Reduce by three quarters the maternal mortality ratio • Achieve universal access to reproductive health	**Achieved** • Maternal mortality ratio per 100,000 live births (1990 = 233 and 2014 = 60) • In 2014, 75.7% of married women 15–49 years old report using some contraceptive method
Goal 6: Combat HIV/AIDS, malaria, and other diseases	• Have halted and begun to reverse the spread of HIV/AIDS • Achieve universal access to treatment for HIV/AIDS for all those who need it • Have halted and begun to reverse the incidence of malaria and other major diseases	**Partially Achieved** • The number of new HIV cases has decreased from 13,815 in 2010 to 10,570 in 2014 and HIV prevalence is under 0.3% of the population • Antiretroviral therapy coverage for 67.6% of those eligible with 90,428 individuals receiving therapy by the end of 2014 (34 times the figure in 2005) • In 2014, nationwide there were 6 reported deaths from malaria • The number of new cases of tuberculosis has declined from 375/100,000 (2000) to 209/100,000 (2014)

Continued on next page

---

[7]   The MDGs are eight international development goals that were established following the Millennium Summit of the United Nations in 2000, following the adoption of the United Nations Millennium Declaration. Viet Nam committed to achieve the MDGs by 2015.

Table 1.22 continued

Goal	Target	Progress
Goal 7: Ensure environmental sustainability	• Integrate the principles of sustainable development into country policies and programs • Reverse the loss of environmental resources, achieving a significant reduction in the rate of loss • Halve the proportion of the population without sustainable access to safe drinking water and basic sanitation • Achieve a significant improvement in the lives of slum dwellers	**Partially Achieved** • Environmental sustainability goals contained in the Strategy for Socioeconomic Development (2011–2020) • Specialized policies and programs focusing on environmental issues (Strategic Orientation for Sustainable Development [2004], the Sustainable Development Strategy for 2011–2020, the National Environmental Protection Strategy until 2012, and the National Strategy for Green Growth 2011–2020) • Funding for environmental protection targeted at least 1% of the total budget • Proportion of the rural population using clean drinking water (2005 = 62% and 2013 = 82.5%) • Proportion of the rural population using hygienic latrines (60%); 87% of targeted school; 92% of health centers • Slum population as percentage of urban (1990 = 60.5% and 2009 = 35.2%)
Goal 8: Develop a global partnership for development	• Develop further an open, rule-based, predictable, nondiscriminatory trading and financial system • Deal comprehensively with developing countries' debt • In cooperation with pharmaceutical companies, provide access to affordable essential drugs • In cooperation with the private sector, make available the benefits of new technologies, especially information and communications	**Partially Achieved** • By 2014, Viet Nam has signed and participated in 9 trade agreements, (6 between ASEAN countries and 3 bilateral); by 2015, signed Free Trade Agreement with the Republic of Korea and negotiation for several other free trade agreements • Between 1990 and 2015 exports grew by 620% and imports by 530% • ODA accounts for 11.4% of total social investment • Public debt including public and publicly guaranteed debt almost doubled since 2000, at around 55% of GDP in 2014 with increases accounted for largely by the increase in domestic debt • Medical expenditure per capita increasing from $6.00 in 2001 to $19.77 in 2009 but the price of drugs a concern • Mobile-cellular subscriptions per 100 inhabitants (1990 = 0 and 2012 = 131) • Internet users per 100 inhabitants (1990 = 0 and 2013 = 43.9)

ASEAN = Association of Southeast Asian Nations, GDP = gross domestic product, NER = net enrollment rate, ODA = official development assistance, PPP = purchasing power parity, SY = school year.
Source: United Nations Development Programme. 2015. *Country Report: 15 Years Achieving the Viet Nam Millennium Development Goals.* New York.

3. Gender Equity

29. Compared with other countries in the region, Viet Nam has a relatively good gender equity performance (see Gender Inequality Index [GII] in Table 1.23).[8] These positive results stem in part from specific measures to promote gender equality which were included in the government's development goals and then incorporated into its Socio-Economic Development Plan (SEDP) 2006–2010, Viet Nam's National Laws on Gender Equality, Domestic Violence Prevention and Control, and the National Program on Gender Equality, which were endorsed in 2006, 2007, and 2011, respectively. A new draft National Strategy on Gender Equality 2011–2020 aims to improve the implementation of these laws.[9] Viet Nam has also ratified the Universal Declaration of Human Rights, and the Convention on the Elimination of All Forms of Discrimination against Women. The 1992 Constitution and the 2013 Amended Constitution guarantee women equal rights in all spheres, including the family, and bans discrimination against women.[10]

Table 1.23: Comparison of Performance Indicators for Women in Viet Nam and in Selected Countries

Country	Gender Inequality Index		Maternal Mortality Ratio (deaths per 100,000 live births)	Adolescent Birth Rate (births per 1,000 women aged 15–19 years)	Share of Seats in Parliament (% held by women)	Population with At Least Some Secondary Education (% of ages 25 and older)		Labor Force Participation Rate (% of ages 15 and older)	
	Value	Rank				Female	Male	Female	Male
	2014	2014	2013	2010/2015	2014	2005–2014	2005–2014	2013	2013
Korea, Rep. of	0.125	23	27	2.2	16.3	77.0	89.1	50.1	72.1
Malaysia	0.209	42	29	5.7	14.2	65.1	71.3	44.4	75.5
PRC	0.191	40	32	8.6	23.6	58.7	71.9	63.9	78.3
Thailand	0.380	76	26	41.0	6.1	35.7	40.8	64.3	80.7
Indonesia	0.494	110	190	48.3	17.1	39.9	49.2	51.4	84.2
Philippines	0.420	89	120	46.8	27.1	65.9	63.7	51.1	79.7
Viet Nam	**0.308**	**60**	**49**	**29.0**	**24.3**	**59.4**	**71.2**	**73.0**	**82.2**
India	0.563	130	190	32.8	12.2	27.0	56.6	27.0	79.9
Lao PDR	...	...	...	65.0	25.0	22.9	37.0	76.3	79.1
Medium human developed countries	0.506	...	168	43.4	18.8	34.8	55.3	37.5	79.8
World	**0.449**	...	210	47.4	21.8	54.5	65.4	50.3	76.7

... = data not available or not applicable, PRC = People's Republic of China, Lao PDR = Lao People's Democratic Republic.
Source: United Nations Development Programme and Viet Nam Academy of Social Sciences. 2016. *Growth that Works for All: Viet Nam Human Development Report 2015 on Inclusive Growth*. Ha Noi.

---

[8]   The GII in UNDP's global Human Development Report measures inequality in achievement between women and men in three dimensions: reproductive health, empowerment, and labor market participation.

[9]   Socialist Republic of Viet Nam, Government Portal. National Strategy on Gender Equality for the 2011–2020 period. http://www.chinhphu.vn/portal/page/portal/English/strategies/strategiesdetails?categoryId=30&articleId=10050924.

[10] Government of Viet Nam. Socio-Economic Development Strategy 2011–2020 Approved by the Eleventh Congress of Viet Nam Communist Party. Ha Noi.

30. However, significant challenges remain, such as low levels of women's participation in public decision-making at local, regional, and national levels; a highly gender-segregated labor market in which women are paid less than men; increased domestic violence against women; an increasing spread of HIV/AIDS among women; rising male sex ratios at birth; and weak implementation of gender equity laws and policies at all levels with little consequence for failure to meet the stated targets (UNDP and VASS 2016). These challenges reflect a deeply rooted cultural social bias against females, particularly in rural areas. Such gender discrimination favors boys over girls, undervalues girls' education and economic potential, places the burden of unpaid housework and childcare disproportionately on women and girls, and increases the vulnerability of females to exploitation. In addition, women are forced out of public service at 55 years compared with 60 years for men, as a result of mandatory retirement laws. This deprives Viet Nam of its most senior and experienced female leaders at the peak of their careers and reduces the likelihood of promotion and training opportunities as women advance in age. Leadership statistics show that only 5% of the presidents of large companies and only under 10% of the vice presidents are women (UNDP and VASS 2016). The fact that some Vietnamese women as well as men are resistant to women taking up leadership roles reflects the strength of traditional gender norms and attitudes held by both sexes.[11]

31. **Labor force participation.** Viet Nam's labor force is generally young and unskilled: over 48% of the labor force is composed of those in the age group of 20–39 years, and only 16% of the labor force has received technical training. Of those employed as unskilled workers, 68% are women and 57% are men (GSO 2017). Men tend to be more educated or skilled; 20% of economically active men compared with 15% of economically active women have undertaken vocational training, and around 5% of men compared with 4% of women have graduated from university (UNDP 2015). Women work mostly in agriculture (50%), followed by services (33%), then industry (17%) where they are commonly employed on an informal or casual basis as a cheap and flexible labor source. In addition, around 54% of female workers are unpaid family workers, often working long hours in informal household businesses with few written contracts and little access to public services, training, or promotion. On average, women earn 25% less than men for the same type of work, with gaps decreasing with level of education and training completed, and the type of education and employment received (UNDP and VASS 2016).

32. **Gender-based violence.** Domestic violence against women is pervasive in Viet Nam. A comprehensive study conducted by the United Nations Population Fund and the Viet Nam's Women Union in 2010 found that among nearly 5,000 women between the ages of 18 and 60, 58% had experienced some form of violence in the hands of an intimate partner at some time in their lives. Since the Domestic Violence Law went into force in 2008, at least two studies have found that the rate of physical violence has not decreased, that both the beneficiaries of the law and those responsible for enforcing it know little about it, and that few women are willing to come forward and confront their abusers. Furthermore, almost 66% of women interviewed think it acceptable for men to beat women because of entrenched gender norms, which consider women subservient to men. Viet Nam's support systems for abuse survivors are very limited, almost always temporary, and often lack any mental health component to help survivors and their families cope with trauma (UNDP and VASS 2016).

33. **HIV/AIDS.** Prevalence of HIV varies considerably by age, sex, sexual orientation or gender identity, occupational group, and location. High-risk groups are people who inject drugs, sex workers, and men who have sex with men. In Viet Nam, the 20–39 age group accounts for 80% of total cases (UNDP

---

[11]   UN Women: Viet Nam Fact Sheet. http://asiapacific.unwomen.org/es/countries/vietnam (accessed 15 July 2017).

2015). Although HIV infection primarily occurs among Vietnamese men (over 73% in 2009), the proportion of infected women has increased. Currently, an estimated 243,000 people in Viet Nam are living with HIV/AIDS of whom 25% are women (UNDP 2015). Some women are infected through injecting drugs and/or sex work, however significant numbers are contracting the disease through sex with infected partners or husbands. Emerging evidence indicates the following link between gender-based violence, unprotected sex, and HIV infection. Sexual violence against girls and women, including within marriage, places women at higher risk of HIV infection not only because forced sex is almost always unprotected sex, but also because violent sex can result in abrasions which facilitate HIV transmission. Moreover, physical and emotional abuse, or fear of it, undermines women's ability to negotiate safer sex with their regular partners. Furthermore, cultural norms about gender and sexuality have given rise to stigma and discrimination within the community against groups most at risk, making it harder for those who become infected to seek information or services for prevention or care and treatment (UNDP 2015).

34. **Sex ratio at birth.** Traditional gender norms including strong son-preference in Viet Nam, combined with access to sex-selective technologies to help with prenatal sex identification and selection, have resulted in the rapid rise in sex ratio at birth. In 1979 and 1989, the ratio was in the normal range of 105–106. Since around 2005 it has risen rapidly, reaching nearly 114 in 2013, placing Viet Nam along with India and the PRC among the countries with the highest sex ratios at birth (World Bank and the Ministry of Planning and Investment 2016). The United Nations Population Fund predicts a 10% surplus of men in 2035 which will likely result in increased demand for sex work, marriage migration, and trafficking of women and girls (UNDP 2015). Disadvantaged groups especially vulnerable to exploitation in such trades currently and in the future, include female domestic migrants and females with lower levels of education.

35. **Formal and nonformal education.** While Viet Nam has good gender parity in education, gender disparities persist in educational outcomes in the rural and mountainous areas of the northwest region, which has the highest levels of poverty. Distance to schools, language of instruction, persistent gender stereotypes, and the lack of gender-sensitive[12] and locally relevant curricula, teaching methods, and qualified teachers, are key concerns. In addition, there is a mismatch between vocational education training, especially for women, and labor market demands (UNDP and VASS 2016).

36. Key issues at the tertiary level include gender imbalances in academic staff and types of study. There are no female leaders as heads of academic institutes, only 20% of appointed professors and associate professors are women, and women earn about half of their male colleagues. Although women in Viet Nam hold half of the bachelor's degrees, only 11% of those with a doctorate or master's degree are women.

37. With regard to career support in the field of science, a recent study on Vietnamese grantees, funded by the International Foundation for Science, found the following differences between men and women scientists. Priorities for women scientists compared with men included (i) support to publish scientific articles (65% versus 47%); (ii) special support programs to women scientists (61% versus 12%); (iii) support to attend scientific conferences (57% versus 69%); (iv) provision of access to up-to-date scientific journal articles (52% versus 67%); (v) support to attend scientific workshops (43% versus 51%); (vi) support to visit a foreign research institution (39% versus 67%); and (vii) support to organize regional networks of scientists (39% versus 24%) (IFS 2009). The study concluded that the International Foundation for Science's female grantees earned less income from

---

[12]   Gender sensitive means that it is free of gender bias and encourages girls to explore different options, including careers in nontraditional and technical areas.

their scientific work, had less research funding, spent less time abroad in training, published less, and were not promoted as often as men. This is not a reflection of women's talent but rather of a scientific and sociocultural system that does not fully take advantage of the capacity of women scientists (Government of Viet Nam 2016). Because science and technology is a key potential growth area for Viet Nam to increase competitiveness regionally and globally, changing discriminatory attitudes to close gender gaps in this arena is necessary to maximize contributions from both sexes.

38. **Gender equality national mechanisms.** A Gender Equality Department in the Ministry of Labour–Invalids and Social Affairs (MOLISA) was established in 2008 to drive gender equality efforts, implement Viet Nam's gender equality laws and the draft National Strategy on Gender Equality and National Program on Gender Equality, and report on the Convention on the Elimination of All Forms of Discrimination against Women. A United Nations (UN)–Government Joint Program on gender equality also serves as an important mechanism to help coordinate government and donor activity in support of gender equality and a network of nongovernment organizations' work in research, training, and advocacy, which feeds into policy discussions. [13]

39. Key social protection strategies and policy frameworks are also in place, including the new National Targeted Program on Poverty Reduction, Resolution No. 80/NQ-CP on Sustainable Poverty Reduction (2011–2020), and a new Master Plan on Social Protection, which together have considerable potential to promote more gender-sensitive social protection interventions. In addition, Viet Nam endorsed a Disability Law in 2010 and ratified the UN Convention on the Rights of Persons with Disabilities in 2014. It is also revising the 2004 Law on Protection, Care and Education of Children and has issued various decrees and interministerial circulars that support inclusive education (UNICEF Viet Nam 2015).

40. However, Viet Nam's national social protection system plays, at best, a limited role in addressing gender risks and vulnerabilities, and there is an urgent need to strengthen the social protection framework (Government of Viet Nam 2016a).

4. Social Development Challenges and Opportunities

41. Although Viet Nam has avoided the large increases in inequality as in other fast-growing countries, the differences between rich and poor are still significant. The government's latest socioeconomic development plan indicates that groups of people still live difficult lives and the poverty gaps between regions and groups of citizens are still large.[14] Further, the plan is concerned that poverty reduction results are not sustainable and the possibility of relapsing into poverty is high.

42. **The global Sustainable Development Goals**. The Sustainable Development Goals (SDGs) were agreed at the UN headquarters in New York on 25 September 2015, with Viet Nam as a signatory (Viet Nam News 2015). There are 17 goals which replace and expand on the MDGs.[15] Over the next 15 years, countries are to mobilize efforts to end all forms of poverty, fight inequality, and tackle climate change, while ensuring that no one is left behind. The new goals are unique in that they call for action by all countries—poor, rich, and middle income—to promote prosperity while protecting the

---

[13]   Government of Viet Nam. Socio-Economic Development Strategy 2011–2020 Approved by the Eleventh Congress of Viet Nam Communist Party. Ha Noi.

[14]   Footnote 13.

[15]   United Nations Department of Economic and Social Affairs. Sustainable Development Knowledge Platform. Sustainable Development Goals. https://sustainabledevelopment.un.org/?menu=1300.

planet. They recognize that ending poverty must go hand in hand with strategies that build economic growth and address a range of social needs including education, health, social protection, and job opportunities, while tackling climate change and environmental protection.[16]

43. **Ethnic minority groups**. Viet Nam has 54 ethnic groups. The ethnic majority Kinh comprise just under 86% of the population, while 53 ethnic minorities account for the rest of the populace. Almost one-fifth of people who live in Viet Nam's rural areas belong to ethnic minority groups. Most of these groups depend primarily on subsistence agriculture for their livelihood and inhabit mountainous, coastal, and remote areas with complex topographies, difficult transportation and communication systems, and harsh climates. While members of ethnic minorities have experienced gains in welfare since the early 1990s, they face a growing gap relative to majority of the population (World Bank and the Ministry of Planning and Investment 2016). With 15% of the population, they now make up half of the poor and, in recent years, progress pertaining to poverty reduction, child mortality, and nutrition have stalled for ethnic minorities. Many ethnic minority citizens remain largely disconnected from the country's larger economic success. Members of ethnic minority groups are more likely to have poor socioeconomic outcomes compared with the Kinh—more poverty, less access to health facilities and formal financial services, lower market access, lower wages, and less schooling and educational resources, especially for females since the gaps between men and women tend to be larger in ethnic minority communities (Dang 2009).

44. Lacking the capability and self-confidence in using the Vietnamese language, ethnic minorities encounter problems accessing education, communicating with others, and attaining high salaried jobs. Furthermore, the custom of early marriage among ethnic minorities and having many children contributes to their prevailing poverty.

45. **Rural to urban migration**. With the rapid economic growth in Viet Nam, more than a third of the population lives in cities or peri-urban areas and this is expected to rise to 50% by 2050. Moreover, these areas account for a major part of the gross domestic product (GDP). Urbanization has helped drive economic growth by supplying sources of labor. The strong pattern of migration from rural to urban areas is expected to grow, which is normal and healthy in growing economies. However, it can put pressure on urban housing, infrastructure, services, and social-welfare systems if not carefully planned and managed, and lead to new forms of multidimensional poverty. In addition, basic infrastructure, such as schools and health care, may not be available in peri-urban areas since development in these areas may be less controlled. Deprivation can develop in terms of basic nonmonetary factors, such as health and education and access to basic services (UNDP 2015).

46. Data from the General Statistics Office (GSO) (2013) indicate that net migration rate in the Red River Delta area dropped slightly in 2013 (–0.3%). In the same year, the Southeast had the highest net migration rate at 8.3% and the largest number of in-migrants of about 243,000 people, which is equivalent to 45% of total in-migrants, suggesting that job opportunity was the most important factor in decisions to migrate to other parts of the country. The Central Highlands also had a positive net migration rate. However, it should be noted that these data include those who have completed upper secondary education (USE) and are moving on to tertiary education in more urban areas. The data show that about two-thirds of migrants have completed lower secondary level or beyond.

47. More than 5 million Vietnamese do not have permanent registration where they live (World Bank and the Ministry of Planning and Investment 2016). Viet Nam's household registration system,

---

[16]   United Nations. Sustainable Development Goals. http://www.un.org/sustainabledevelopment (accessed 13 July 2017).

although loosely implemented with respect to employment, restricts access to both education and basic services for migrants (UNDP and VASS 2016).

48. Migrant households have fewer assets, live in worse housing conditions in areas less well served by public schools (Cameron 2012). Migrant adults have lower educational levels than those in urban "native" households; and educational expenditure and achievement were lower for children from migrant households than for urban natives. Various studies have reported different rates of school attendance for children from domestic migrant families. The Urban Poverty Survey in 2009 indicated that only 35% of children from poor migrant families enrolled in schools where 88% of children from poor urban households enrolled (Thanh, Anh, and Phuong 2013). Another study by UNDP and VASS (2016) found that 64.6% of migrant students attended public schools, compared with 82.1% among permanent residents. A third study by the GSO (2012) found 82.7% of migrant children attending a public school compared with 95.7% of permanent residents. Both studies clearly show that migrant children have difficulty accessing education because of the registration system.

49. **Persons with a disability.** There is a clear relationship between poverty and disability. It was indicated in 2006 that poverty rates among households that have a person with disability are 20% higher than those without one (UNDP and VASS 2016). Disability affects women more than men. Viet Nam's policies for people with disabilities are highly inclusive but have substantial shortcomings in implementing a broad agenda (World Bank and the Ministry of Planning and Investment 2016). According to the 2009 Viet Nam Population Census, there are around 6.1 million people with disabilities (including 385,000 have severe disabilities). The assessment by the National Assembly Committee on Social Affairs in 2008 reported that only 36.8% of children with disabilities ever attended primary or secondary schools. According to the Ministry of Education and Training, in SY2017/18,   only 17,034 students with a disability attended lower secondary education (LSE) which is 0.3% of the student population at this level, and 1,520 or 0.1% of students at USE.[17] The data reveal that education opportunities for disabled people are still very limited. While the government has provided financial support programs to the disabled, education opportunities remain restricted for youth with a disability, leading to few job opportunities and limiting integration in the community. Providing such basic opportunities is crucial to enable the youth to participate in society and engendering attitudes of inclusion among others (World Bank and the Ministry of Planning and Investment 2016).

50. **Multidimensional poverty reduction**. Viet Nam is experiencing a significant policy shift in relation to sustainable poverty reduction and the focus on education as one of the main five dimensions. Under the direction of Resolution No. 80 and Resolution No. 76, the National Assembly and Central Poverty Reduction Steering Committee is encouraging line ministries to look at poverty in a concerted and multidimensional way. Better and more effective measurement and targeting of poverty is anticipated with the evolution of this approach and experience from other middle-income countries such as Mexico, Colombia, Brazil, and Malaysia. This methodology has been integrated into the design of a new poverty survey that was applied by the Ministry of Labour–Invalids and Social Affairs (MOLISA) and the GSO in 2015.[18]

---

[17] Government of Viet Nam. Department of Planning and Finance, Ministry of Education and Training.

[18] The Multidimensional Poverty Index complements monetary measures of poverty by considering overlapping deprivations suffered by people at the same time. The index shows the number of people who are multidimensionally poor and the number of deprivations with which poor households typically contend with. It can be deconstructed by region, ethnicity, and other groupings as well as by dimension (UNDP).

51. In many ways this revolutionary move away from the traditional income measurement will have far-reaching effects on the coordination and concerted approaches and interventions of line ministries. The MOLISA Poverty Reduction Coordinating Office is leading this move with support from the Party, the National Assembly, and the government. The Ministry of Education and Training (MOET) is part of this development and the Department of Student Affairs has been involved in the development of indicators (attendance at primary school and lower secondary school) for the education dimension.

52. Policy makers, researchers, and statistical sections need to understand this policy shift in a comprehensive way to tailor support to poor and near poor, ethnic minority, disadvantaged, and migrant students/families as well as mainstream groups. The development of broader and more inclusive indicators and strategic restructuring of policy responses are key to MOET inputs into this transition. The transition to middle-income country status has "moved the goal posts" in relation to attitudes to poverty and targeted responses by line ministries (Ross 2015). Figure 1.10 attempts to capture the impact of selected "multidimensional" elements of the disadvantaged in Viet Nam.

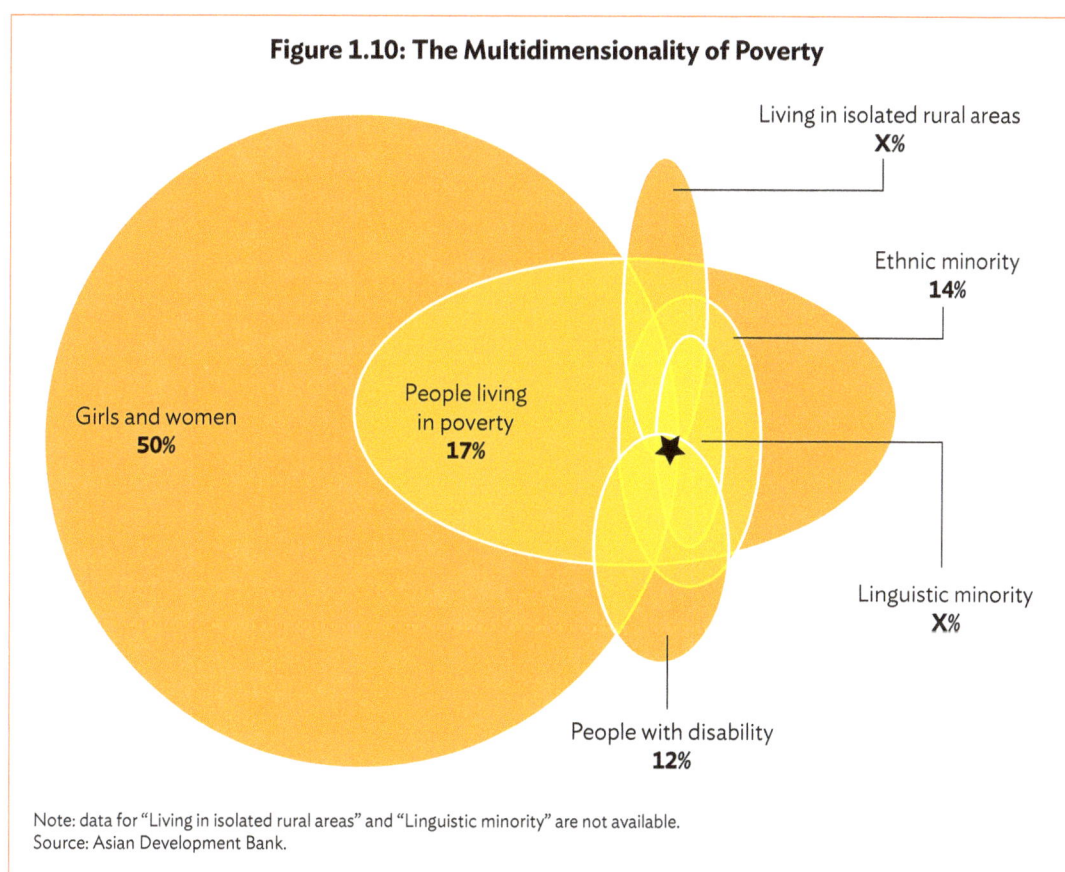

Figure 1.10: The Multidimensionality of Poverty

Living in isolated rural areas
X%

Ethnic minority
14%

Girls and women
50%

People living
in poverty
17%

Linguistic minority
X%

People with disability
12%

Note: data for "Living in isolated rural areas" and "Linguistic minority" are not available.
Source: Asian Development Bank.

53. Table 1.24 reveals major disparities among different neighboring developing countries. Between 2010 and 2012, multidimensional poverty waned overall in Viet Nam. Regional Multidimensional Poverty Index levels vary considerably, with the Mekong River Delta having the highest proportion of multidimensionally poor households at 41.6%. In contrast, the Red River Delta had the lowest proportion of multidimensionally poor households at 5.7%. There are major variations across ethnicity, income groups, and rural and urban areas.

Table 1.24: Multidimensional Poverty Index, Selected Developing Countries

Country	Population in Multidimensional Poverty			Population Near Poverty	Population in Severe Poverty	Population Living Below Income Poverty Line (%)	
	Index Value	Headcount (%)	Intensity (%)	(%)	(%)	National poverty line 2004–2014	PPP $1.25 a day 2002–2012
Cambodia	0.211	46.8	45.1	20.4	16.4	17.7	10.1
India	0.282	55.3	51.1	18.2	27.8	21.9	23.6
Indonesia	0.024	5.9	41.3	8.1	1.1	11.3	16.2
Philippines	0.033	6.3	51.9	8.4	4.2	25.2	19.0
Thailand	0.004	1.0	38.8	4.4	0.1	12.6	0.3
Viet Nam	**0.026**	**6.4**	**40.7**	**8.7**	**1.3**	**17.2**	**2.4**

PPP = purchasing power parity.
Source: United Nations Development Programme and Viet Nam Academy of Social Sciences. 2016. *Growth that Works for All: Viet Nam Human Development Report 2015 on Inclusive Growth.* Ha Noi.

54. The single biggest disadvantaged group in Viet Nam consists of women and girls (slightly under 50% of the population). However, Figure 1.10 also shows other disadvantaged groups. For example, approximately 17% of the population live in poverty, over half of these female. A combination of being female and being poor means being doubly disadvantaged. "Free education" may not be free to the poor, where both direct and indirect costs can lead to exclusion from education. Add other elements such as being from an ethnic minority and the deprivation is compounded. Thus, for example, a Muong girl with a disability living in a poor, isolated rural area could suffer severely from the overlapping, multiple dimensions of poverty.

55. Various disadvantaged groups warrant special attention from the perspective of multidimensional poverty. This reality has been reflected in the design of recent Asian Development Bank (ADB) education projects in Viet Nam. For example, the ADB-supported Lower Secondary Most Disadvantaged Regions Project and the follow-on Second Lower Secondary Education Project for Most Disadvantaged Areas Project specifically targeted the poorest areas with concentrations of ethnic minority groups, focusing strongly on girls' education because of the significant statistical disparities in educational outcomes between male and female students in those geographic areas. Thus such projects can be seen as "multidimensional." While many issues have yet to be resolved with respect to these groups, they are at least highly visible on the government agenda, and as such are attracting attention and budgetary support—whether directly from the government, or through support from development partners. Other aspects, such as disability, have not yet been fully addressed—especially at secondary level.

56. Viet Nam has achieved significant progress in universal education in the primary level. In 2014, the net enrollment rate (NER) in primary school was 99.0% (MOET 2014). However, the Ministry of Planning and Investment (2013) indicated that the speed of improvement in the education sector has lagged behind national economic growth and a fast-changing society. Inequality in educational access

and quality persists among different ethnic groups and disparate geographic regions, and among children with disabilities, for example. Education reform in teaching and learning and improvement in school facilities are still needed.

C. Contribution of the Education System to Economic and Social Development

57. Learning throughout life is becoming one of the keys to sustainable development, poverty alleviation, and social development. Many education and development policies are based on the assumption that literacy and primary education play a key role in poverty reduction, while secondary and higher education is crucial for economic development in the global knowledge society (Maclean, Jagannathan, and Sarvi 2013). Knowledge has become the heart and soul of development in the 21st century economy. Comparative advantages in national institutional capacities to access, assess, adapt, and adopt knowledge now drive the innovation that leads to productivity gains and economic growth.

58. There is growing international consensus that education, even at the early stage of childhood development, is critical to economic growth and development (Boocock 1995, Cohen and Soto 2007). Cost–benefit studies of high-quality child education programs have consistently found substantial long-term benefits derived over the course of many years and decades. Studies have found that increasing investment in good quality education for child development is one of the most cost-effective strategies for breaking the intergenerational transmission of poverty and improving productivity and social cohesion in the long run. These education programs contribute to strengthening the prospects of children achieving their full potential and enable the country to improve its future competitiveness, overcome the challenges of an aging population, and transition from a middle- to high-income economy (Kin, Young, and Cai 2012). The effects are positive, long-lasting, and largest for the most disadvantaged. Education is especially vital in developing economies where an expansion of the supply of skilled workers allows the economy and industries to modernize, adopt new technologies, attract foreign investment, increase productivity and trade competitiveness, and better respond to new opportunities created by shifting markets. Education also promotes inclusive growth.

59. For individuals with low skill levels, having the opportunity to acquire skills for employability at strategic points throughout their lives is a crucial factor in improving their prospects for gaining employment and securing income, and thus combat poverty and improve the quality of life for themselves and their families (Maclean, Jagannathan, and Sarvi 2013). Many economic development studies have demonstrated significant wage returns to education, with most finding that one additional year of schooling raises an individual's earnings by about 10% (Psacharopoulos and Patrinos 2004). The returns to primary and secondary schooling are particularly high in less developed countries, and secondary education appears particularly important in rapidly growing economies, including those in Asia (Barro and Lee 2010). Many studies have found that completion of secondary education by girls has a large impact on wages, as well as broader impacts such as participation in the formal labor market and nonagriculture sectors (Spohr 2003). Table 1.25 shows that the average monthly wage in Viet Nam increases with the amount of education.

**Table 1.25: Average Monthly Earnings of Wage Earners in Viet Nam
Aged 15 Years and Over, 2018**

Professional and Technical Qualification	Monthly Earning (VND thousand)
No qualification	4,704
Vocation training	5,680
Secondary vocational school	5,297
College	5,838
University and over	7,345

Source: Ministry of Planning and Investment, General Statistics Office. 2018. *Report on Labor Force Survey (Quarter 1, 2018)*. Ha Noi.

D. Education System and Structure in Viet Nam

60. In Viet Nam, two ministries oversee the education sector. The first is the Ministry of Education and Training (MOET), which has responsibility for preprimary, primary, secondary, and higher education. The second is the Ministry of Labour–Invalids and Social Affairs (MOLISA), which has primary responsibility for managing the technical and vocational education and training (TVET) sector with a focus on training students to enter the workforce.

61. MOET is responsible for preprimary programs catering for students from age 1 to 5 years, primary education which provides 5 years of schooling starting at age 6, secondary education, higher education, and continuing education. Preprimary consists of nursery school for 1- and 2-year olds and kindergarten for 3- to 5-year olds. Secondary education is provided at two levels: lower secondary covering grades 6 to 9 and catering for students in the 11 to 14 age group; and upper secondary for grades 10 to 12 with a focus on continuing to higher education. A third level of secondary education is called professional secondary education for grades 10 to 12 or 13 with a focus on TVET. Professional secondary education was transferred from MOET to be under MOLISA effective January 2017.[19]

62. TVET is administered principally by MOLISA, but TVET is provided by various education and training institutions and is still administrated by multiple owners at both central and local levels, including (i) various line ministries such as Ministry of Industry and Trade, Ministry of Agriculture and Rural Development, Ministry of Transport, Ministry of Construction, Ministry of Defense, and Ministry of Culture, Sports and Tourism; (ii) provincial, city, and district governments through their Provincial People's Committees; (iii) enterprises and cooperatives; and (iv) social and economic organizations like the Viet Nam Women's Union and the Viet Nam Labor Federation. The Ministry of Industry and Trade (MOIT), state-owned enterprises, and local governments, also manage training institutions. About half the vocational colleges and 25% of vocational secondary schools are administered at the national level. TVET is provided mostly in schools and training institutions, rather than in the workplace.

63. Higher education consists of colleges providing 3- to 3.5-year programs, and universities that offer undergraduate and postgraduate degrees. These programs are offered in over 428 institutions that range from small highly specialized units to large multicampus institutions. Although still dominated by smaller specialized institutions, the system has become more multidisciplinary with the formation of larger universities in regional centers. Research units and institutes have also been reorganized to help integrate research activities within universities.

---

[19]   Government of Viet Nam. Law No. 74/2014/QH13 on Vocational Education enacted 17 November 2014.

64. Figure 1.11 illustrates the structure of the Viet Nam education system. Within MOLISA, TVET programs are managed through the Directorate of Vocational Education and Training (DVET). The figure also shows the role of nonformal education programs within TVET programs. In addition, MOET provides extensive nonformal education programs through community education centers where out-of-school youth participate in bridging programs that enable them to reenter the formal schooling system or undertake short-term training programs.

Figure 1.11: Structure of the Viet Nam Education System

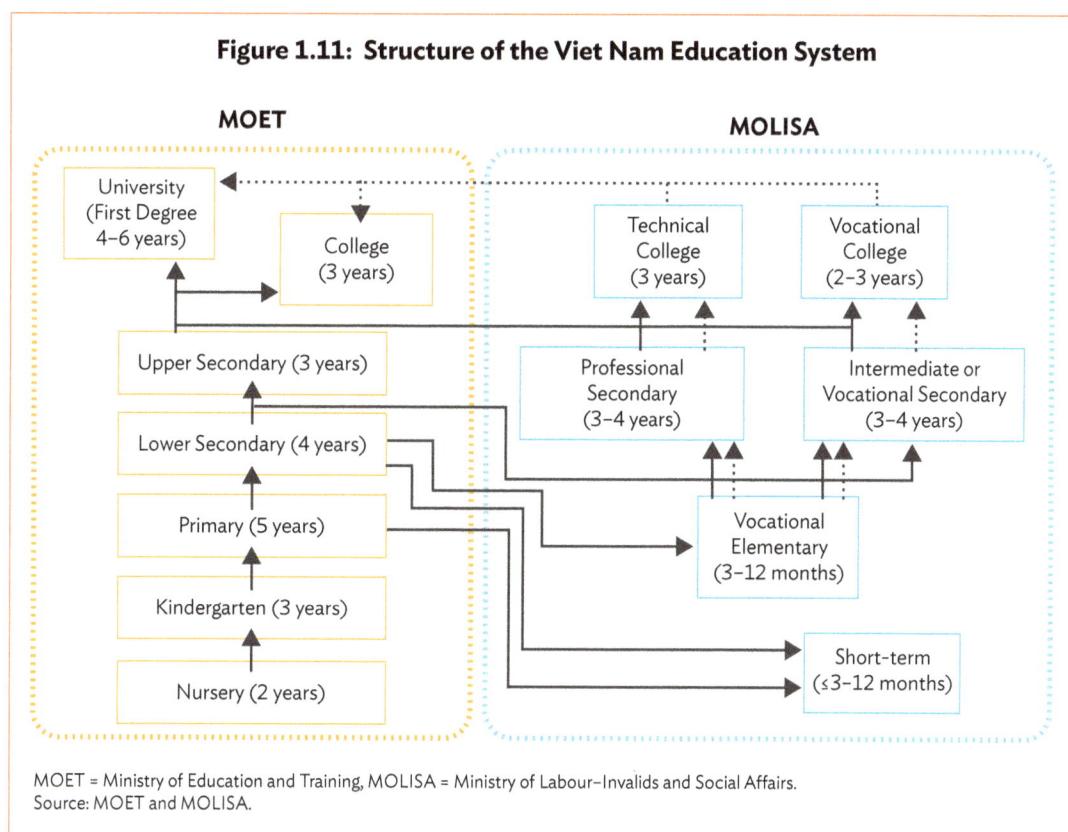

MOET = Ministry of Education and Training, MOLISA = Ministry of Labour–Invalids and Social Affairs.
Source: MOET and MOLISA.

E. Subsector Profiles

65. **Preprimary education**. This subsector consists of nursery school for 3-month-old children to 3-year-old children and kindergarten for children aged 3, 4, and 5 years. Preprimary education is established under the Education Law 2005 as revised and supplemented by the Law of Education 2009.[20]

66. Although attendance in preprimary is not compulsory in Viet Nam, as can be seen in Table 1.27, the majority of children, particularly 5-year olds, do attend kindergarten. The majority of schools have both nursery and kindergarten students. As can be seen in in Table 1.26, the number of schools increased by 15.8% between SY2011/12 and SY2017/18. During this period, the number of nursery school students increased by 28.0% and kindergarten students by 38.5%. Over this same period, the number of nursery school teachers increased by 27.7%, while the number of kindergarten teachers jumped by 58.2%.

---

[20]   Government of Viet Nam. Law No. 38/2005/QH11 on Education approved by the National Assembly.

**Table 1.26: Number of Preprimary Schools, Students, and Teachers,
SY2011/12 to SY2017/18**

	2011/12	2012/13	2013/14	2014/15	2015/16	2016/17	2017/18
Number of schools	13,172	13,548	13,867	14,203	14,532	14,881	15,256
Number of nursery students	553,117	597,274	612,981	661,877	648,795	676,059	707,990
Number of kindergarten students	3,320,328	3,551,082	3,614,066	3,754,975	3,978,521	4,409,576	4,598,546
Number of nursery teachers	55,715	56,302	58,555	62,166	62,742	65,825	71,142
Number of kindergarten teachers	174,009	188,176	204,944	215,518	231,931	250,791	266,346

Source: Ministry of Education and Training. 2018. *Education Statistics 2017–2018*. Ha Noi.

Table 1.27: Enrollment Rate for Preprimary Education, SY2013/14

Age Group	Rate
2 years old	13.5
3–5 years old	83.1
5 years old	96.9

SY = school year.
Source: Ministry of Education and Training. 2017. *Education Statistics 2015–2016*. Ha Noi.

67. MOET regulates the curriculum and instructional materials for preprimary education.[21]

68. **Requirements for preprimary teachers.** The requirement to become a nursery school or kindergarten teacher is successful completion of 2 years at a teacher training school. According to the Department of Planning and Finance, about 98% of preprimary teachers met this qualification in 2015. MOET and the departments of education and training (DOETs) regulate the in-service training programs for preprimary teachers.[22] MOET specifies compulsory content to meet the requirements each school year of about 30 periods (each period is 45 minutes) and the DOETs designate compulsory content to meet the requirements for development of local education annually and for another 30 periods. In addition, teachers are expected to complete optional content for self-study for continuing professional development which is regulated by MOET and is about 60 periods with 44 topics for preprimary.[23]

69. Table 1.28 shows the amount of funds expended on preprimary education.

---

[21]   Circular No. 17/2009/TT-BGDĐT dated 25 July 2009 issues the preprimary education curriculum, Circular No. 32/2012/TT-BGDĐT dated 14 September 2012 issues the list of equipment and outdoor toys for preprimary educational level, and Decision No. 4045/QD-BGDDT dated 16 September 2010 approves the Development of Self-Made Teaching Equipment at Preprimary and General Education, Period 2010–2015.

[22]   Circular No. 26 /2012/TT-BGDĐT dated 10 July 2012: Regulations on regular training for preprimary teachers, teachers of general education, and teachers of continuing education.

[23]   Circular No. 36/2011/TT-BGDĐT.

Table 1.28: Trends in Expenditure for Preprimary Education, 2009-2013

Item	2009	2010	2011	2012	2013
Total government expenditure on preprimary (VND billion)	10,621	14,259	18,405	26,839	31,922
Total capital expenditure (VND billion)	7,171	9,001	12,081	18,800	22,939
Total recurrent cost (VND billion)	3,450	5,258	6,325	8,039	8,983
Total education and training expenditure (VND billion)	88,421	115,676	136,840	185,951	202,909
Total preprimary expenditure as proportion of government education and training expenditure (%)	12.0	12.3	13.5	14.4	15.7

Notes:
Capital expenditure includes new goods and civil works and rehabilitation.
Recurrent expenditure includes wages and benefits, subsidies, and services payment.
Source: Data were provided by Department of Finance and Planning and Ministry of Education and Training, based on data from the Ministry of Finance. Only budget estimates are available for 2014 and 2015.

70. The government has indicated how it envisions preprimary education will be improved over the coming years in Resolution No. 29-NQ/TW 8 on Comprehensive Innovations of Education and Training.[24] This resolution has set the following targets for preprimary education: (i) help children develop their physical health, mental health, knowledge, and perception, and go through the first stages of personality development; (ii) prepare children for primary education; (iii) ensure primary completion at the age of 5 by 2015; (iv) improve the quality of primary completion over the next years and exempt tuition fees by 2020; (v) standardize the system of preschools; and (vi) ensure that the quality of preschool education for children under the age of 5 is suitable for the conditions of each locality and educational institution. The 2016 UNDP and VASS report calls for increased emphasis being put on preprimary education as a means to achieve above average development relative to other expenditures in education (UNDP and VASS 2016). By nurturing and supporting capability development during the crucial early years, many issues related to developmental disparity can be overcome.

71. **Primary education** This subsector consists of grades 1 to 5. Children enter grade 1 when they are 6 years old. Primary education is established under the Education Law 2005 as revised and supplemented by the Law of Education 2009.[25] Circular No. 41/2010/TT-BGDDT dated 30 December 2010 issues principles for primary school outlining the following: (i) tasks and rights of primary schools; (ii) implementation of curriculum; (iii) decentralization of management; (iv) inclusive education for disabled students in primary schools; (v) organization and operation of semi-boarding primary schools and classes at primary level in specialized schools; (vi) organization and management of primary schools; and (vii) relationships between schools, students' families, and society. Decision No. 16/2006/QD/BGDDT set the curriculum for general education including primary. Circular No. 36/2009/TT-BGDĐT dated 4 December 2009 issues regulations on assessment and recognition of primary education and universalization. Circular No. 14/2011/TT-BGDĐT issues regulations on standards for principals of primary schools. Circular No. 14/2007/TT-BGDĐT issues regulations on standards for teachers at the primary educational level. Circular No. 15/2009/TT-BGDĐT issues the list of minimum teaching equipment for the primary educational level. Circular No. 30/2014/TT-BGDĐT issues regulations on assessment of primary students.

---

[24]   Issued by the Central Committee of the Communist Party of Viet Nam at the Central Conference XI dated 4 November 2013.

[25]   Government of Viet Nam. Law No. 38/2005/QH11 on Education approved by the National Assembly.

72. The number of students in primary school has been constantly increased since SY2011/12 (Table 1.29). Universal primary education is one of the Millennium Development Goals and Viet Nam has made significant progress in achieving this MDG. In 2014, the net enrollment rate (NER) in primary school was 99.0% and in 2013, 97.5% of children who entered grade 1 completed 5 years of primary education (MOET 2017). Between SY2011/12 and SY2017/18, enrollment increased by 13.2%, while the number of schools decreased by about 3%, reflecting that extra schools were not needed because the system had been built to accommodate a larger primary school population. During this period, the number of primary teachers increased by 8.3% which was less than the change in number of students.

Table 1.29: Number of Primary Schools, Students, and Teachers, SY2011/12 to SY2017/18

	2011/12	2012/13	2013/14	2014/15	2015/16	2016/17	2017/18
Number of schools	15,337	15,361	15,337	15,277	15,254	15,052	14,937
Number of students	7,100,950	7,202,767	7,435,600	7,543,632	7,790,009	7,801,560	8,041,842
Number of teachers	366,045	381,432	387,196	392,136	396,843	397,098	396,600

SY = school year.
Source: Ministry of Education and Training. 2018. *Education Statistics 2017–2018*. Ha Noi.

73. **Requirement for primary school teachers**. The requirement to become a primary school teacher is the successful completion of 2 years at a teacher training school. About 99% of primary teachers meet this qualification.[26] MOET and the DOETs regulate the in-service training programs for primary teachers.[27] MOET indicates compulsory content to meet the requirements each school year of about 30 periods (each period is 45 minutes) and the DOETs indicate compulsory content to meet the requirements for development of local education for each school year and another 30 periods. In addition, teachers are expected to complete optional content for self-study for continuing professional development which is regulated by MOET and is about 60 periods with 45 topics for primary.[28]

74. Table 1.30 shows the amount of money spent on primary education and reflects that this subsector receives the largest share of the education budget.

Table 1.30: Trends in Expenditure for Primary Education, 2009–2013

Item	2009	2010	2011	2012	2013
Total government expenditure on primary education (VND billion)	26,147	32,467	38,314	52,326	57,310
Total capital expenditure (VND billion)	20,699	24,689	29,945	42,358	47,792
Total recurrent cost (VND billion)	5448	7,778	8,369	9,968	9,518
Total education and training expenditure (VND billion)	88,421	115,676	136,840	185,951	202,909
Total primary education expenditure as proportion of government education and training expenditure (%)	29.6	28.1	28.0	28.1	28.2

Notes:
Capital expenditure includes new goods and civil works and rehabilitation.
Recurrent expenditure includes wages and benefits, subsidies, and services payment.
Source: Data were provided by the Department of Finance and Planning and the Ministry of Education and Training, based on data from the Ministry of Finance. Only budget estimates are available for 2014 and 2015.

---

[26]   Department of Planning and Finance (2015), MOET.

[27]   Circular No. 26 /2012/TT-BGDĐT dated 10 July 2012: Regulations on regular training for preprimary teachers, teachers of general education, and teachers of continuing education.

[28]   Circular No. 32/2011/TT-BGDĐT.

75. The government has a few primary school-related initiatives. The most major change is the development of a new curriculum for all levels of general education including primary schools. The Education Development Strategy 2011–2020 has set the following primary education targets to be achieved by 2020: (i) ensure adequate supply of teachers to teach full-day schooling (emphasis on teachers of foreign languages, counseling, special needs, and continuing education); (ii) 100% of primary school teachers will achieve training standard; (iii) the NER will be 99%; (iv) 70% of students with a disability will attend school; (v) 90% of lower secondary schools (LSSs) will implement full-day schooling; and (vi) increased support for the most disadvantaged and ethnic minority areas and for social policy beneficiaries. Resolution No. 29 seeks to improve the quality of educators and administrative officers so that every teacher in primary schools has at least a bachelor's degree.

76. **Lower secondary education.** This subsector consists of grades 6 to 9 and most students are between 11 and 14 years of age. Lower secondary education (LSE) is established under the Education Law 2005 as revised and supplemented by the Law of Education 2009.[29] Decision No. 12/2011/TT-BGDĐT issues the principles for lower secondary schools, upper secondary schools (USSs), and multilevel secondary schools covering the following: (i) tasks and rights of secondary schools; (ii) types and systems of secondary schools; (iii) decentralization in management of schools; (iv) organization and management of schools; (iv) curriculum, educational activities, and textbooks; (v) teacher's books; (vi) workbooks; (vii) teaching equipment; (viii) reference materials; (ix) filing systems for educational activities; (x) student assessment; (xi) preservation and promotion of traditions of each school; and (xii) relationship between schools, students' families, and society. Circular No. 47/2012/TT-BGDĐT issues regulations to recognize LSSs, USSs, and multilevel secondary schools meeting national standards. Circular No. 29/2009/TT-BGDĐT issues regulations on standards and criteria for principals of LSSs, USSs, and multilevel secondary schools. Circular No. 30/2009/TT-BGDĐT issues standards for lower secondary and upper secondary school teachers. Instruction No. 3008/CT-BGDĐT provides the focus of preprimary education, general education, continuing education, and professional education in SY2014/15.

77. At the LSE level, enrollment of 4,926,401 in SY2011/12, declined slightly to 4,869,839 in SY2012/13, and reflecting the increase in primary school enrollment, has increased constantly since then. The government has established a target that by 2020 the NER for LSE will be 95%. As of SY2015/16 the NER was 92.3% (Table 1.31). Between SY2011/12 and SY2017/18, enrollment increased by 9.1% while the number of schools and the number of teachers decreased by 1.5% and 2.5%, respectively. LSE schools (in particular in rural areas) were merged due to migration of people and rural infrastructure development.

Table 1.31: Number of Lower Secondary Education Schools, Students, and Teachers, SY2011/12 to SY2017/18

	2011/12	2012/13	2013/14	2014/15	2015/16	2016/17	2017/18
Number of schools	10,243	10,290	10,290	10,293	10,312	10,155	10,091
Number of students	4,926,401	4,869,839	4,932,390	5,098,830	5,138,646	5,235,524	5,373,312
Number of teachers	311,970	315,405	315,593	312,587	313,526	310,953	303,947

SY = school year.
Source: Ministry of Education and Training. 2018. *Education Statistics 2017–2018*. Ha Noi.

---

[29]   Government of Viet Nam. Law No. 38/2005/QH11 on Education Approved by the National Assembly.

78. To become an LSE teacher, successful completion of 3 years at a teacher college is required. Table 2.3 shows the percentage of LSE teachers by qualification. MOET and DOETs regulate the in-service training programs for LSE teachers.[30] MOET indicates compulsory content to meet the requirements each school year of about 30 periods (each period is 45 minutes) and DOETs define compulsory content to meet the requirements for development of local education of each school year and another 30 periods. In addition, teachers are expected to complete optional content for self-study for continuing professional development which is regulated by MOET and is about 60 periods with 41 topics for LSE.[31]

79. Table 1.32 shows the amount of funding used for LSE.

Table 1.32: Trends in the Expenditure for Lower Secondary Education, 2010–2015

Item	2010	2011	2012	2013	2014	2015
Total government expenditure on LSE (VND billion)	26,336	30,489	41,799	44,804	48,796	50,376
Total capital expenditure (VND billion)	6,764	7,677	8,728	7,860	6,652	7,268
Total recurrent cost (VND billion)	19,572	22,812	33,071	36,944	42,144	43,108
Total education and training expenditure (VND billion)	115,676	136,840	185,951	202,909	218,375	229,592
Total LSE expenditure as proportion of government education and training expenditure (%)	22.8	22.8	23.4	21.5	23.4	24.2

LSE = lower secondary education.
Notes:
Capital expenditure includes new goods and civil works and rehabilitation.
Recurrent expenditure includes wages and benefits, subsidies, and services payment.
Source: Data were provided by the Department of Finance and Planning and the Ministry of Education and Training, based on data from the Ministry of Finance.

80. The major government initiative that will have a potential major impact on LSE is the development of a new curriculum for all levels of general education including lower secondary schools. This will also entail a significant shift in teaching and learning methods. The Education Development Strategy (EDS) 2011–2020 has set the following LSE-related targets to be achieved by 2020: (i) ensure that students graduated from lower secondary have the fundamental knowledge to meet the requirements after lower secondary education; (ii) ensure adequate supply of teachers to teach full-day schooling (emphasis on teachers of foreign languages, counseling, special needs, and continuing education); (iii) 88% of lower secondary teachers will achieve the training standard; (iv) the NER will be 95%; (v) 70% of students with a disability will attend school; (vi) 50% of lower secondary schools will implement full-day schooling; and (vii) support will increase for the most disadvantaged and ethnic minority areas and for social policy beneficiaries. Resolution No. 29 seeks to improve the quality of educators and administrative officers so that every teacher in LSE has at least a bachelor's degree.

81. **Upper secondary education.** This subsector consists of grades 10 to 12 and most students are between 15 and 18 years of age. Upper secondary education (USE) is established under the Education Law 2005 as revised and supplemented by the Law of Education 2009.[32] Decision No. 12/2011/TT-

---

[30] Circular No. 26/2012/TT-BGDĐT dated 10 July 2012 on Regulations on Regular Training for Preprimary Teachers, Teachers of General Education, and Teachers of Continuing Education.

[31] Circular No. 31/2011/TT-BGDĐT.

[32] Government of Viet Nam. Law No. 38/2005/QH11 on Education Approved by the National Assembly.

BGDĐT issues the principles for lower secondary schools, upper secondary schools, and multilevel secondary schools covering the following: (i) tasks and rights of secondary schools; (ii) types and systems of secondary schools; (iii) decentralization in management of schools; (iv) organization and management of schools; (v) curriculum, educational activities, and textbooks; (vi) teacher's books; (vii) workbooks; (viii) teaching equipment; (ix) reference materials; (x) filing systems for educational activities; (xi) student assessment; (xii) preservation and promotion of traditions of each school; and (xiii) relationship between schools, students' families, and society. Circular No. 47/2012/TT-BGDĐT issues regulations to recognize LSSs, USSs, and multilevel secondary schools meeting national standards. Circular No. 29/2009/TT-BGDĐT issues regulations on standards and criteria for principals of LSSs, USSs, and multilevel secondary schools. Circular No. 30/2009/TT-BGDĐT issues standards for lower secondary and upper secondary teachers. Instruction No. 3008/CT-BGDĐT instructs the focus of preprimary education, general education, continuing education, and professional education in SY2014/15.

82. USE enrollment peaked in SY2006/07 at 3,111,280 and has since steadily declined to 2,425130 in SY2015/16 but started increased again in recent years. Between SY2011/12 and SY2017/18, enrollment decreased by 9.0%, while the number of schools increased by 2.0% and the number of teachers remained almost the same. The NER in USE is lower than in many of Viet Nam's economic competitors. The government has established a target that by 2020, 80% of youngsters over 18 years of age will have completed secondary education or equivalent. In SY2015/16, the NER for USE is 63.0% (Table 1.33).

Table 1.33: Number of Upper Secondary Education Schools, Students, and Teachers, SY2011/12 to SY2017/18

	2011/12	2012/13	2013/14	2014/15	2015/16	2016/17	2017/18
Number of schools	2,350	2,425	2,404	2,386	2,399	2,391	2,398
Number of students	2,755,210	2,675,320	2,532,696	2,439,919	2,425,130	2,477,175	2,508,564
Number of teachers	150,133	150,915	152,689	152,007	150,900	150,721	150,288

SY = school year.
Source: Ministry of Education and Training. 2018. *Education Statistics 2017–2018*. Ha Noi.

83. To become a USE teacher, successful completion of 4 years at a teacher training university is required. Table 2.3 shows the percentage of USE teachers by qualification. MOET and DOETs regulate the in-service training programs for USE teachers.[33] MOET dictates compulsory content to meet the requirements each school year of about 30 periods (each period is 45 minutes) and DOETs define compulsory content to meet the requirements for development of local education of each school year for another 30 periods. In addition, teachers are expected to complete optional content for self-study for continuing professional development which is regulated by MOET and is about 60 periods with 41 topics for USE.[34]

84. Table 1.34 shows the amount of funding being expended on USE.

---

[33] Circular No. 26 /2012/TT-BGDĐT dated 10 July 2012: Regulations on regular training for preprimary teachers, teachers of general education, and teachers of continuing education.

[34] Circular No. 30/2011/TT-BGDĐT.

Table 1.34: Trends in the Financing of Upper Secondary Education, 2010–2015

Item	2010	2011	2012	2013	2014	2015
Total government expenditure on USE (VND billion)	13,593	15,421	19,772	21,093	28,610	29,637
Total capital expenditure (VND billion)	4,485	4,488	5,072	5,139	5,111	5,617
Total recurrent cost (VND billion)	9,108	10,933	14,700	15,954	23,499	24,020
Total education and training expenditure (VND billion)	115,676	136,840	185,951	202,909	218,375	229,592
Total USE expenditure as a proportion of government education and training expenditure (%)	11.8	11.5	11.5	11.1	10.1	13.7

USE = upper secondary education.
Notes:
Capital expenditure includes new goods and civil works and rehabilitation.
Recurrent expenditure includes wages and benefits, subsidies, and services payment.
Source: Data were provided by the Department of Finance and Planning and the Ministry of Education and Training, based on data from the Ministry of Finance.

85. The government sees improvement of the quality of and access to USE as a major component of its drive to better prepare students for the labor market. The initiative to develop and implement new curriculum and textbooks with the concomitant significant shift in teaching and learning methods will have a major impact on USE. The EDS 2011–2020 has set the following USE-related targets to be achieved by 2020: (i) ensure that upper secondary students have vocational guidance and are prepared for post high school; (ii) ensure adequate supply of teachers to teach full-day schooling (emphasis on teachers of foreign languages, counseling, special needs, and continuing education); (iii) 16.6% of upper secondary teachers will achieve the training standard; (iv) 70% of students with a disability will attend school; and (v) support will increase for the most disadvantaged and ethnic minority areas and for social policy beneficiaries. Among the key tasks and primary solutions contained in Resolution No. 29, the following pertain to USE: (i) categorize students after secondary education and provide career guidance during compulsory education; (ii) improve the quality of educators and administrative officers so that every teacher in USE has at least a bachelor's degree; and (iii) 80% of youths within the age range for upper secondary education will obtain upper secondary education or equivalent level. Resolution No. 44 has the following specific primary solution designed specifically for USE: (i) change the form and methods for examination and evaluation of the results of learning (combine the overall evaluation with the term and year evaluations); and (ii) change the organization of the General Certificate of Secondary Education examination by organizing integrated examinations whose result can be used for recognition of the high school graduation and admission to universities and colleges.

86. **Colleges and universities.** Higher education consists of colleges providing 3- to 3 1/2-year programs and universities that offer undergraduate and postgraduate degrees. These programs are offered in over 442 institutions that range from small highly specialized units to large multi-campus institutions. Although still dominated by smaller specialized institutions, the system has become more multidisciplinary with the formation of larger universities in regional centers. Research units and institutes have also been reorganized to help integrate research activities within universities.

87. Resolution No. 14/2005 on Comprehensive and Fundamental Reform of Higher Education in Viet Nam 2006–2020 (Higher Education Action Agenda or HERA) was the most ambitious higher education reform effort to that date and represented an important commitment by the government to the higher education sector. It set the following targets to be achieved by 2020: (i) increasing

enrollment in universities and colleges by 10% annually and reaching a level of 450 students per 10,000 people; (ii) revenue from science and technology activities increased to 25%; (iii) the proportion of university teaching staff with master's level degrees increased to 60%; (iv) the proportion of university teaching staff with doctoral level degrees increased to 35%; (v) ratio of university students to teaching staff reduced to 20:1; (vi) encouraging the establishment of private institutions including high-quality accredited and 100% foreign-invested institutions in science, technology, and economic management; and (vii) encouraging foreign scientific and educational experts and Vietnamese expatriates to teach in Viet Nam. The goals and strategies of the HERA were updated in 2013 in Decision No. 37/2013/QDTTg on Adjusting the Master Plan on the University and College Network during 2006–2020.

88. Viet Nam's Law on Higher Education 2012 was the country's first law dedicated specifically to the higher education sector.[35] The law aims to reform and regulate higher education to develop human resources needed for Viet Nam's move toward a knowledge-based economy. The law covers areas not previously mentioned in legislation, e.g., institutional autonomy, quality assurance, international cooperation, university research mission, university mission in science and technology, private universities, national and regional universities, and university classification and ranking. Decree No. 141/2013/ND-CP provided detail on the implementation of the Law on Higher Education and was followed by Decision No. 70/2014/QD-TTg promulgating the University Charter. The charter specifies the new duties, authority, autonomy, and responsibilities of universities. It also defines the organization and management structure of public and private universities.

89. Enrollment in colleges peaked in SY2011/12 when a little more than twice as many students were enrolled compared with SY2003/04. However, college enrollment in SY2013/14 dropped considerably and this trend continued in SY2015/16. With the large drop in enrollment in SY2013/14, the number of teaching staff started to decline a year later in SY2014/15. Notwithstanding the decline in the number of students in USE, enrollment in university has shown steady growth over the past 10 years. The number of teaching staff in universities increased by 22.0% between SY2011/12 and SY2017/18 while the student population grew by 22.0% with a large jump up in SY2014/15 and then a dip in SY2015/16. As set out in HERA 2006–2020, the government aimed to have 17–20 university and college students per lecturer by 2020. The ratio in SY2015/16 was 18.5 to 1 instructor at the college level and has been steadily decreasing. However, the ratio at university was 27.8 to 1 in SY2014/15 up from 22.4 to 1 the previous year and 24.2 in SY2017/18 (Table 1.35). This reflects the MOET's difficulty in accurately and centrally anticipating enrollments and planning for the required staffing.

Table 1.35: Number of College and University Institutions, Students, and Instructors, SY2011/12 to SY2016/17

	2011/12	2012/13	2013/14	2014/15	2015/16	2016/17	2017/18
Number of colleges	215	214	214	217	219	N/A	N/A
College students	756,292	724,232	599,802	539,614	449,558	N/A	N/A
Graduating college	169,400	176,917	161,398	200,122	150,851	N/A	N/A
Teaching staff	24,437	26,008	26,427	25,519	24,260	N/A	N/A
Number of universities	204	204	214	219	223	235	N/A
University students	1,448,021	1,447,167	1,461,839	1,824,328	1,753,174	1,767,879	N/A
Graduating university	232,877	248291	244,880	353,936	352,789	305,601	N/A
Teaching staff	59,672	61,674	65,206	65,664	69,591	72,792	N/A

N/A = data not available, SY = school year.
Source: Ministry of Education and Training. 2018. *Education Statistics 2016–2017*. Ha Noi.

---

[35] Government of Viet Nam. Law on Higher Education No. 08/2012/QH13 Approved by the National Assembly 18 June 2012.

90. The minimum requirement to become a college or university staff member is graduation from a teacher training college or university. The EDS 2011–2020 has targeted that by 2020, 60% of college lecturers and 100% of university lecturers hold a master's or higher degree. In SY2015/16, 2.6% of college lecturers and 19.5% of university lecturers hold a doctoral degree while 51.0% of college and 58.1% of university lecturers hold a master's degree. There is an additional target that 100% of college and university lecturers are fluent in one foreign language.

91. The curriuclum framework for higher education is regulated by MOET. Based on this framework, each college and university is responsible for identifying the course content. The rectors of the colleges and universities are responsible for organizing the development and approval of textbooks and training materials. Principals establish asessment councils to perform this function.

92. Table 1.36 shows the amount of money being spent for colleges and universities. The total amount spent on education and training declined by D7,000 billion between 2012 and 2013 but the amount spent on higher education declined by about D14,000 billion. The amount budgeted for higher education did not reflect the large increase in actual expenditure for the years 2010, 2011, and 2012. The total expenditure in 2013 was higher than the budget allocation of D4,658 billion.

Table 1.36: Trends in Financing of Colleges and Universities, 2009–2013

Item	2009	2010	2011	2012	2013
Total government expenditure on higher education (VND billion)	2,985	14,749	18,624	21,400	6,476
Total capital expenditure (VND billion)	1,921	11,581	14,323	16,582	4,421
Total recurrent cost (VND billion)	1,065	3,167	4,302	4,818	2,055
Total education and training expenditure (VND billion)	88,421	115,676	136,840	185,951	202,909
Total higher education expenditure as proportion of government education and training expenditure (%)	3.4	12.8	13.6	11.5	3.2

Notes:
Capital expenditure includes new goods and civil works and rehabilitation.
Recurrent expenditure includes wages and benefits, subsidies, and services payment.
Only budget estimates are available for 2014 and 2015.
Source: Data were provided by Department of Finance and Planning and Ministry of Education and Training, based on data from Ministry of Finance.

93. The government's educational reform agenda sees improvement of the quality and access to colleges and universities as a major component to better preparing students to contribute to economic growth. The EDS 2011–2020 set the following strategies to improve higher education: (i) implement policies to support higher education institutions; (ii) enhance linkage among education with utilization, science research, and technology transfer; and (iii) enhance effectiveness in international cooperation. Resolution No. 29 lists among its key tasks and primary solutions, (i) to raise the quality and effectiveness of research and application of science and technology, especially the science of education and administration; and (ii) to focus on investment in building technical education universities and some universities that provide training in key disciplines. Resolution No. 44 specifies the following primary solutions for higher education: (i) introduce policies that encourage researchers to take part in teaching and encourage teachers to conduct scientific research; (ii) enhance the private sector involvement in education, particularly in the preschool, vocational, and higher education; and (iii) classify universities as those specialized in research, application, and practice.

94. **Technical and vocational education and training.** The 2006 TVET law identifies the Ministry of Labour–Invalids and Social Affairs (MOLISA) as being tasked with coordinating the training provision of all entities. With a new TVET law, effective January 2017, MOLISA's GDVT became the single central "state management" agency for TVET. Before the new TVET law, MOET was responsible for professional secondary education. Operationally, this merger should lead to substantial alignments regarding school accreditation and program certification.[36] Due to the diversity of institutions, the general directorate has intensified its focus on stipulating standard procedures and criteria by issuing circulars and decrees. All institutions maintain thick books of orders and regulations that they are to follow. However, there is often little or even no coordination between national and provincial administrative levels and among ministries, as each sector agency handles its own institutions. Unfortunately, there is still no central database or management system providing consistent and reliable data on vocational education and training (VET) institutions across all levels and agencies.[37]

95. In 2017, the central ministries owned almost a third (32%) of the institutions at the college level, while provincial People's Committees managed about 40% of them. At the intermediate level, the central government managed only 6% of the institutions, while 21% are known to be directly managed by People's Committees.[38] At the elementary level, local governments and sociopolitical organizations directly managed approximately 70% of the institutions (vocational training centers [VTCs]), and more than 30% were run by private owners (14%) or enterprises (17%).

96. Getting a clear picture of the network of VET institutions is difficult because many institutions not only offer programs from both tracks but also provide different levels of VET courses at their facilities (Figure 1.12). Higher-level institutions can offer lower-level training and this is regulated by Article 23 of the TVET Law. For instance, some universities offer college-level as well as secondary-level VET and provide even elementary-level training as well as short-term courses. Colleges tend to offer also intermediate-level VET, elementary training, and short-term courses, while vocational secondary schools can also offer elementary-level courses and short-term training. Since teachers and lecturers of these institutions sometimes teach at more than one level, it is also difficult to obtain relevant statistical data on staff distributions.

---

[36] According to MOLISA's 2015 TVET Report, the network of TVET institutes, professional secondary schools, and colleges under MOET did not change much. Due to a lack of guiding documents, these institutes still followed regulations established under the Education Law, the Law on Higher Education, and the 2006 TVET Law. The merger is expected to take a couple of years to be fully implemented.

[37] MOLISA is working on collecting data from previous MOET institutions but announced during a meeting in July 2017 that respective data will be available only around 2020.

[38] For about 50% of vocational secondary schools the current ownership status could not be clearly identified by the GDVT.

Figure 1.12: Forms of TVET Schools

University plus Affiliated VET Institutions

University

Technical College (3 years)

Vocational College (2–3 years)

Professional Secondary (3–4 years)

Vocational Secondary (1–4 years)

Vocational Elementary (3–12 months)

Short-term (≤3–12 months)

VET College including VET School and Vocational Training Center

Technical College (3 years)

Vocational College (2–3 years)

Professional Secondary (3–4 years)

Vocational Secondary (1–4 years)

Vocational Elementary (3–12 months)

Short-term (≤3–12 months)

Vocational Training Center

Vocational Elementary (3–12 months)

Short-term (<3–12 months)

TVET = technical and vocational education and training, VET = vocational education and training.
Source: Ministry of Labour–Invalids and Social Affairs.

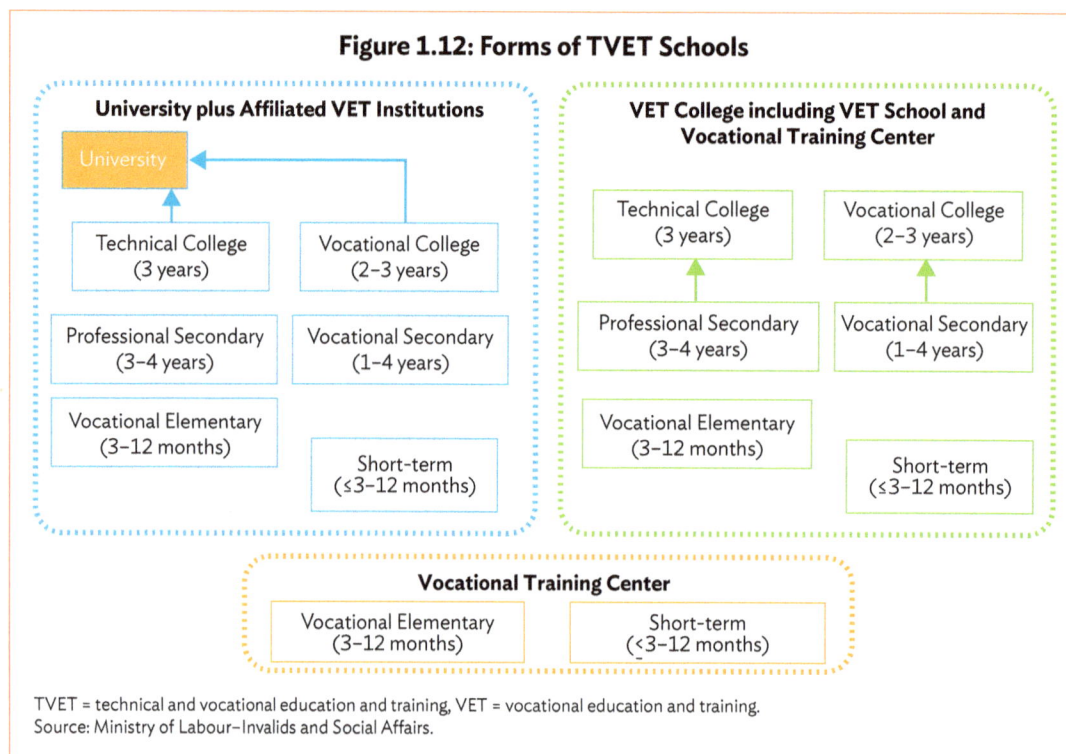

97. Table 1.37 displays the qualifications that can be earned in TVET programs.

Table 1.37: Vocational Training Alternatives

Level	Vocational Training Institution	Other Education and Training Institutions	Required Training Period	Prerequisite	Certificate
College	Vocational colleges	Universities Colleges	1–2 years	Professional or vocational secondary	College diploma
			2–3 years	Upper secondary school	
Secondary	Vocational colleges, Vocational secondary schools	Universities Colleges Professional secondary schools	1–2 years	Upper secondary school	Professional/ Vocational secondary education diploma or intermediate certificate
			3–4 years	Lower secondary school	
Primary	Vocational colleges and training centers	Universities Colleges Professional schools Employment service centers	3 months–1 year	Youth, unskilled workers	Elementary certificate

Source: Ministry of Labour–Invalids and Social Affairs.

98. Since 2011, the network of TVET institutes has been considerably expanded and partly aligned to particular economic sectors, regions, and localities. For 2017, MOLISA reported a total of 388 vocational and technical colleges—which include 199 technical colleges formerly supervised under MOET—of which 22% (84) are private. On the secondary level, there are 551 intermediate vocational

and professional schools (covering 279 institutions from MOLISA and 272 professional schools formerly supervised by MOET)— almost half of them (243) are privately run. Vocational training centers (VTCs) still make up the bulk of Viet Nam's VET institutions, accounting for a total number of 1,036, of which 240 are private.[39] Figure 1.13 shows the changes in the number of TVET institutions between 2012 and 2016.

Figure 1.13: Number of TVET Institutions by Type, 2012–2016

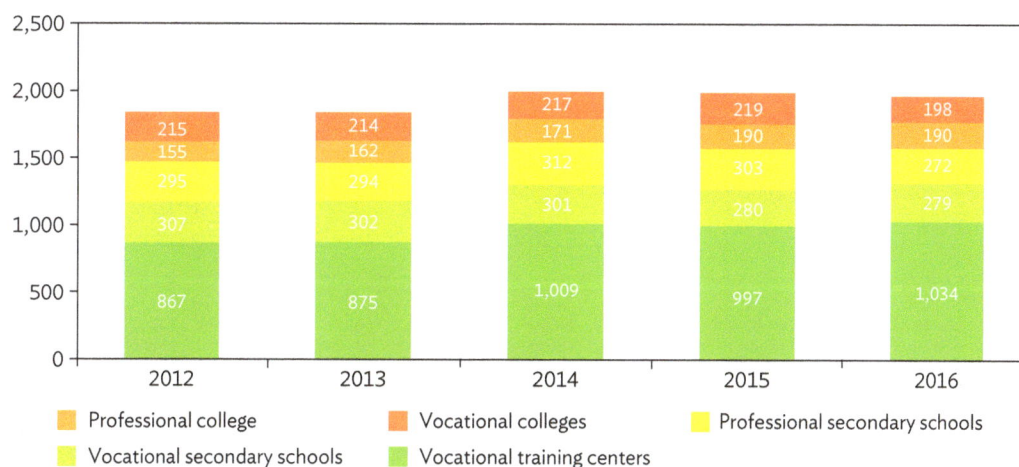

Year	Vocational training centers	Vocational secondary schools	Professional secondary schools	Professional college	Vocational colleges
2012	867	307	295	155	215
2013	875	302	294	162	214
2014	1,009	301	312	171	217
2015	997	280	303	190	219
2016	1,034	279	272	190	198

TVET = technical and vocational education and training.
Sources: Directorate of Vocational Education and Training, National Institute for Vocational Education and Training. 2017. *Viet Nam Vocational Education and Training Report 2015.* Ha Noi; and MOLISA. 2017. Project on Renovation and Improvement of the Quality of Technical and Vocational Education and Training – Up to 2020, with Orientation to 2030 (Draft October 2017). Ha Noi.

99. In 2015, 303,854 students were enrolled in Viet Nam's vocational and professional secondary schools, which was about 12.3% of total upper secondary enrollments under MOET (Figure 1.14). In the tertiary subsector, vocational and technical colleges enrolled 219,885 students, which accounts for only 9.5% of enrollments in higher education in the same year. Yet, enrollments in both TVET subsectors declined between 2011 and 2015, particularly in the professional schools and technical colleges formerly governed by MOET[40] (Figure 1.5).

100. A different situation applies to TVET enrollments at elementary level and in short-term courses offered by VTCs (1,769,095 in 2015). Between 2011 and 2015, total enrollments in these centers accounted for a share of 88% of all TVET enrollments (7.8 million) in the country. In more than half of the cases (4.1 million) students were granted access to these trainings through the National Target Program for Rural Vocational Training (Project 1956), which included financial support for over 2.7 million people. This has led to a dramatic increase in the enrollments for short-term courses (under 3 months), while enrollments in formal elementary training (3–12 months) significantly decreased (Figure 1.16). Moreover, MOLISA reported that some rural provinces have difficulty enrolling students in formal intermediate and higher level VET programs.[41] Although MOLISA had to conclude in recent

---

[39] These figures, however, should be taken with care, as they are not congruent with the actual number of VET facilities, which often comprise institutional units on several VET levels (Cf. section above).

[40] During this period, annual student enrollments in MOET's professional secondary schools decreased by 35.6% and in its technical colleges by 38.4%. At the same time, annual enrollment in vocational secondary schools and vocational colleges under MOLISA decreased by 8.9% and 1.8%, respectively.

[41] MOLISA. Report on Vocational Training in the Northern Midland and Mountainous Region. Unpublished.

Figure 1.14: Number of Students Enrolled in VET Institutions by Supervising Ministry, SY2010/11 to SY2014/15

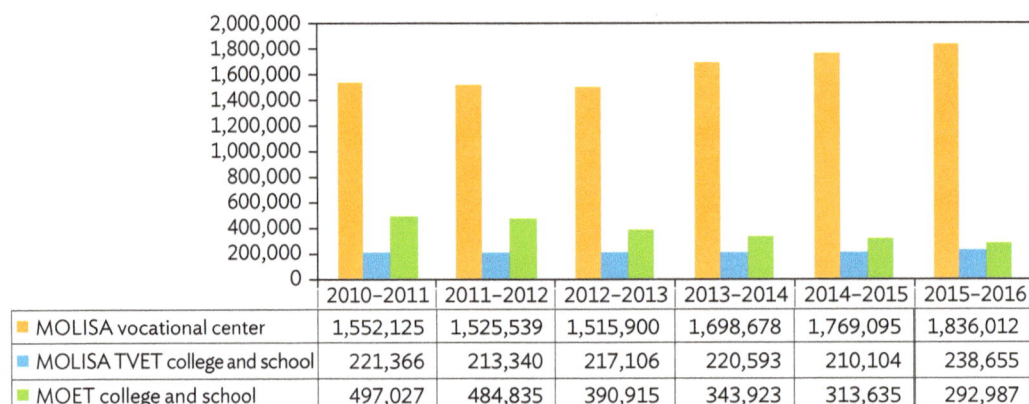

	2010-2011	2011-2012	2012-2013	2013-2014	2014-2015	2015-2016
■ MOLISA vocational center	1,552,125	1,525,539	1,515,900	1,698,678	1,769,095	1,836,012
■ MOLISA TVET college and school	221,366	213,340	217,106	220,593	210,104	238,655
■ MOET college and school	497,027	484,835	390,915	343,923	313,635	292,987

MOET = Ministry of Education and Training, MOLISA = Ministry of Labour–Invalids and Social Affairs, SY = school year, VET = vocational education and training.
Sources: Directorate of Vocational Education and Training, National Institute for Vocational Education and Training. 2017. *Viet Nam Vocational Education and Training Report 2015*. Ha Noi; and MOLISA. 2017. Project on Renovation and Improvement of the Quality of Technical and Vocational Education and Training – Up to 2020, with Orientation to 2030 (Draft October 2017). Ha Noi.

Figure 1.15: Development of Enrollments in VET Institutions at Intermediate and Diploma Levels, SY2010/11 to SY2014/15

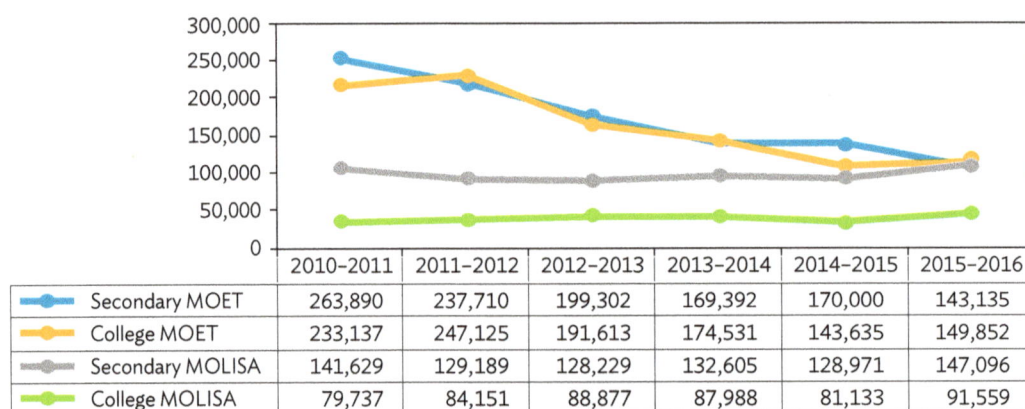

	2010-2011	2011-2012	2012-2013	2013-2014	2014-2015	2015-2016
●— Secondary MOET	263,890	237,710	199,302	169,392	170,000	143,135
●— College MOET	233,137	247,125	191,613	174,531	143,635	149,852
●— Secondary MOLISA	141,629	129,189	128,229	132,605	128,971	147,096
●— College MOLISA	79,737	84,151	88,877	87,988	81,133	91,559

MOET = Ministry of Education and Training, MOLISA = Ministry of Labour–Invalids and Social Affairs, SY = school year, VET = vocational education and training.
Sources: Directorate of Vocational Education and Training, National Institute for Vocational Education and Training. 2017. *Viet Nam Vocational Education and Training Report 2015*. Ha Noi; and MOLISA. 2017. Project on Renovation and Improvement of the Quality of Technical and Vocational Education and Training – Up to 2020, with Orientation to 2030 (Draft October 2017). Ha Noi.

reviews that "vocational training for rural laborers was not really efficient," the program has been continued in 2016 for another 1.72 million people and shall enroll a total of 5.73 million–7.9 million people between 2017 and 2020.[42]

---

[42] According to MOLISA (2017), "the number of unemployed graduates was high (about 30%) and tended to increase…". Other recent MOLISA reports indicate that the vast majority of training graduates (>80%) become self-employed after the training: "the number of rural workers who, after the vocational training, were employed by enterprises through working contracts (...) by enterprises was still small. The number of workers studying nonagricultural occupations to change their jobs into industry and service sectors was low. Most of them participated in agricultural training and after the vocational training continued to work in agriculture sector. Due to difficult natural, socioeconomic and trading conditions, their jobs were not sustainable" (MOLISA Report on Vocational Training in the Northern Midland and Mountainous Region).

Figure 1.16: Development of Enrollments in Vocational Training Centers by Type of Training

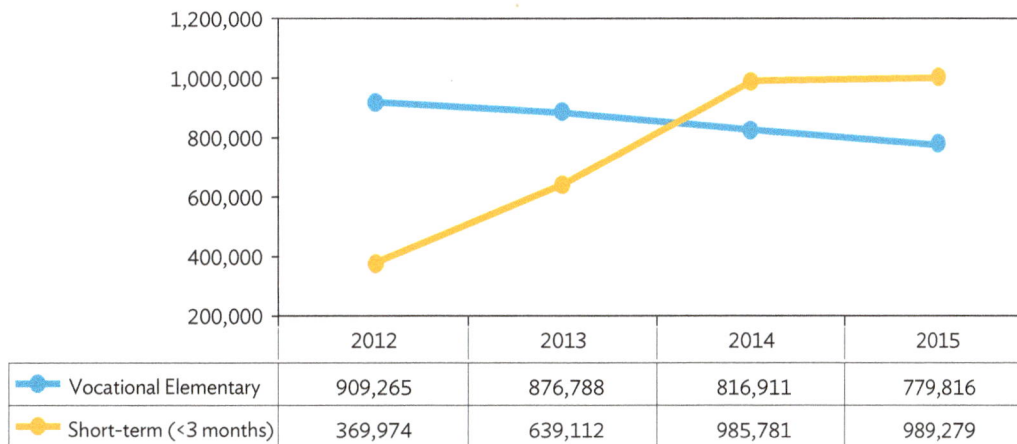

	2012	2013	2014	2015
Vocational Elementary	909,265	876,788	816,911	779,816
Short-term (<3 months)	369,974	639,112	985,781	989,279

Source: Directorate of Vocational Education and Training, National Institute for Vocational Education and Training. 2017. *Viet Nam Vocational Education and Training Report 2015*. Ha Noi.

101. Under the centrally managed economy, several state-owned sectors had their own training institutions. A few of these remain and are currently under the Ministry of Industry portfolio. With the withdrawal of separate state funding, many have closed. The Vocational Training Report – Viet Nam 2012 reports an increase in the number of trainees attending the training conducted by school corporations: 15,300 trainees attended long-term training in 1998, 60,102 trainees in 2006, and about 100,000 trainees in 2010 (GDVT 2014).

102. Many schools in the large economic conglomerates have large-scale training in their corporate field. VINASHIN (shipbuilding) trains between 6,000 and 7,000 technical workers annually. The Lilama Corporation (mixed manufacturing) has an annual training rate of 3,000 to 4,500 vocational college and vocational secondary qualified graduates. After nearly 40 years of operation, the Petroleum Vocational College has trained more than 70,000 people including 15,000 technical workers in 27 different professional skills areas.

103. GDVT (2014) also indicates that as of 2011, over 283 industrial parks, export processing zones, and economic zones (hereinafter, referred to as industrial parks) employed nearly 2 million workers directly and around the industrial area. In addition to getting labor from vocational schools, some businesses in the industrial park have implemented vocational training for newly recruited workers while organizing retraining for, or retraining skilled workers. A number of industrial parks have created vocational schools or vocational training centers, such as the Vinh Phuc Industrial Zone, Bac Ninh Industrial Zone, Dung Quat industrial Zone, and Binh Duong in Ha Noi.

104. Enterprises organize vocational training for employees under three main forms: coaching at work, focused training, and training in business outside the enterprise focus, including vocational mentoring which accounts for 63.6% of the total number of trainees. No clear data are available on total numbers of trainees in these enterprise schools although both MOLISA and the Ministry of Industry and Trade (MOIT) feel that the numbers are stable. The Viet Nam Chamber of Commerce and Industry feels that the number of these schools may be increasing but data are not available to the government.

105. MOIT is responsible for 49 institutions made up of 10 universities and 39 colleges. In 2014, enrollment reached 470,000 full-time students. As in MOLISA and MOET institutions, there appears to be no record of part-time enrollment. Up to June 2014, 202,000 students graduated from MOIT schools. This number is expected to decline to 199,000 in 2015 and increase to 263,000 in 2020. It could be concluded that MOIT schools provide about 30% of the labor training needed in Viet Nam. However, with the increase in in-industry schools this may be a conservative estimate.

106. MOIT institutions were built on links to single industries and, thus, when they were placed in the general public sector and supported by the government rather than individual industries, they brought with them their links to those industries. These institutions believe that their strong links with their historic partners can lead to work placement for students and graduates. MOIT courses tend to target specific job families rather than the general technology targeted by MOLISA schools. Although MOIT schools believe their job placement rate to be superior to other colleges or universities, there are no data to support job placement outcomes from any institution.

107. MOIT institutions fall under the regulatory environment of either MOET or MOLISA. Some MOIT schools have courses in both regulatory ministries, and certification is issued through MOLISA or MOET. Thus, in the data given by these regulatory ministries, MOIT institutions are included even though they may have their own unique programs and curriculum.[43]

---

[43]   Interview with Pham Van Quan of the Human Resources Department of MOIT on May 2015.

II. Sector Assessment and Analysis

A. Key Sector Achievements

108. **Summary of secondary education achievements.** Viet Nam's achievements in education have been impressive. The government has placed a high priority on education by setting a goal of spending 20% of the total government budget on education.[44] As of 2015, the actual expenditures on education and training were 15.3% of total government spending. In 2015, the proportion of total government expenditure on education and training was 5.5% of gross domestic product (GDP). The general quality of education has improved; national and international student assessments have been introduced; professional certificates and quality teacher standards have been developed; teachers have been trained; student-centered teaching has been introduced; based on the national standards, school accreditation has been established; and access to education for disadvantaged groups including girls, ethnic minorities, children from poor households and children with disabilities has been increased (MPI 2011).

1. Quality

109. **Student learnings are assessed nationwide.** Using reliable assessment methodology supported by international testing experts can provide data which allow decision makers to know relative to standards how well students are learning. These data can then be used to evaluate the effectiveness of program interventions and provide data for policy making.

110. In school year (SY) 2008/09, the Ministry of Education and Training (MOET) introduced the National Achievement Monitoring (NAM) for grade 9 (Table 2.19) and readministered this assessment in SY2012/13 (Table 2.20). Administered by the Center of Education Quality Assurance of MOET, the national assessment is administered to a nationally significant sample of students. The SY2008/09 test was designed to assess knowledge and skills relative to national standards, and the SY2012/13 test was designed to assess students' literacy (competency based) relative to national standards. The test items in both cycles were not homogenous in difficulty. However, test equating using common test items was used to compare the SY2012/13 results with the SY2008/09 results. In SY2011/12, MOET introduced the NAM for grade 11 (Table 2.21), and administered a revised test in SY2014/2015 (Table 2.22). To compare student performance between the two tests, the results were equated using a common item methodology.

111. The Programme for International Student Assessment (PISA) is an international assessment of 15-year-old students administered in 75 countries and is sponsored by the Organisation for Economic Co-operation and Development (OECD). In April 2012, Viet Nam participated for the first time in

---

44   Prime Minister's Decision No. 711/QD-TTg dated 13 June 2012 Approving the Education Development Strategy 2011–2020.

PISA and again in 2015 and in 2018. Figure 2.22 and Table 2.23 provide a summary of PISA results for Viet Nam in 2012 and 2015. Viet Nam country report on the 2018 PISA results will be available in March 2020.

112. The expertise regarding modern standardized assessment developed through participating in PISA and NAM can also be used to assist with planned changes to the Upper Secondary Graduation Examination. Since PISA is a competency-based assessment, the large number of teachers trained for PISA will be useful for implementing the new competency-based curriculum. MOET is intending to continue and possibly expand the grade 9 and 11 NAM and has registered to participate in PISA 2018.

113. **A systematic curriculum development is adopted.** MOET established a committee to prepare a comprehensive proposal to develop the new curriculum and textbooks to be used for primary, lower secondary education (LSE), and upper secondary education (USE). Resolution No. 29-NQ/TW 8 on Comprehensive Innovations of Education and Training indicates the key features of the new curriculum, and Resolution No. 44/NQ-CP on Radical Changes in Education and Training to Meet Requirements of Industrialization and Modernization Economy provides the tasks the government sees as needed to ensure the implementation of the curriculum. Decision No. 404/QD-TTg approved by the Prime Minister on 27 March 2015 indicates how the general education curriculum and textbooks will be reformed. The new curriculum, which is expected to be adopted in SY2018/19, will integrate or unify separate subjects under a broader theme of studies relevant to the needs of learners and the local conditions of different regions in the country. This approach will also allow some of the curriculum to be localized to ensure that its scope and contents are relevant to the needs of different population groups in different areas of the country. Subsequently, localized textbooks will adopt competency-based education principles and incorporate innovative and active teaching and learning activities to equip students with the knowledge and skills to function effectively in their communities and in society at large.

114. **Improved qualifications of teachers.** The nationwide teacher assessment for secondary teachers was implemented in SY2011/12. Teachers are assessed as excellent, good, average, or unqualified according to six standards subdivided into 25 criteria. Around 95% of secondary teachers were assessed in SY2013/14 (Table 2.1). Table 2.2 shows the results of secondary teacher assessments for the last 3 years.

Table 2.1: Number and Percentage of Secondary Teachers Assessed, SY2013/14

Number of lower secondary teachers assessed	94,063
Total number of lower secondary teachers in provinces reporting	100,538
Number of provinces reporting	24
Percentage of lower secondary teachers assessed in provinces reporting (%)	93.6
Number of upper secondary teachers assessed	44,426
Total number of upper secondary teachers in provinces reporting	45,892
Number of provinces reporting	24
Percentage of upper secondary teachers assessed in provinces reporting (%)	96.8

SY = school year.
Source: Ministry of Education and Training, Department of Teachers and Managers of Educational Institutes.

Table 2.2: Percentage of Lower Secondary and Upper Secondary Teachers by Assessment Category, SY2011/12 to SY2013/14

School Year	Excellent	Good	Fair	Unqualified
2011/12	49.3	42.9	7.0	0.1
2012/13	52.2	41.7	5.0	0.1
2013/14	54.3	41.6	4.0	0.1

SY = school year.
Source: Ministry of Education and Training, Department of Teachers and Managers of Educational Institutes.

115. The qualifications of teachers have been steadily improving (Tables 2.3 and 2.4) and are closing in on the targets set in the Education Development Strategy (EDS) 2011–2020.

Table 2.3: Percentage of Teachers with Academic Qualifications by Level of Education

Level	Qualification	2005	2010	2013
Lower secondary teachers	Teacher training college	70	60	34
	Teacher training university or above	30	40	65
Upper secondary teachers	Teacher training university	95	90	89
	Teacher training university (with master's degree) or above	5	10	10

Source: Ministry of Education and Training, Department of Planning and Finance.

Table 2.4: Number of Teachers in Vocational Education and Training Institutions by Formal Qualification in 2015

Subsector and Training Level	Total	Qualifications				Technical Skills	
		Postgraduate Degree (Master's, PhD)	Bachelor's Degree	College Diploma	Others		Integrative Teaching Ability
MOLISA	**39,152**	**7,342**	**17,430**	**4,962**	**9,418**	**16,052**	**41.0%**
Vocational colleges	15,986	4,670	9,246	1,271	799	3,053	19.1%
Vocational secondary schools (intermediate level)	9,254	2,406	4,720	925	1,203	2,797	30.2%
Vocational training centers (elementary level)	13,912	266	3,464	2,766	7,416	10,202	73.3%
MOET	**34,460**	**17,014**	**12,022**	**4,844**	**580**	**n/a**	**n/a**
Technical colleges	24,260	13,542	7,350	3,160	208	n/a	n/a
Professional secondary schools	10,200	3,472	4,672	1,684	372	n/a	n/a
	73,612	24,356	29,452	9,806	9,998		

n/a = not applicable, MOET = Ministry of Education and Training, MOLISA = Ministry of Labour–Invalids and Social Affairs.
Sources: Directorate of Vocational Education and Training, National Institute for Vocational Education and Training. 2017. *Viet Nam Vocational Education and Training Report 2015*. Ha Noi; and MOLISA. 2017. Project on Renovation and Improvement of the Quality of Technical and Vocational Education and Training – Up to 2020, with Orientation to 2030 (Draft October 2017). Ha Noi.

116. **Improved quantity and quality of facilities.** In spite of an increase in student enrollment in LSE, the number of schools has decreased in LSE while it is the opposite for USE (Table 2.5).

Table 2.5: Number of Schools and Percentage Change in Number, SY2011/12 to SY2017/18

	2011/12	2012/13	2013/14	2014/15	2015/16	2016/17	2017/18	Percentage Difference in SY2011/12 and SY2017/18
Lower secondary education	10,243	10,290	10,882	10,293	10,312	10,155	10,091	(1.5%)
Upper secondary education	2,350	2,425	2,758	2,386	2,399	2,391	2,398	2.0%

( ) = negative, SY = school year.
Source: Ministry of Education and Training. 2018. *Education Statistics 2017–2018.* Ha Noi.

117. MOET developed and approved national standards for secondary schools to ensure all schools have quality school buildings and facilities and adequate number of teachers and instructional materials.[45] These standards are especially important in rural areas, where costs are often higher but incomes lower. All schools, no matter where they are built, must meet the national standards for effective teaching and learning. The performance target indicator was for 25% of public secondary schools to be accredited using the new national standards by 2015. Schools complete the "self-evaluation" section of the evaluation and then an external evaluation team completes their reports. The accreditation profiles include the self-evaluation report, the external report, and the certificate of accreditation.

Table 2.6: Number of Secondary Schools Completing Evaluation as of the End of SY2014/15

	Total Number of Schools	Number of Schools Completed Internal Evaluation	Percentage of Completed Internal Evaluation	Number of Schools Completed External Evaluation	Percentage of Completed External Evaluation
Lower secondary	10,752	10,262	95.4%	2,059	19.3%
Upper secondary	2,708	2,419	89.3%	501	18.5%

SY = school year.
Source: Ministry of Education and Training.

118. As shown in Table 2.6, most secondary schools have completed their self-evaluation, but only about one-fifth have completed the external evaluation and have been accredited as meeting national standards. It is possible that once schools have completed an internal evaluation, they determine that they would not meet national standards and do not proceed to undergo an external examination, which would indicate that facilities need upgrading. Alternatively, it could be that the availability of external evaluators and the costs for an external evaluation have held back the completion of external evaluations. MOET is seeking to train additional external evaluators and has issued guidelines on how to finance expenses for external teams.

---

[45]   Circular No. 67/2011/TT-BGDDT dated 30 December 2011 on Evaluation Standards of Primary Schools and Circular No.13/2012/TT-BGD dated 6 April 2012 Approving the Updated National Secondary Standards for Schools.

2. Access and Equity

119. **Increased access to education.** Figure 2.1 plots the number of students enrolled in each educational subsector from 2005 to 2016 and Table 2.7 shows the percentage change over this period. Viet Nam has been experiencing a decline in birth rate, which is reflected in the dip in the total number of students in the educational system, seen around SY2008/09. The total number of students served by the education sector has not changed significantly over the past 10 years, but the enrollment by subsector has shown different patterns. Over this time period, preprimary schools have had a steady increase in number of children and serve about twice as many students. The number of students in primary school declined from a high of 8,350,191 in SY2003/04 to a low of 6,745,016 in SY2008/09 and has since rebounded to 7,790,009 in SY2015/16. At the LSE level, the enrollment peaked at 6,670,714 in SY2005/06 and then declined to 4,869,839 in SY2012/13 and has shown some growth in SY2015/16. The USE enrollment peaked in SY2006/07 at 3,111,280 and has since steadily declined to 2,425,130 in SY2015/16. Enrollment in professional secondary jumped from 360,392 in SY2003/04 to 614,516 in SY2007/08 but has since steadily declined to 315,000 in SY2015/16. Enrollment in colleges declined by 274,674 between SY2012/13 and SY 2015/16 after having seen very significant growth over the previous 9 years. Enrollment in university showed significant steady growth from 2005 to 2016.

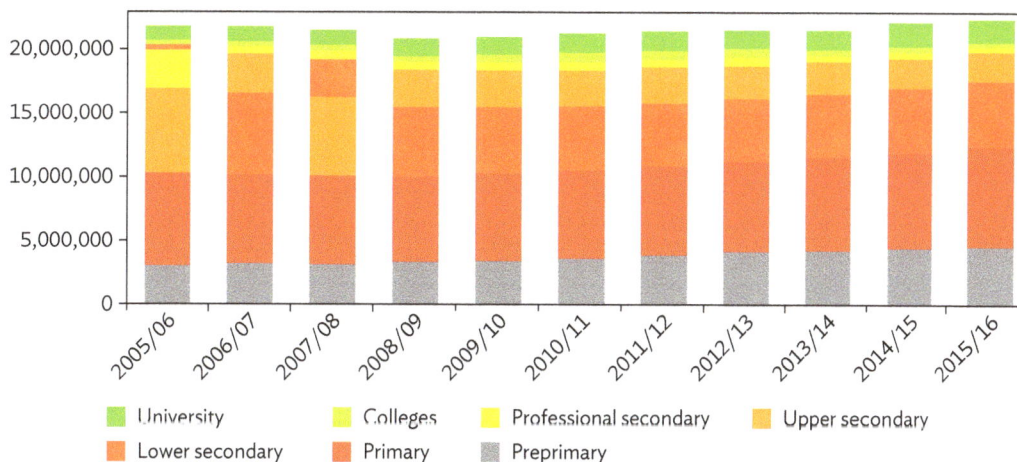

Figure 2.1: Number of Students in School, SY2005/06 to SY2015/16

SY = school year.
Source: Ministry of Education and Training. 2017. *Education Statistics 2015–2016*. Ha Noi.

Table 2.7: Change in Student Enrollment, SY2005/06 to SY2015/16

Education Subsector	Change in Number of Students	Percentage Change (%)
Preprimary	1,602,654	53.0
Primary	468,270	6.4
Lower secondary	(1,532,068)	(23.0)
Upper secondary	(551,742)	(18.5)
Professional secondary	(185,252)	(37.0)
College	150,264	50.2
University	665,361	61.2

( ) = decrease in enrollment, SY = school year.
Source: Ministry of Education. 2017. *Education Statistics 2015–2016*. Ha Noi.

120. Primary education is almost universal. The net enrollment rate was 99.4%, and 97.5% of children in grade 1 completed 5 years of primary education in 2016.[46] In most provinces, the targets of 99% net enrollment rate and 90% completion rate have been achieved.

121. Since SY2010/11, all provinces have achieved MOET's universalization targets for LSE. However, the EDS 2011–2020 target of a 95% net enrollment rate (NER) by 2020 has not yet been realized (Table 2.8). The NER for USE has likewise improved but also falls short of the 80% EDS target for youths within the age range attaining USE or equivalent level by 2020. Table 2.9 shows considerable variation in the NER by province, with a very low rate for some provinces particularly at USE.

Table 2.8: Net Enrollment Rate, SY2005/06 to SY2015/2016

Educational Level	2006	2008	2010	2011	2012	2013	2014	2015	2016
Primary	89.3	88.3	94.9	95.3	96.5	96.6	99.0	99.4	99.4
Lower secondary	78.8	78.4	81.9	82.5	83.9	88.0	89.9	90.9	92.3
Upper secondary	53.9	54.2	58.1	60.2	62.5	64.4	58.6	61.0	63.0

SY = school year.
Notes: By agreement with the Asian Development Bank, figures for this table are taken from General Statistics Office for 2006 to 2012 and from the Ministry of Education and Training (MOET) for 2013 to 2016. MOET uses a slightly different methodology for calculating (different dates) net enrollment rate (NER). For example, for SY2015/16 MOET reported NER for lower secondary as 92.3, while GSO reported 91.4 and at the upper secondary MOET reported 63.0 and GSO reported 68.9. However, MOET does not provide NER with a gender breakdown (Tables 2.9, 2.14, 2.15). Sources: General Statistics Office of Viet Nam (GSO). 2011. *Viet Nam Population and Housing Census 2009 – Education in Viet Nam: An Analysis of Key Indicators.* Ha Noi; GSO. 2010, 2011, 2013. The April Time-Point Population Change and Family Planning Survey. Ha Noi; and MOET. 2017. *Education Statistics Yearbook 2015–2016.* Ha Noi.

Table 2.9: Net Enrollment Rate in 10 Lowest and Highest Provinces or Cities

	Ten Lowest			Ten Highest	
Province/City	Lower Secondary	Upper Secondary	Province/City	Lower Secondary	Upper Secondary
Soc Trang	72.6	33.1	Nam Dinh	98.2	89.3
Gia Lai	74.4	37.7	Thai Binh	97.9	87.1
Bac Lieu	75.3	40.7	Hai Phong	97.8	84.3
Ca Mau	75.8	42.1	Ha Noi	97.6	84.2
Ha Giang	76.4	42.2	Ha Nam	97.6	83.9
Ninh Thuan	77.1	42.4	Phu Tho	97.5	83.2
Lai Chau	77.2	42.5	Hung Yen	97.5	82.0
Kien Giang	78.7	43.7	Bac Ninh	97.2	81.5
Cao Bang	80.8	45.5	Vinh Phuc	97.0	81.0
Son La	81.4	46.9	Thai Nguyen	97.0	81.0

Source: General Statistics Office. 2016. Major Findings: The 1/4/2015 Time-Point Population Change and Family Planning Survey. Ha Noi.

122. **Gender parity in education is being achieved**. As can be seen in Table 2.10 between SY2009/10 and SY2015/16 the percentage of female students enrolled in primary and lower secondary remained about the same. More males than females were enrolled in primary and lower secondary because there were more males of school age in those years. For SY2015/16, females made up 48.8% of the children of LSE age. In USE, the percentage of female students enrolled remained above 53.0%.

---

[46]   NER is defined by the UNESCO Institute for Statistics as enrollment of the official age group for a given level of education expressed as a percentage of the corresponding population.

More females than males were enrolled in USE even though there were fewer females in the upper secondary school-aged population. The percentage of females enrolled in colleges and university consistently hovers around 50%.

Table 2.10: Student Enrollment by Gender by School Level, SY2009/10 to SY2015/16

	2009/10	2010/11	2011/12	2012/13	2013/14	2014/15	2015/16
Primary	6,922,624	7,048,493	7,100,950	7,202,767	7,435,600	7,543,632	7,790,009
Female	3,271,858	3,337,266	3,447,654	3,438,338	3,688,413	3,611,152	3,735,231
	47.3%	47.3%	48.6%	47.7%	49.6%	47.9%	47.9%
Lower secondary	5,214,045	4,968,302	4,926,401	4,869,839	4,932,390	5,098,830	5,138,646
Female	2,598,267	2,395,682	2,388,172	2,363,611	2,401,840	2,489,545	2,506,551
	49.8%	48.2%	48.5%	48.5%	48.7%	48.8%	48.8%
Upper secondary	2,886,090	2,835,025	2,755,210	2,675,320	2,532,696	2,439,919	2,425,130
Female	1,521,326	1,492,238	1,466,155	1,417,899	1,339,558	1,296,153	1,298,292
	52.7%	52.6%	53.2%	53.0%	52.9%	53.1%	53.5%
Tertiary	1,935,739	2,162,106	2,204,313	2,171,399	2,061,641	2,363,942	2,202,732
Female	965,733	1,079,440	1,092,433	1,082,805	n/a	1,165,104	1,203,677
	49.9%	49.9%	49.6%	49.9%		49.3%	54.6%

n/a = not applicable, SY = school year.
Sources: Ministry of Education and Training. 2017. *Education Statistics 2015–2016*. Ha Noi; and MOET. 2012. *Education Statistics 1999–2010*. Ha Noi.

123. Table 2.11 shows that the NER in all levels of general education improved between 2006 and 2014 for both the male and female populations, but the increase was greater for females at the LSE and USE levels. The 2014 NER is higher for females at LSE and USE levels. However, further analysis shows that the situation is not uniform across provinces. In the rural parts of the Northern Midland and Mountainous region, the NER for females was 1.9 percentage points lower than for males at the primary level and 2.1 percentage points lower at the LSE level in 2013. Table 2.12 shows the difference between genders at the LSE level—some provinces favor females and others favor males. Issues relating to poverty and membership in an ethnic minority appear to inhibit females of these groups from attending school while in other locales the pressure for males to be economically productive limits their ability to attend school. This difference is not apparent at the USE level, which could be because poor and ethnic minority children from both sexes are equally not in attendance.

Table 2.11: Net Enrollment Rate by Gender for Viet Nam Secondary Schools

	Primary			Lower Secondary			Upper Secondary		
	Total	Boys	Girls	Total	Boys	Girls	Total	Boys	Girls
2006	89.3	89.3	89.2	78.8	78.3	79.2	53.9	51.5	56.4
2008	88.3	88.7	87.9	78.4	77.3	79.5	54.2	50.3	58.5
2010	91.9	92.3	91.5	81.3	80.1	82.6	58.2	53.7	63.1
2012	92.4	92.2	92.7	83.9	79.8	83.0	62.5	55.2	63.9
2014	93.0	93.4	92.6	84.4	83.8	85.1	63.1	58.2	68.3
% Change 2006 to 2014	3.7	4.1	3.4	5.6	5.5	5.9	9.2	6.7	11.9

Source: General Statistics Office of Viet Nam. 2016). *Household Living Standards Survey 2014*. Ha Noi.

Table 2.12: Net Enrollment in Lower Secondary Education for 10 Provinces with Largest Difference between Males and Females, 2015

(%)

Province	Total NER	Male NER	Female NER	Female–Male Difference
Kon Tum	81.7	76.6	86.8	10.2
Lam Dong	86.1	81.9	90.2	8.3
Binh Duong	84.1	80.6	88.2	7.6
Soc Trang	72.6	68.8	76.3	7.4
Kien Giang	78.7	75.2	82.5	7.3
Cao Bang	80.8	82.4	79.2	–3.2
Lai Chau	77.2	79.6	74.6	–5.0
Ha Giang	76.4	79.5	73.2	–6.3
Son La	81.4	85.1	77.4	–7.7
Dien Bien	84.1	89.0	79.0	–10.0

NER = net enrollment rate.
Source: General Statistics Office of Viet Nam. 2016. *Major Findings: The 1/4/2015 Time-Point Population Change and Family Planning Survey.* Ha Noi.

124. Another area for equality for females appears to be related to the ratio of female staff in schools. As shown in Table 2.13, most general education teachers are female. There has been some discussion that even though the majority of teachers are female, the percentage of school, institution, provincial, and MOET senior staff who are females is not equivalent.

Table 2.13: Number and Percentage of Teachers/Instructors by Level and Gender, SY2009/10 to SY2015/16

	2009/10	2010/11	2011/12	2012/13	2013/14	2014/15	2015/16
Primary	347,840	359,039	366,045	381,432	387,196	392,136	396,843
Female	270,912	276,896	283,361	291,228	292,515	304,391	308,883
Percentage of female	77.9%	77.1%	77.4%	76.4%	75.5%	77.6%	77.8%
Lower secondary	313,911	312,710	311,970	315,405	315,593	312,587	313,526
Female	216,961	211,035	213,072	212,184	214,030	213,625	214,427
Percentage of female	69.1%	67.5%	68.3%	67.3%	67.8%	68.3%	68.4%
Upper secondary	142,432	146,789	150,133	150,915	152,689	152,007	150,900
Female	90,488	87,345	92,004	91,418	93,932	95,900	95,534
Percentage of female	63.5%	59.5%	61.3%	60.6%	61.5%	63.1%	63.3%

SY = school year.
Sources: Ministry of Education and Training (MOET). 2017. *Education Statistics 2015–2016.* Ha Noi; and MOET. 2012. *Education Statistics 1999–2010.* Ha Noi.

125. The results for PISA 2015 related to gender indicated the following: (i) in mathematics, the OECD average gender difference (boys–girls) was 8 score points but in Viet Nam girls outscored boys by 3 score points which is not considered statistically significant; (ii) in reading, in all countries that participated, girls outperformed boys with an average gender difference (boys–girls) of –27 score points while for Viet Nam the gender difference was –25 points; (iii) in science, the OECD average

gender difference (boys–girls) was 4 score points, but in Viet Nam girls outscored boys by 3 score points which was not considered statistically different.

126. The NAM results (Table 2.20 and Table 2.22) show that males and female performance at grade 9 is very similar but girls outperform boys in all subjects at grade 11.

127. In 2014, the NER was higher for females at all levels, which means that a higher percentage of females were attending school than boys or the gap in attendance was in favor of females. Results from the NAM and PISA indicate that in Viet Nam females are either outperforming males or performance is not statistically different.

128. **Improved access for students from an ethnic minority.** As can be seen in Table 2.14, the percentage of ethnic minority students enrolled in LSE and USE between SY2011/12 and SY2017/18 increased. While the percentage of ethnic minority students has held steady at around 17.5% in primary, there is a slight increase by 0.5% in LSE and 1.3% in USE.

Table 2.14: Enrollment of Students from Ethnic Minorities, SY2011/12 to SY2017/18

	2011/12	2012/13	2013/14	2014/15	2015/16	2016/17	2017/18
Primary	7,100,950	7,202,767	7,435,600	7,543,632	7,790,009	7,801,560	8,041,842
Ethnic minority	1,244,771	1,265,096	1,446,147	1,319,029	1,354,009	1,381,917	1,416,710
Percentage of ethnic minority	17.5%	17.6%	19.4%	17.5%	17.4%	17.7%	17.6%
Lower secondary	4,926,401	4,869,839	4,932,390	5,098,830	5,138,646	5,235,524	5,373,312
Ethnic minority	774,358	777,521	794,439	816,995	834,429	853,573	875,977
Percentage of ethnic minority	15.7%	16.0%	16.1%	16.0%	16.2%	16.3%	16.3%
Upper secondary	2,755,210	2,675,320	2,532,696	2,439,919	2,425,130	2,477,175	2,508,564
Ethnic minority	299,602	296,854	299,594	296,868	299,394	301,502	306,091
Percentage of ethnic minority	10.9%	11.1%	11.8%	12.2%	12.3%	12.2%	12.2%

SY = school year.
Source: Ministry of Education and Training. 2018. *Education Statistics 2017–2018*. Ha Noi.

129. Table 2.15 shows the NER for all groups with a substantial increase at both LSE and USE levels between 2008 and 2012. However, the NER is still lower for ethnic minority students than for Kinh/Hoa, and the NER for minority students in USE is particularly low. Table 2.16 shows a more detailed breakdown by ethnic group and illustrates the differences among groups. The NER among the H'mong and Dao are particularly low at the USE level.

Table 2.15: Net Enrollment Rate by Ethnic Group

Year	Lower Secondary			Upper Secondary		
	Total	Kinh/Hoa	Other ethnic group	Total	Kinh/Hoa	Other ethnic group
2008	78.4	81.2	64.1	54.2	58.6	29.4
2012	82.3	84.8	71.1	60.3	65.3	37.7

Source: General Statistics Office of Viet Nam. 2013. *Vietnam Household Living Standards Survey 2012*. Ha Noi.

Table 2.16: Net Enrollment by Ethnic Group and Level, 2014

	Primary	Lower Secondary	Upper Secondary
Kinh	93.4	86.9	69.0
Tay	93.4	89.6	66.3
Thai	93.2	81.3	32.8
Hoa	95.6	90.3	65.0
Khome	89.1	59.9	24.1
Muong	89.2	90.3	62.7
Nung	96.5	89.2	51.2
H'mong	89.4	57.3	18.3
Dao	90.5	71.5	19.5
Others	90.5	66.7	32.9

Source: General Statistics Office of Viet Nam. 2016. *The 1/4/2015 Time-Point Population Change and Family Planning Survey.* Ha Noi.

130. Through the government's efforts, the number and percentage of teachers from an ethnic minority increased at the primary and secondary levels (Table 2.17) between SY2011/12 and SY2017/18. However, there is still a need to attract more teachers from ethnic minority backgrounds, particularly to support the efforts of MOET in encouraging the development of textbooks and learning materials suitable for the local context. Also, having more teachers of an ethnic minority at the USE level will encourage more students from an ethnic minority to enroll in USE.

Table 2.17: Number and Percentage of Primary and Secondary Ethnic Minority Teachers, SY2011/12 to SY2017/18

	2011/12	2012/13	2013/14	2014/15	2015/16	2016/17	2017/18
No. of primary	366,045	381,432	387,196	392,136	396,843	397,098	396,600
No. of ethnic minority	46,739	47,096	47,075	49,713	50,634	N/A	N/A
Percentage of ethnic minority	12.8%	12.3%	12.1%	12.7%	12.8%	N/A	N/A
No. of lower secondary	311,970	315,405	315,593	312,587	313,526	310,953	303,947
No. of ethnic minority	24,770	24,668	24,867	24,850	24,978	N/A	N/A
Percentage of ethnic minority	7.9%	7.8%	7.9%	7.9%	8.0%	N/A	N/A
No. of upper secondary	150,133	150,915	152,689	152,007	150,900	150,721	150,288
No. of ethnic minority	7,842	7,947	8,661	8,728	8,636	N/A	N/A
Percentage of ethnic minority	5.2%	5.3%	5.7%	5.7%	5.7%	N/A	N/A

N/A = not applicable, SY = school year.
Source: Ministry of Education and Training. 2018. *Education Statistics 2017–2018.* Ha Noi.

3. Governance

131. **The education strategy has been integrated into the national development strategy.** The policy framework for long-term development of the education sector has been defined and guided by the following key government strategies and plans: the Socio-Economic Development

Strategy (SEDS) 2011–2020,[47]Socio-Economic Development Plan (SEDP) 2011–2015,[48] Human Resources Development Strategy 2011–2020,[49] Human Resources Development Master Plan 2011–2020,[50] Human Resources Development for Education Sector during 2011–2020,[51] and Education Development Strategy (EDS) 2011–2020.[52] In accordance with the EDS, MOET issued the strategy action plan in April 2013 and started implementation to achieve, by 2020, the following targets: (i) 80% of children of kindergarten age will be in preschools; (ii) net enrollment rate for primary, LSE, and USE will be 99%, 95%, and 80%, respectively; (iii) 70% of children with a disability attend school; and (iv) 70% of laborers receive skills training.

132. In November 2013, the Central Committee of the Communist Party issued the Resolution on the Comprehensive Renovation of Education and Training.[53] This commitment from the highest level of government is for comprehensive renovation to promote quality education and training to enhance integration of all youth and competitiveness in the labor market. The resolution covers the development of the new curriculum, textbooks, and teacher training based on the regional needs and competency-based approach. This resolution is one of the milestone reforms for Viet Nam's education which had been very much centralized and standardized by the central government. Now, each region can propose educational content that is more responsive to local needs as well as have more options for selecting textbooks that can attract students. These new curricula and textbooks are expected to help develop competencies as well as reduce the dropout rate and increase the retention of academically disadvantaged students.

133. **Sustainable public expenditure on education and training**. The government increased annual spending on education and training from VND115,676 billion in 2010 to VND229,592 billion in 2015, or a total of about 98.5% over the period (Table 2.18).[54] Reflecting the importance of education and training in the government's integrated strategy for economic development, education and training expenditure is targeted to be 20% of total government expenditures.[55] In 2015, the government budget for education and training was to be 19.1% of the total government budget but as seen in Table 2.18 the actual expenditure was 15.3%. As a percentage of the country's gross national product, annual expenditure on education and training remained fairly constant from 2010 to 2015 at around 5.5%.

---

[47]   Approved by the Eleventh Congress of the Viet Nam Communist Party.

[48]   Resolution No. 10/2011/QH13 Approved at the National Assembly 8 November 2011.

[49]   Prime Minister's Decision No. 579/QD-TTg dated 19 April 2011 Approving the Strategy on Development of Vietnamese Human Resources during 2011–2020.

[50]   Prime Minister's Decision No. 1216/QD-TTg dated 22 July 2011 Approving the Master Plan on Development of Vietnam's Human Resources during 2011–2020.

[51]   Approved by MOET in Decision No. 6639 dated 29 December 2011 Approving the Human Resources Development for Education Sector during 2011–2020.

[52]   Prime Minister's Decision No. 711/QD-TTg dated 13 June 2012 Approving the Education Development Strategy 2011–2020.

[53]   Issued by the Central Committee of the Communist Party of Viet Nam at the Central Conference XI dated 4 November 2013.

[54]   The value of total government expenditure on education and training for 2013 is based on a MOET estimate.

[55]   Prime Minister's Decision No. 711/QD-TTg Approving the Education Development Strategy 2011–2020. Ha Noi.

Table 2.18: Trends in the Financing of Education in Viet Nam, 2010–2015

Item	2010	2011	2012	2013	2014	2105
Government expenditure on education and training (VND billion)[a]	115,676	133,914	178,751	208,087	218,375	229,592
Government annual expenditure (VND billion)[b]	850,874	1,034,244	1,170,924	1,277,710	1,339,489	1,502,189
Total education and training expenditure as % of total expenditure	13.6%	12.9%	15.3%	16.3%	16.3%	15.3%
Total Viet Nam gross domestic product (GDP) (VND billion, current price)[c]	2,157,828	2,779,881	3,245,419	3,584,262	3,937,856	4,192,862
Annual growth rate of GDP (%)	19.3%	28.8%	16.7%	10.4%	9.9%	6.5%
Annual inflation (%)	12.9%	22.6%	11.5%	3.2%	3.2%	3.2%
Proportion of total government education and training expenditure to GDP (%)	5.4%	4.8%	5.5%	5.8%	5.5%	5.5%
Annual growth rates (%)						
Government education and training expenditure	22.6%	15.8%	33.5%	16.4%	4.9%	5.1%

Sources:
[a] Data provided by Ministry of Education and Training.
[b] Government annual expenditure data are collected from Ministry of Finance. http://www.mof.gov.vn (accessed 26 August 2017).
[c] World Bank. http://data.worldbank.org/indicator/NY.GDP.MKTP.CN (retrieved on 15 April 2016).

B. Key Sector Development Needs

134. While Viet Nam's education sector is now better organized, more diversified, and better funded, many issues still limit the sector's capacity to respond to the needs of a growing economy—poor quality, limited access, inequities, and ineffective governance remain. A 2016 World Bank report indicated that Viet Nam's education system is inclusive, high-quality, and largely equitable through lower secondary education but above that level it is exclusive, inequitable, and mediocre (World Bank Group 2016). The system provides students with an excellent foundation for success, but then fails to build on that foundation. Too many students fail to enter and graduate from high school and too few continue to tertiary education and those who do continue often do not receive a high-quality, relevant education. The 2016 United Nations Development Programme (UNDP)–Viet Nam Academy of Social Sciences (VASS) report echoes these findings in that outside of primary and lower secondary schooling, serious disparities have emerged and, while vocational training and higher education are fundamental for inclusive growth there is evidence of social stratification and exclusion at these levels (UNDP and VASS 2016). The lack of relevance and the slowness to respond to changing needs are major problems at all levels.

135. The government is aware of the development needs for the education sector, noting in its review of the progress toward achievement of the Millennium Development Goals that the speed of improvement in education has lagged behind national economic growth and a fast-changing society. Inequality in educational access and quality persists among different ethnic groups and disparate

geographic regions. The Education Development Strategy (EDS) 2011–2020 identifies some of the education system's constraints: (i) the national education system is not comprehensive and lacks strategic links among education subsectors and training qualifications; (ii) the quality and effectiveness of education are still low compared with the development requirements of the country and with those of other developing countries; (iii) the management of education and training is not consistent with the responsibilities and duties in human resources and financial management; (iv) teaching staff and education managers are not yet capable of meeting the requirement of educational tasks in the new period; (v) the content, the teaching and learning methods, and the examination and evaluation activities have been slow to change and are not suitable for different regions and different learners; (vi) temporary, old, and ruined classrooms still exist, especially in the remote areas, and the number of libraries, laboratories, subject-based rooms, and teaching and learning equipment is insufficient; and (vii) the quality and effectiveness of scientific research are inadequate and not linked to training or economic needs.

136. A problem tree analysis carried out based on the analysis of secondary education sector constraints (Appendix 1), identified the core problem: not enough graduates and early school leavers have the required competencies for the middle-income inclusive labor market. The three main root causes were identified as follows: (i) the quality of secondary education is weak and not relevant to the labor market, (ii) equitable access to quality education is insufficient to meet student and national needs, and (iii) education resource management is ineffective and inefficient.

137. A problem tree analysis conducted for a parallel ADB (2018) study on technical and vocational education and training (TVET) identified the core sector problem: most TVET institutions provide graduates with insufficient skills to increase productivity and competitiveness of companies. This study indicated that the root causes were (i) ineffective management of skills development, (ii) inequitable access to advanced skills acquisition, (iii) weak accountability structures, (iv) insufficient enterprise-based training, (v) skills not properly taught, and (vi) wrong skills taught.

138. The competencies of those leaving the education sector, either upon graduation from USE, secondary TVET institution, or of those leaving before graduation, are not the competencies deemed critical to function in a modern society. In addition to not producing the quality graduates needed, the sector is not educating enough students to be able to fill the needs for development and societal stability. Low quality is a result of weak systems for curriculum development and implementation, a shortage of qualified teachers and instructors at all levels, weak linkage with industry and higher education, little emphasis on noncognitive skills, and poor creative thinking and higher order skills development. The inequities in quality and access result partly from financial and cultural barriers to basic education for ethnic minority youth, disabled children, and youth from domestic migrant families. Weak sector management and governance arise mainly from poor quality assurance of public and private institutions, and overly centralized and inflexible governance structures.

1. Secondary Education Is Weak and Not Relevant to the Labor Market

139. **School leavers do not have required competencies.** Despite the relative success of Viet Nam's students in the Programme for International Student Assessment (PISA) there is a persistent perception that students are receiving a low quality of education, and that the competencies of the graduates or those leaving the system before graduation are not meeting the country's needs either in the labor market and economic development, or in social development. The EDS 2011–2020

confirms that the quality and effectiveness of the education sector are low relative to the development requirements of the country and with those of other developed countries, and the qualification of undergraduates are not meeting the requirements of the job market. Resolution No. 29 on Fundamental and Comprehensive Innovation in Education noted that the quality and effectiveness of education are still lower than expected especially in higher education. Besides lacking in continuity between levels and education methods, the education system is theoretical rather than practical. Further, training is not well associated with scientific research, manufacturing, business, and labor market demands. Education about ethics, lifestyles, and working skills are underestimated. The methods of education, testing, and assessment are still obsolete and imprecise.

140. The data from national and international assessments indicate that although students perform relatively well against international standards they are not performing as well as many of Viet Nam's neighboring economic competitors—the results are declining in some subjects and, in most subjects, students are not meeting national standards. Between SY2008/09 (Table 2.19) and SY2012/13 (Table 2.20), grade 9 students' NAM performance in three subjects (mathematics, literature, and English) declined significantly. Different areas of science were tested in the two cycles and cannot be directly compared. Further, on the 2012/13 assessments, only around half of the grade 9 students were considered to have met the required standard.

Table 2.19: Results for Grade 9 (SY2008/09) National Achievement Monitoring
(Percentage meeting the acceptable standard)

	Total Population	Males	Females	Kinh	Other
Mathematics	58.7	57.7	59.9	62.2	38.5
Literature	66.4	58.1	74.2	69.4	49.3
English	57.5	53.9	60.4	59.5	46.5
Physics	58.1			60.6	49.3

SY = school year.
Source: Ministry of Education and Training, Center of Education Quality Assurance.

Table 2.20: Results for Grade 9 (SY2012/13) National Achievement Monitoring
(Percentage meeting the acceptable standard)

	Total Population	Males	Females	Kinh	Other
Mathematics	46.7	46.7	46.6	50.5	24.0
Literature	51.4	52.9	49.9	55.6	27.1
English	42.9	43.2	42.7	45.6	27.4
Biology	51.5	52.0	51.0	53.7	39.0

SY = school year.
Source: Ministry of Education and Training, Center of Education Quality Assurance.

141. At the grade 11 level, student performance declined slightly in mathematics between SY2011/12 (Table 2.21) and SY2014/15 (Table 2.22) but improved significantly in literature and English. Other than in literature in 2014/15, only around 50% of the students met the national expectations.

Table 2.21: Results for Grade 11 (SY2011/12) National Achievement Monitoring
(Percentage meeting the acceptable standard)

	Total Population	Males	Females	Kinh	Other
Mathematics	54.8	52.0	57.2	58.1	27.3
Literature	53.5	43.0	62.3	56.3	30.0
English	24.2	20.3	27.5	25.6	12.2

SY = school year.
Source: Ministry of Education and Training, Center of Education Quality Assurance.

Table 2.22: Results for Grade 11 (SY2014/15) National Achievement Monitoring
(Percentage meeting the acceptable standard)

	Total Population	Males	Females	Kinh	Other
Mathematics	52.2	48.0	55.8	54.4	30.0
Literature					
Multiple Choice	72.5	66.9	77.4	74.2	55.2
Open-ended	76.7	68.2	84.1	77.7	66.2
English	40.4	38.5	45.2	41.9	25.2

SY = school year.
Source: Ministry of Education and Training, Center of Education Quality Assurance.

142. The results from PISA 2012 showed that Vietnamese students were exceeding international standards in all three areas of assessment, but their performance declined significantly on the PISA 2015 assessment in reading and mathematics (Figure 2.2 and Table 2.23). It should be noted that even in 2015, the average student performance in these two subjects was still at the OECD average and that their performance in science was among the highest in the world. The results in 2015 in mathematics and reading are similar to the OECD average but the mathematics results are lower than many of its Asian neighbors. The results in science are above both the OECD average and most of its neighbors.

Figure 2.2: Summary of PISA Results, 2012 and 2015

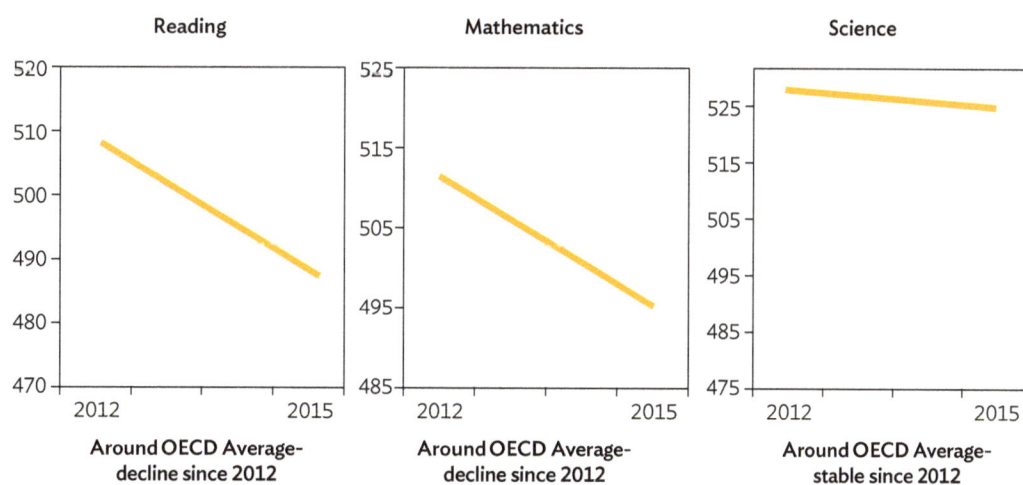

Reading — Around OECD Average-decline since 2012

Mathematics — Around OECD Average-decline since 2012

Science — Around OECD Average-stable since 2012

OECD = Organisation for Economic Co-operation and Development, PISA = Programme for International Student Assessment.
Sources: OECD. 2013. *PISA 2012 Results: What Students Know and Can Do – Student Performance in Mathematics, Reading and Science (Volume I)*. Paris; and OECD. 2016. *PISA 2015 Results: Excellence and Equity in Education (Volume I)*. Paris.

Table 2.23: Comparison of Viet Nam PISA Results, 2012 and 2015

	Performance in 2012	Performance 2015	Trend
Reading	Average score of 508 is significantly above the OECD average and its performance was not statistically different from the following economies: Austria; Australia; Belgium; Estonia; France; Germany; Liechtenstein; Macau, China; the Netherlands; New Zealand; Norway; Poland; Switzerland; the United Kingdom; and the United States (ranked 19th out of 65)	Average score of 487 is not significantly different from the OECD average and its performance was not statistically different from the following countries: Argentina, Austria, the People's Republic of China, Croatia, Czech Republic, Iceland, Israel, Italy, Luxembourg, the Russian Federation, and Switzerland (ranked 32nd of 75 participating countries)	Significant decline
Mathematics	Average score of 511 is significantly above the OECD average and its performance was not statistically different from the following countries: Austria, Australia, Belgium, Canada, Estonia, Finland, Germany, Ireland, the Netherlands, and Poland (ranked 17th out of 65 participating countries)	Average score of 495 is not significantly different from the OECD average and its performance was not statistically different from the following countries: Austria, Australia, Czech Republic, France, Iceland, Ireland, Italy, Luxembourg, New Zealand, Norway, Portugal, the Russian Federation, Spain, Sweden, and the United Kingdom (ranked 22nd of 75)	Significant decline
Science	Average score of 528 is significantly above the OECD average and its performance was not statistically different from the following economies: Australia; Canada; Taipei,China; Germany; Ireland; the Republic of Korea; Liechtenstein; Macau, China; the Netherlands; and Poland (ranked 8th out of 65)	Average score of 525 is significantly above the OECD average and its performance was not statistically different from the following economies: Canada; the People's Republic of China; Taipei,China; Finland; Hong Kong, China; the Republic of Korea; Macau, China; the Netherlands; and Poland (ranked 8th out of 75)	Stable

OECD = Organisation for Economic Co-operation and Development, PISA = Programme for International Student Assessment.
Sources: OECD. 2013. *PISA 2012 Results: What Students Know and Can Do – Student Performance in Mathematics, Reading and Science (Volume I)*. Paris; and OECD. 2016. *PISA 2015 Results: Excellence and Equity in Education (Volume I)*. Paris.

143. Table 2.24 shows that the performance of students in Viet Nam relative to students from more developed Asian economies is lower in mathematics and reading. In 2015, Vietnamese students' performance in science was only significantly lower than students from Singapore.

Table 2.24: Performance of Asian Economies in Mathematics, Reading, and Science in PISA, 2012 and 2015

	Mathematics		Reading		Science	
	2012	2015	2012	2015	2012	2015
Shanghai, PRC	613		570		580	
Singapore	573	564	570	535	551	556
Hong Kong, China	561	548	545	527	555	523
Macau, China	538	544	509	509	521	529
Taipei,China	560	542	523	497	523	532
Japan	536	532	538	516	547	538
B-S-J-G (PRC)[a]		531		484		518
Korea, Rep. of	554	524	536	517	538	516
Viet Nam	**511**	**495**	**508**	**487**	**528**	**525**
OECD average	494	490	496	483	501	493
Malaysia	421	446	398	431	420	443
Thailand	427	415	441	409	444	421
Indonesia	375	396	396	397	382	403

OECD = Organisation for Economic Co-operation and Development, PISA = Programme for International Student Assessment, PRC = People's Republic of China.
[a] B-S-J-G (PRC) refers to the four provinces in the PRC: Beijing, Shanghai, Jiangsu, and Guangdong.
Sources: OECD. 2013. *PISA 2012 Results: What Students Know and Can Do – Student Performance in Mathematics, Reading and Science (Volume I)*. Paris; and OECD. 2016. *PISA 2015 Results: Excellence and Equity in Education (Volume I)*. Paris.

144. Six proficiency levels are defined in the PISA assessments, with level 6 as the highest and level 1 as the lowest. Students at level 6 can successfully complete the most difficult PISA items. Level 2 is considered the baseline level of proficiency that is required to participate fully in modern society. Table 2.25 shows the percentage of Vietnamese students at or above level 2 in each subject for 2012 and 2015. PISA does not capture ethnicity. However, in Viet Nam the language of test is Vietnamese and most students from an ethnic minority speak another language at home so the last column does give an indication of how well ethnic minority students did on PISA. Student performance at this level is significantly better than the NAM results at both grades 9 and 11.

Table 2.25: Percentage of Students Meeting Baseline Level of Proficiency (Level 2 or Higher), Viet Nam PISA 2012 and 2015

	Total Population		Males		Females		Language of Test		Other Language	
	2012	2015	2012	2015	2012	2015	2012	2015	2012	2015
Mathematics	85.8	79.9	85.7	79.2	85.7	82.5	86.6	83.0	63.0	65.2
Reading	90.4	86.1	86.1	80.9	94.5	91.2	90.9	88.0	80.2	78.5
Science	93.3	94.1	92.3	93.4	94.3	94.7	94.1	94.9	80.3	91.4

PISA = Programme for International Student Assessment.
Source: Ministry of Education and Training, Center of Education Quality Assurance.

145. Having a low percentage of students performing at the top levels could signal the absence of a highly educated talent pool for the future. In 2012 and 2015, in mathematics and science, Viet Nam had about the same percentage of students achieving levels 5 and 6 as the OECD average but less than the high-performing Asian economies (Tables 2.26 to 2.29). In reading, the results at the upper two levels were not as good as the OECD average and much below the neighboring economies (Tables 2.30 and 2.31). Having few students achieving at the top levels can also indicate that students in Viet Nam are not acquiring the desired high-level competencies. This observation is reinforced by students' report that they seldom had the opportunity to participate in activities that would facilitate the acquisition of higher-level science competencies (Figure 2.5). Low performance among top performers coupled with high overall performance could be due to rote learning and proficient test-taking skills, rather than meaningful learning or the ability to use knowledge in new situations (Iyer 2017).

Table 2.26: Percentage of Students at Each Proficiency Level – Mathematics 2012

	Below Level 1	Level 1	Level 2	Level 3	Level 4	Level 5	Level 6
Shanghai, PRC	0.8	2.9	7.5	13.1	20.2	24.6	30.8
Singapore	2.2	6.1	12.2	17.5	22.0	21.0	19.0
Hong Kong, China	2.6	5.9	12.0	19.7	26.1	21.4	12.3
Taipei,China	4.5	8.3	13.1	17.1	19.7	19.2	18.0
Korea, Rep. of	2.7	6.4	14.7	21.4	23.9	18.8	12.1
Macau, China	3.2	7.6	16.4	24.0	24.4	16.8	7.6
Japan	3.2	7.9	16.9	24.7	21.7	16.0	7.6
Viet Nam	**3.6**	**10.6**	**22.8**	**28.4**	**21.3**	**9.8**	**3.5**
OECD average	8.0	15.0	22.5	23.7	18.2	9.3	3.3
Thailand	19.1	30.6	27.3	14.5	5.8	2.0	0.5
Malaysia	23.0	28.8	26.0	14.9	6.0	1.2	0.1
Indonesia	42.3	33.4	16.8	5.7	1.5	0.3	0.0

OECD = Organisation for Economic Co-operation and Development, PRC = People's Republic of China.
Source: OECD. 2013. *PISA 2012 Results: What Students Know and Can Do – Student Performance in Mathematics, Reading and Science (Volume I)*. Paris.

Table 2.27: Percentage of Students at Each Proficiency Level – Mathematics 2015

	Below Level 1	Level 1	Level 2	Level 3	Level 4	Level 5	Level 6
Singapore	2.0	5.3	12.4	20.0	25.1	21.7	13.1
Hong Kong, China	2.5	6.4	13.6	23.4	22.4	18.8	7.7
Macau, China	1.3	5.3	15.1	27.3	29.1	16.9	5.0
Taipei,China	4.4	8.3	14.6	21.2	23.3	18.0	10.1
Japan	2.9	7.8	17.2	25.8	25.9	15.0	5.3
B-S-J-G (PRC)[a]	5.8	10.0	16.3	20.5	21.8	16.6	9.0
Korea, Rep. of	5.4	10.0	17.2	23.7	22.7	14.3	6.6
Viet Nam	**4.5**	**14.6**	**26.4**	**27.0**	**18.2**	**7.2**	**2.1**
OECD average	8.5	14.9	22.5	24.8	18.6	8.4	2.3
Thailand	24.2	29.6	26.1	13.8	4.8	1.2	0.2
Indonesia	37.9	30.7	19.6	8.4	2.7	0.6	0.1

OECD = Organisation for Economic Co-operation and Development, PRC = People's Republic of China.
[a] B-S-J-G (PRC) refers to the four provinces in the PRC: Beijing, Shanghai, Jiangsu, and Guangdong.
Source: OECD. 2016. *PISA 2015 Results: Excellence and Equity in Education (Volume I)*. Paris.

Table 2.28: Percentage of Students at Each Proficiency Level – Science 2012

	Below Level 1	Level 1	Level 2	Level 3	Level 4	Level 5	Level 6
Shanghai, PRC	0.3	2.4	10.0	24.6	35.5	23.0	4.2
Singapore	2.2	7.4	16.7	24.0	27.0	16.9	5.8
Hong Kong, China	1.2	4.4	13.0	29.8	34.9	14.9	1.8
Taipei,China	1.6	8.2	20.8	33.7	27.3	7.8	0.6
Korea, Rep. of	1.2	5.5	18.0	33.6	30.1	10.6	1.1
Macau, China	1.4	7.4	22.2	36.2	26.2	6.2	0.4
Japan	2.0	6.4	16.3	27.5	29.5	14.8	3.4
Viet Nam	**0.9**	**5.8**	**20.7**	**37.5**	**27.0**	**7.3**	**1.0**
OECD average	4.8	13.0	24.5	28.8	20.5	7.2	1.2
Thailand	7.0	26.6	37.5	21.6	6.4	0.9	0.1
Malaysia	14.5	31.0	33.9	16.5	3.7	0.3	0.0
Indonesia	24.7	41.9	26.3	6.5	0.6	0.0	0.0

OECD = Organisation for Economic Co-operation and Development, PRC = People's Republic of China.
Source: OECD. 2013. *PISA 2012 Results: What Students Know and Can Do – Student Performance in Mathematics, Reading and Science (Volume I)*. Paris.

Table 2.29: Percentage of Students at Each Proficiency Level – Science 2015

	Below Level 1	Level 1a	Level 1b	Level 2	Level 3	Level 4	Level 5	Level 6
Singapore	0.2	2.0	7.5	15.1	23.4	27.7	18.6	5.6
Hong Kong, China	0.1	1.6	7.8	19.7	36.1	27.4	6.9	0.4
Macau, China	0.1	1.1	6.9	20.6	34.2	28.0	8.3	0.9
Taipei,China	0.3	2.7	9.4	18.1	27.0	27.1	12.7	2.7
Japan	0.2	1.7	7.7	18.1	28.2	28.8	12.9	2.4
B-S-J-G (PRC)[a]	0.6	3.8	11.8	20.7	25.8	23.8	11.5	2.1
Korea, Rep. of	0.4	2.9	11.1	21.7	29.2	24.0	9.2	1.4
Viet Nam	**0.0**	**0.2**	**5.7**	**25.3**	**36.6**	**23.9**	**7.1**	**1.2**
OECD average	0.6	5.4	17.5	24.8	27.2	19.0	6.7	1.1
Thailand	1.1	11.9	33.7	32.2	16.0	4.6	0.4	0.0
Indonesia	1.2	14.4	40.4	31.7	10.6	1.6	0.1	0.0

OECD = Organisation for Economic Co-operation and Development, PRC = People's Republic of China.
[a] B-S-J-G (PRC) refers to the four provinces in the PRC: Beijing, Shanghai, Jiangsu, and Guangdong.
Source: OECD. 2016. *PISA 2015 Results: Excellence and Equity in Education (Volume I)*. Paris.

Table 2.30: Percentage of Students at Each Proficiency Level – Reading 2012

	Below Level 1	Level 1a+1b	Level 2	Level 3	Level 4	Level 5	Level 6
Shanghai, PRC	0.3	2.8	11.0	25.3	35.7	21.3	3.8
Singapore	0.5	9.4	16.7	25.4	26.8	16.2	5.0
Hong Kong, China	0.2	6.6	14.3	29.2	32.9	14.9	1.9
Taipei,China	0.6	10.9	18.1	29.9	28.7	10.4	1.4
Korea, Rep. of	0.4	7.2	16.4	30.8	31.0	12.6	1.6
Macau, China	0.3	11.1	23.3	34.3	24.0	6.4	0.6
Japan	0.6	9.1	16.6	26.7	28.4	14.6	3.9
Viet Nam	**0.3**	**9.3**	**23.7**	**39.0**	**23.4**	**4.2**	**0.4**
OECD average	1.3	16.7	23.5	29.1	21.0	7.3	1.1
Thailand	1.2	31.8	36.0	23.5	6.7	0.8	0.3
Malaysia	5.8	46.9	31.0	13.6	2.5	0.1	0.0
Indonesia	4.1	51.1	31.6	11.5	1.5	0.1	0.0

OECD = Organisation for Economic Co-operation and Development, PRC = People's Republic of China.
Source: OECD. 2013. *PISA 2012 Results: What Students Know and Can Do – Student Performance in Mathematics, Reading and Science (Volume I).* Paris.

Table 2.31: Percentage of Students at Each Proficiency Level – Reading 2015

	Below Level 1	Level 1a	Level 1b	Level 2	Level 3	Level 4	Level 5	Level 6
Singapore	0.3	2.5	8.3	16.9	26.2	27.4	14.7	3.6
Hong Kong, China	0.3	2.0	7.0	18.1	32.1	29.0	10.4	1.1
Macau, China	0.3	2.3	9.3	23.1	34.2	24.4	6.2	0.5
Taipei,China	1.0	4.4	11.8	22.4	31.3	22.1	6.3	0.6
Japan	0.6	3.0	9.2	19.8	30.5	26.0	9.5	1.3
B-S-J-G (PRC)[a]	2.1	6.2	13.5	20.9	25.4	20.9	9.1	1.8
Korea, Rep. of	0.7	3.4	9.5	19.3	28.9	25.5	10.8	1.9
Viet Nam	**0.1**	**1.7**	**12.1**	**32.5**	**35.2**	**15.8**	**2.5**	**0.1**
OECD average	1.3	5.2	13.6	23.2	27.9	20.5	7.2	1.1
Thailand	2.8	15.1	32.1	31.1	15.0	3.7	0.3	0.0
Indonesia	3.8	16.8	34.8	30.9	11.7	1.9	0.1	0.0

OECD = Organisation for Economic Co-operation and Development, PRC = People's Republic of China.
[a] B-S-J-G (PRC) refers to the four provinces in the PRC: Beijing, Shanghai, Jiangsu, and Guangdong.
Source. OECD. 2016. *PISA 2015 Results. Excellence and Equity in Education (Volume I).* Paris.

146. Researchers are still trying to determine the reasons for the success of Viet Nam's students in PISA and for the decline between 2012 and 2015 in mathematics and reading. It is possible that positive student performance could have more to do with strong parental commitment to education and positive attitudes of students than the quality of the education system. Further, in both 2012 and 2015, Viet Nam had the lowest rate of 15-year-old students enrolled in school (Table 2.40). OECD has pointed out that if all of the 15-year-old students in Viet Nam were included in the analysis of PISA 2012, then the mathematics results would fall from being ranked 17th out of 64 participating countries and significantly above the average to 41st and significantly below the average (OECD 2013b). One would expect a similar result for science in 2015.

147. The Viet Nam Young Lives secondary school survey Wave 2 was conducted for SY2016/17. The samples (total of 8,740) were from grade 10 in five provinces: Ben Tre, Da Nang, Hung Yen, Lao Cai, and Phu Yen (Iyer, Azubuike, and Rolleston 2017). Students were assessed in mathematics and English at the beginning of school year and in problem-solving and critical-thinking at the end of their school

year. Figure 2.3 shows the student's performance in mathematics in Wave 1 (conducted in SY2011-12) and Wave 2. The results show that the performance varies across the provinces. Tables 2.23 and 2.33 show the variation by gender, ethnic status, and rural/urban. The tables indicate that the girls' scores were higher than the boys' and the ethnic majority (Kinh) performed better in both mathematics and English in both Waves.

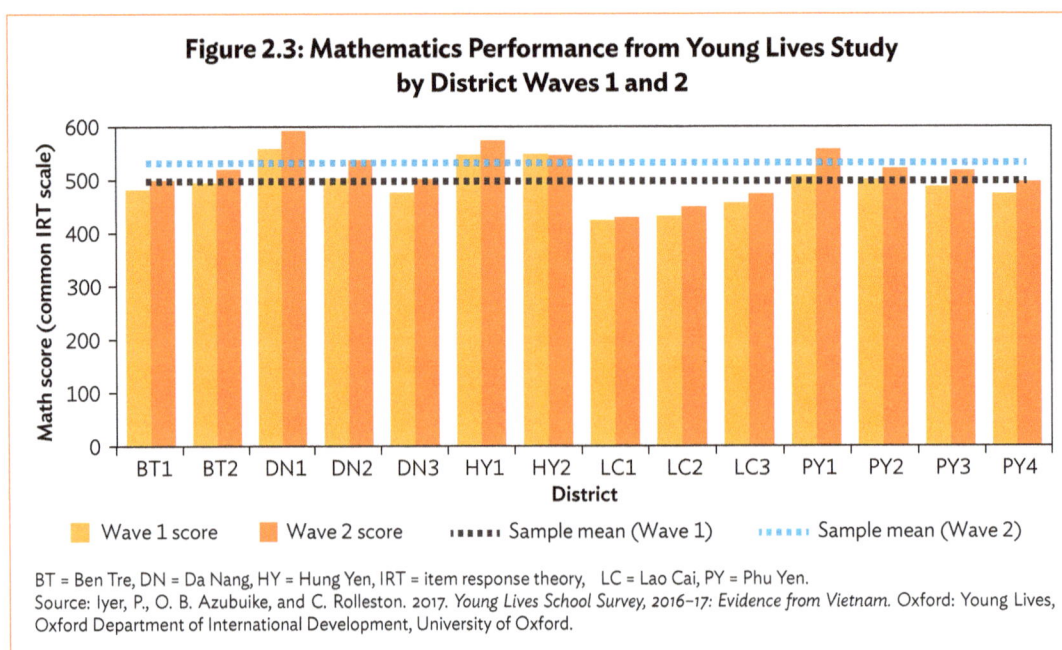

Figure 2.3: Mathematics Performance from Young Lives Study by District Waves 1 and 2

BT = Ben Tre, DN = Da Nang, HY = Hung Yen, IRT = item response theory,   LC = Lao Cai, PY = Phu Yen.
Source: Iyer, P., O. B. Azubuike, and C. Rolleston. 2017. *Young Lives School Survey, 2016–17: Evidence from Vietnam.* Oxford: Young Lives, Oxford Department of International Development, University of Oxford.

Table 2.32: Young Lives Mathematics Performance in Waves 1 and 2, by Gender, Ethnic Status, and Locality

	Female	Male	Ethnic Minority	Ethnic Majority (Kinh)	Rural	Urban	Total
Wave 1 score	504	497	409	509	505	497	500
Wave 2 score	532	523	423	528	528	527	527
Mean learning gain	28***	26***	14***	26***	23***	30***	27***

Notes: t-test (of difference in Wave 1 and Wave 2 means) significant *** p<0.01, ** p<0.05, * p<0.10.
Source: Iyer, P., O. B. Azubuike, and C. Rolleston. 2017. *Young Lives School Survey, 2016–17: Evidence from Vietnam.* Oxford: Young Lives.

Table 2.33: Young Lives English Performance in Waves 1 and 2, by Gender, Ethnic Status, and Locality

	Female	Male	Ethnic Minority	Ethnic Majority (Kinh)	Rural	Urban	Total
Wave 1 score	518	479	400	509	487	508	500
Wave 2 score	529	485	402	518	499	515	509
Mean learning gain	11***	6**	2	9***	12***	7***	9***

Notes: t-test (of difference in Wave 1 and Wave 2 means) significant *** p<0.01, ** p<0.05, * p<0.10.
Source: Iyer, P., O. B. Azubuike, and C. Rolleston. 2017. *Young Lives School Survey, 2016–17: Evidence from Vietnam.* Oxford: Young Lives.

148. The results of problem-solving and critical-thinking performance is shown in Figure 2.4, which indicates that results vary by provinces. The survey report also informed that girls performed significantly better than boys and the ethnic majority scored significantly better than the ethnic minority. Similar to the mathematics results, rural students performed significantly better than urban students.

Figure 2.4: Problem-Solving Performance from Young Lives Study by District

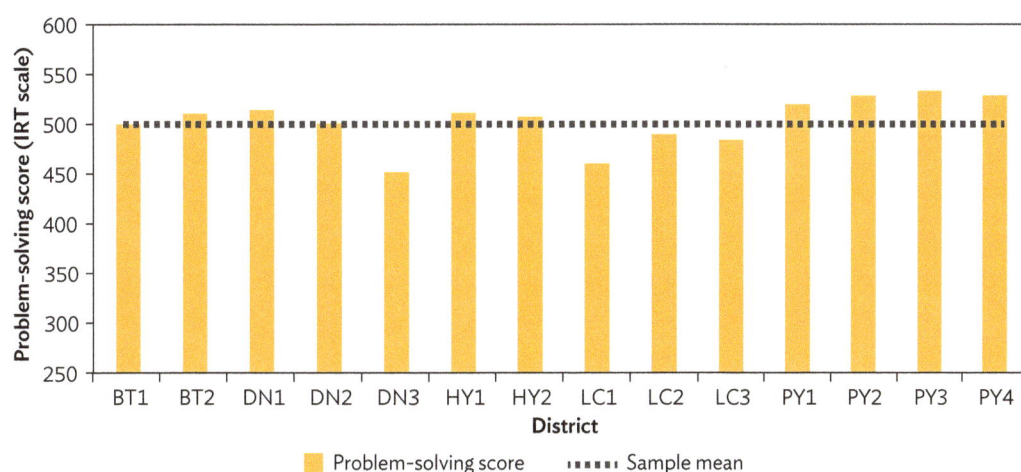

BT = Ben Tre, DN = Da Nang, HY = Hung Yen, IRT = item response theory, LC = Lao Cai, PY = Phu Yen.
Source: Iyer, P., O. B. Azubuike, and C. Rolleston. 2017. *Young Lives School Survey, 2016–17: Evidence from Vietnam.* Oxford: Young Lives.

149. Asked for their opinion of the quality of various education and skills subsectors (Tables 2.34 and 2.35), executives of Viet Nam firms viewed equality of education and skills to be lower than their colleagues in other nations, and ranked Viet Nam 97th of 135 countries in 2016 and the same rank out of 140 countries in 2018 for the education and skills pillar of competitiveness. In particular, these executives have a low opinion of the quality of management schools and specialized training services.

Table 2.34: Global Competitiveness Index for Education, 2016

In your country, how would you assess the quality of	Value (7 maximum)	Rank (out of 135)
Education system	3.6	76
Math and science education	3.9	78
Management schools	3.4	122
Internet access in schools	4.2	71
Availability of specialized training services	3.7	110
Extent of staff training	3.9	70

Source: World Economic Forum. 2016. *The Global Competitiveness Report 2016–2017.* Geneva.

Table 2.35: Global Competitiveness Index for Skills, 2018

	Value	Scores (0-100)	Rank (out of 140)
Mean years of schooling (years)	7.6	50.7	98
Extent of staff training (1-7)	3.7	45.8	81
Quality of vocational training	3.5	41.0	115
Skillset of graduates (1-7)	3.3	38.6	128
Digital skills among population (1-70)	3.7	44.6	98
Ease of finding skilled employees (1-7)	3.7	44.6	104
School life expectancy (years)	12.6	70.0	91
Critical thinking teaching (1-7)	2.9	31.4	113
Pupil-to-teacher ratio in primary education (Ratio)	19.6	75.9	76

Source: World Economic Forum. 2018. *The Global Competitiveness Report 2018.* Geneva.

150. In Tran et al. (2014) the Vietnamese education system is less strong at the upper secondary educational levels than at basic education, and it is weaker still in higher and vocational education, where much training is not relevant to the economy's needs, and scientific research and social research of genuine world standards are minimal, even in the country's leading universities. It is common practice for students to study without much critical reflection and without learning knowledge that is challenging. Most students find it hard to think creatively or to respond flexibly to emerging challenges.

151. Prime Minister's Decision No. 1982/QD-TTg approved in October 2016 a national qualification framework (NQF), which specifies eight levels of TVET qualifications by generic work task-related descriptions of competencies and minimum academic loads (credit points) for each level to achieve them.[56] The framework provides the essential basis for mapping recognized occupations and respective skills standards to regulative arrangements that stipulate minimum outputs and outcomes of vocational training programs consistently at different institutional levels. Currently, such regulations are largely input-oriented by prescriptions of training objectives, content, methods, and unit duration in curricula to be followed by teachers and used for school-based student assessments.[57]

152. Based on provisions in the 2006 TVET Law, the government launched the development of national occupational skills standards (NOSS) by establishing a lead agency for this task in GDVT and by endorsing respective regulations, which specified key agents including diverse line ministries and employer representatives and guided the processes, operative procedures, and expected outcomes of this endeavor. A major achievement was the establishment of national skills standards development committees and appraisal subcommittees, which initially enjoyed the active participation of industry representatives and employers. However, a 2012 GDVT study reported that active participation in these committees had basically shrunk to contributions of training institutions, "whereas the role of enterprises is passive and dim." The study concluded that the quality of these standards would be "limited in terms of relevance for labor market" (MOLISA 2012). Parallel initiatives supported by the

---

[56] Government of Viet Nam. Prime Minister Decision No. 1982/QD-TTg (18 October 2016) on Approval for Vietnamese Qualifications Framework.

[57] Although, reportedly, the development of such curriculum frameworks has been also based on an "extensive analysis of occupational requirements," these frameworks specify 70% of the content and time requirements of respective training programs.

Australian government and the Asia-Pacific Economic Cooperation focused on the development of common competence standards for selected occupational fields across different Asian countries.[58]

153. According to the 2017 report of the Ministry of Labour–Invalids and Social Affairs (MOLISA) 191 NOSS have been so far established and promulgated for 189 occupations, 36 centers for assessment and certification of NOSS were granted certificates, a respective contingent of accreditors was developed, and occupational skills assessment for workers was conducted for 22 national occupations and 4 occupations following Japanese standards.[59] By 2015, a total of 83 occupations had NOSS examinations compiled but only 62 examinations could be deployed, as the rest had not been appraised for promulgation. Hence, by the end of 2015, occupational skills assessment could be conducted only for 8,407 workers, with less than half of them (49.7%) actually meeting the assessment requirements.

154. MOLISA's 2017 report provides more indications for a piecemeal perpetuation of the traditional input-oriented approach by stating that only "some parts of the training curricula were developed on basis of occupational skills standards" and adding that "for international focal occupations" 8 curricula from Malaysia and 12 curricula from Australia have been "transferred," partly piloted, and tested at some colleges. How these foreign curricula will comply with national occupational standards and compete with national certificates on the labor market remains unclear. Managers of vocational education and training (VET) colleges implementing those curricula indicated that the actual cost of course delivery at this level will be about seven times higher than the current VND14 million–VND16 million, which the Prime Minister in 2016 endorsed for three pilot VET colleges as the maximum limit of tuition fees to be charged from students per academic year.[60]

155. The adoption of VET curricula from abroad follows the government's policy objective for 2020 to obtain around 70 high-quality vocational schools qualified for training in some vocations recognized by the advanced countries in the Association of Southeast Asian Nations (ASEAN) region or in the world. This shall contribute "to the basic and comprehensive innovation of vocational training in Vietnam" and meet "the requirement of high-quality human resources for socio-economic development of the country."[61]

156. Moreover, the new TVET law has no specifications on NOSS and its systemic relation to the NQF. According to the new regulations, the development, assessment, and certification of NOSS are to be

---

[58] Under the project, Development and Comparison of TVET Standards, within the Australia–Viet Nam Government Partnership Program for Development, Viet Nam, the Philippines, and Australia collaborated to establish common competency standards in the four fields of automobile (auto mechanics), agriculture (aquaculture team leader), construction (elementary engineering), and manufacturing (mechanics and welding). Within the framework of the APEC project, Comparing the Training Levels in Transportation and Logistics, Australia, Indonesia, the Philippines, the People's Republic of China (PRC), and Viet Nam developed generic competency standards for five occupations of the logistics sector: warehouse operator, logistics administrative officer, freight forwarder, warehouse supervisor, and supply chain manager.

[59] Further, 275 standards shall be developed from 2016 to 2020 while 264 shall be updated during this period.

[60] Prime Minister's Decision Nos. 538, 539, and 540 issued on 4 April 2016 to approve a pilot project for the period 2016–2019, which provides autonomy to three colleges (HCMC Technical College, LILAMA 2 Industrial College, and Quy Nhon Vocational College) and includes the establishment of independent fee structures and college management.

[61] Government of Viet Nam. Prime Minister Decision No. 761/2014/QD-TTg Approving the High Quality Vocational School Development Project by 2020.

adjusted in accordance with the Employment Law.[62] While MOLISA and GDVT (2017) appreciates this as a "positive change in the perception of the role and position of occupational skills assessment in the world of work" and expects that it will make "the assessment and certification of occupational skills more practically relevant," severe structural challenges concerning the future alignment of NOSS and the NQF are indicated by the following statement: "The Law on TVET identified three training levels of the TVET system, however, compared with the labor market demand and the national education system structure framework as well as the national qualifications framework, this revealed shortcomings."

157. MOLISA's 2010 Circular on Criteria and Standards for Quality Accreditation of Vocational Education envisages the need for NQF and NOSS alignment of vocational training programs only in its enhanced requirements for program accreditation at elementary level. Colleges and intermediate schools are apparently not as yet subjected to such regulations.

158. **Science and technology education not emphasized.** Relative to the OECD average, Vietnamese students do well on the PISA mathematics and science assessments (Figure 2.2) but do not perform as well as other high performing Asian economies in mathematics (Table 2.24). Of concern is the fact that students from Viet Nam do not perform well relative to the top performing students from other Asian economies (Table 2.27 to Table 2.31). For example, in the Republic of Korea on the mathematics PISA assessment in 2015, 20.9% of the students scored at level 5 or 6, while in Viet Nam only 9.3% scored at this level. In science in 2015, the overall performance of students in Viet Nam and Taipei,China was not significantly different, but in Taipei,China, 15.7% of students scored either 5 or 6 while only 8.4% of the students in Viet Nam scored at this level. In Singapore, 24.2% of the students were top performers in science.

159. Despite relatively good results in PISA, employers in Viet Nam think that the quality of the mathematics and science education is only fair, ranking it 78th out of 135 economies (Table 2.24). The government's SEDS 2011–2020 identified the need to develop human resources associated with science and technology development and application.[63] The EDS 2011–2020 calls for education development associated with science and technology development.[64]

160. Viet Nam will need to increase the number of secondary and higher education graduates who have the capacity to use technology to increase productivity and use science to be innovative. Recent United Nations Educational, Scientific and Cultural Organization (UNESCO) data indicate that most European countries and upper-income East Asian countries have high school graduates enrolling in science and technology fields with around 20% and 30%, with often one-third in sciences. Another 25% to 35% in social science, business and law, and the remaining 35% to 55% enrolled in a variety of disciplines, such as education and humanities and the arts. By contrast, in Viet Nam, nearly 50% of all students enrolled in higher education are enrolled in the two academic majors of economics/business

---

[62]   Government of Viet Nam. Decree No. 31/2015/ND-CP Regulating the Details of the Implementation of a Number of Articles in the Employment Law Regarding the Assessment and Certification of National Occupational Skills; MOLISA. Circular No. 56/2015/TT-BLDTBXH (24 December 2015) Guiding the Formulation, Appraisal, and Promulgation of the NOSS.

[63]   Government of Viet Nam. Socio-Economic Development Strategy 2011–2020 Approved by the Eleventh Congress of Viet Nam Communist Party. Ha Noi.

[64]   Government of Viet Nam. Prime Minister's Decision No. 711/QD-TTg Approving the Education Development Strategy 2011–2020. Ha Noi.

and education, with only about 15% of students enrolled in technology and almost none in the hard sciences. If industry is to be innovative and have the ability to develop new approaches and products, it is critical that Viet Nam develops a national strategy to increase the number of students studying the "hard sciences."

161. Students also need to be made aware of the potential and desirability of careers in science and technology. Most upper secondary school students avoid advanced mathematics and science and opt instead for the basic education stream. As can be seen in Table 2.36, 15-year-old students in Viet Nam are less likely to select a career in science than students from other Asian economies and less than the average across the OECD. Of particular concern is that this is also the case among Viet Nam's top performing science students, which could be in part because science and technology education has lost relevance by not being able to adapt to current scientific and technological developments. Developing students' interest and competencies in science and technology will need to start in at least lower secondary school if not primary.

Table 2.36: Science Career Expectations from PISA 2015

	Science and Engineering Professions	Health Professionals	ICT Professionals	Science-Related Technicians
Singapore	14.1	11.7	1.7	0.5
Hong Kong, China	8.5	13.0	1.7	0.3
Macau, China	5.4	12.4	2.6	0.5
Taipei,China	7.9	7.2	3.4	2.4
Japan	4.8	9.9	2.4	0.9
B-S-J-G (PRC)[a]	6.7	7.5	2.1	0.4
Korea, Rep. of	6.3	8.3	2.5	2.3
Viet Nam	**4.8**	**13.4**	**1.0**	**0.4**
OECD Average	8.8	11.6	2.6	1.5
Thailand	4.0	14.0	1.4	0.2
Indonesia	1.9	12.7	0.6	0.1

ICT = information and communication technology, OECD = Organisation for Economic Co-operation and Development, PISA = Programme for International Student Assessment, PRC = People's Republic of China.
[a] B-S-J-G (PRC) refers to the four provinces in the PRC: Beijing, Shanghai, Jiangsu, and Guangdong.
Source: OECD. 2016. *PISA 2015 Results: Excellence and Equity in Education (Volume I)*. Paris.

162. At the secondary school level Viet Nam needs to have a multidisciplinary approach to science and technology education that gives particular attention to providing basic knowledge, life skills, and scientific literacy for all, as well as preparing them for the world of work. In a rapidly evolving world, science and technology education is an important instrument to sustaining development and reducing poverty.

163. **Private sector participation for better education relevance and quality**. At upper secondary education (USE), industry needs to be more directly involved in identifying current and future needs and in designing programs to meet these needs. The 2010 research studies conducted by the Viet Nam National Institute of Education and Science concluded the quality of USE schooling and the relevance and quality of learning outcomes must be improved for USE graduates to have access to, and successfully undertake higher education to prepare them for the labor market in future (VNIES 2010). The studies have identified inflexible curriculum and poor quality of pre-service teaching training as major causes for the poor learning outcomes of USE students.

164. TVET graduates must meet the requirements of industry or they will not be hired; thus, building the partnership between employers and TVET institutions is a priority. Involvement of Viet Nam's enterprises in TVET delivery has become a more prominent aspect in the process of quality accreditation, especially in the ongoing efforts to establish a network of high-quality schools. Basically, the approach holds all VET institutions responsible for engaging employers in their training delivery as well as in their quality assurance and for establishing and developing respective enduring relationships. Some VET colleges have already managed to establish intensive and highly productive relationships with enterprises in their vicinities (ADB 2018).

165. However, comprehensive data on a nationwide scale regarding school collaborations with industry partners are lacking. A representative employer survey conducted in 2011 revealed that industry cooperation with Viet Nam's VET institutions has been largely confined to graduate recruitment procedures and providing internship to students. Only 10% of employers stated their involvement in curriculum development and only 5% took part in student assessments (World Bank and CIEM 2012). Still missing are reasonable strategies and incentives for employers to support and collaborate also with VET institutions that do not yet perform well in the demand orientation of their training delivery due to various organizational and financial constraints. MOLISA's new quality accreditation model seems to emphasize unilateral obligations for VET institutions to solve this chicken-and-egg problem. However, unless public VET suppliers gain the basic capacity (including appropriate training facilities and equipment as well as competent staff) to make themselves more attractive, the demand side will likely remain skeptic and stay reluctant to contribute actively.

166. Despite the data reflecting employers' difficulty in locating and recruiting skilled workers, the expansion of industry especially in the economic zones suggests that companies are growing and are therefore meeting their skills needs. Clearly, large employers and especially those in the economic zones have significant in-house training programs not only targeting new employees but also upgrading existing workers to more complex technologies and jobs. For instance, the active worker training programs in foreign-owned companies such as Toyota and Canon range from entry-level skills training to university-level engineering programs supported by the Japan International Cooperation Agency (JICA) and with graduates going to Japanese industry in Viet Nam. The JICA/Mechanical Engineering Partnership at Hanoi University of Industry is a long-standing model of this program.

167. **Lack of vocational knowledge and the required cognitive skills for vocations.** Employers have identified the required cognitive skills for employment. The new curriculum has been designed to better match marketplace needs. However, lower secondary students tend to be unaware of career alternatives and the type of education required for the variety of options. The majority of upper secondary students who plan on continuing their education assume that their best option is to enroll in a university but do not know of or consider the alternatives. Approaches need to be developed to make students aware of vocational options and the required cognitive skills for finding jobs. Further, students need to understand the training preparations for different career paths.

168. **The curriculum does not meet labor market needs**. There are concerns that the current curriculum was never fully implemented in classrooms as intended and it may not have had the desired impact on student learning. The National Curriculum of Basic Education (covering primary and lower secondary education [LSE]) was developed and implemented between 1996 and 2000. Under the ADB-funded First and Second Lower Secondary Education Development Project, the LSE curriculum was revised and textbooks were developed to improve students' problem-solving skills with the idea that teachers would be trained to employ more creative and dynamic learning approaches (MOET

2012). The USE curriculum was revised between SY2006/07 and SY2008/09 (UNESCO 2011). The plan was to bring in a broader curriculum that would be more relevant to labor market needs by introducing new textbooks and teaching methods that involved a more active and student-centered learning environment (ADB 2013b). The Upper Secondary Education Development Project provided 47,592 copies of textbooks, 57 titles of teaching subjects for training, 66 CD titles for teacher training workshops, and training to 15,346 trainers with the departments of education and training (DOETs) providing nationwide training programs to 83,824 teachers.

169. Despite all efforts to implement the new curriculum, the Viet Nam National Institute of Education Sciences' 2010 study concluded that the curriculum did not equip students with the knowledge and skills needed for their future careers and that the limited relevance and quality of secondary education constrained the development of a skilled labor force (VNIES 2010). From primary to upper secondary education, direct instruction continued to be the main technique, rather than learning approaches that are more appropriate for developing desired student competencies.

170. The Ministry of Education and Training (MOET) has recognized the need to comprehensively revise the curriculum and textbooks to be implemented after 2018 and has moved to make this occur. The challenge will be to find a professional development strategy that will change teachers' classroom behavior so that students will in fact acquire the desired competencies. The current model of collecting teachers in large groups and providing a series of lectures has not proven successful.

171. **Too few teachers have the required skills.** There is a growing concern in Viet Nam that workers are not equipped to think critically and creatively, and their command of a foreign language and business skill abilities are insufficient to help companies succeed in the increasingly competitive environment.

172. At all educational levels, one-way teaching is still the basic instructional method used, in which learners are asked to memorize knowledge and criticism, creativity, and self-study are discouraged. Early childhood teachers continue to favor direct instruction over more appropriate teaching practices for early childhood (Thao and Boyd 2014). The grade 11 NAM found that educational environment and teaching methods, among other factors, have the greatest positive impact on students' academic achievement; in fact, students of teachers who wrote math exercise answers for them on the board had lower academic achievement.

173. When asked during the 2015 PISA about science activities, students reported that most often there would be some kind of discussion, or an explanation by the teacher of a science idea or its relevance to life, or students would be given opportunities to explain their ideas or draw conclusions from an experiment they conducted (Figure 2.5). On the other hand, students reported much less often being actively involved in investigating or testing ideas, performing practical experiments in the laboratory, designing their own experiments, and other similar activities that are associated with developing higher-level thinking skills.

174. The lack of a master plan for teacher training for all levels has led to shortages in some areas, redundancy, and inconsistency. Teacher training and recruitment processes have been slow to change. As discussed in this report under section II on sector achievements, teachers have been successfully assessed relative to professional standards. However, the ratings (Table 2.2) appear to overestimate their true abilities. Many see the ratings as not being a valid representation of teachers' skills. The perception that the expertise of some teachers hardly meets minimum requirements and that a small

Figure 2.5: Inquiry-Based Instruction in Science Lessons (Results Based on Students' Reports that these Happen in "Most" or "All" Science Lessons)

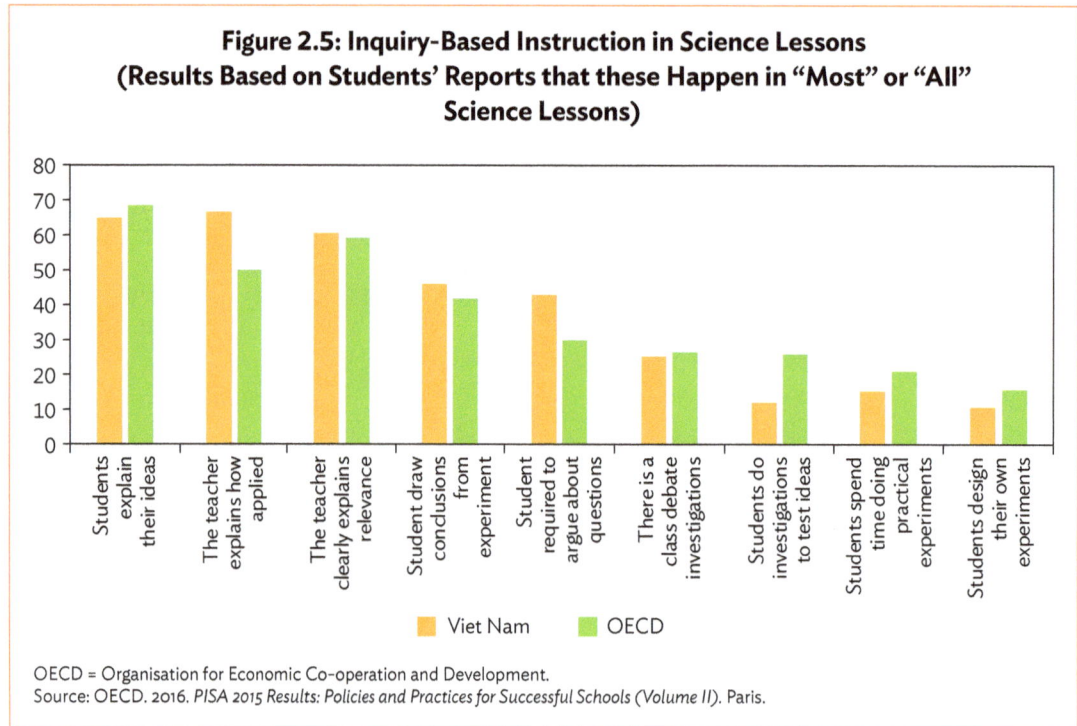

OECD = Organisation for Economic Co-operation and Development.
Source: OECD. 2016. *PISA 2015 Results: Policies and Practices for Successful Schools (Volume II)*. Paris.

group of teachers lack commitment and live unethical lifestyles negatively affects teachers' reputation in the society. Also, MOET officials have indicated the need to update teacher standards based on the new Resolution on Comprehensive Education Renovation and are looking for support for upgrading the teacher standards. In applying the new standards, direction and training will be needed to make criterion-referenced assessments so that teachers are ranked based on behavioral evidence rather than subjective judgments.

175. As mentioned, the current professional development model for teachers does not appear to have resulted in the desired changes to teacher behavior. Teacher training and expertise improvement are still seen as being ineffective. Policies and compensations for teachers and managing staff are not satisfactory, failing to motivate teachers to provide students with effective instruction and make efforts in improving their profession skills. Alternative decentralized professional development models need to be considered, especially those that utilize individual school plans, including evidence of the characteristics of local communities and students which can be used to inform the professional growth plans of teachers and principals and teachers' involvement in experimenting with innovative techniques as part of their individual growth through collegial collaboration activities.

176. To foster excellent secondary teachers, the teacher training programs in teacher training universities and teacher training colleges need to be accredited and made consistent and with more continuity. At present, the programs used by MOET's teacher training universities to train USE teachers and the programs that teacher training colleges use to train the provincial governments' LSE teachers are not connected to each other.

177. Table 2.37 lists the number of teachers by level. Although enrollments in USE education have declined in recent years, the number of teachers has increased, partly as a result of government efforts to provide full-day programs for lower secondary students. Despite shortages in specific areas,

the number of teachers overall is adequate for the preprimary, primary, LSE, and USE levels. PISA 2012 and 2015 found that teacher shortage was not a significant factor in Viet Nam at the USE level.

Table 2.37: Number of Teachers by Level of Education

	2000/01	2005/06	2010/11	2013/14	2014/15	2015/16	2016/17	2017/18
Primary	373,783	339,090	359,039	387,196	392,136	396,843	397,098	396,600
Lower secondary	275,958	301,752	312,710	315,593	312,587	313,526	310,953	303,947
Upper secondary	102,528	137,962	146,789	152,689	152,007	150,900	150,721	150,288
Professional secondary	10,189	14,230	18,085	11,515	10,911	10,200	N/A	N/A

N/A = not available.
Source: Ministry of Education and Training. 2018. *Education Statistics 2017–2018*. Ha Noi.

178. Expanding the TVET system based on its present components may not be effective. Industry wants TVET graduates to have both a theoretical knowledge of the technology they are studying and job skills to apply their learning in the workplace. As few teachers have any industrial, hands-on skills, most students can meet only half of the requirement when they graduate. To overcome this deficit, in-industry, on-the-job, work release and cooperative training for students have been instigated where industry/education partnerships are possible. This, however, is not the rule. Most TVET teachers in the region have not worked in the industry for which they are preparing graduates. They complete university and then take teacher training or integrate technology education with teacher education. The product is teacher training graduates with little preparation for working in industry and with little understanding of the industrial work environment. As a consequence, industry is critical of school preparation and graduates of vocational institutions are disenchanted with their employment. Further, in-service teacher training focused on theory and pedagogy has little impact on this. Experience suggests that the upgrading of TVET teachers in technical (not pedagogical) skills is extraordinarily difficult.

179. A major concern regarding vocational education and training (VET) teacher qualification standards results from the vague definition of "certificates of professional skills" as the only mandatory legal requirement for teaching practical lessons. Awards of such certificates are often based only on some more or less preliminary exercises to be accomplished during formal vocational training (obligatory short-term industry placements and internships); hence, they do not necessarily assert in-depth professional work experience and profound occupational competence. Beyond that, teachers can voluntarily sign up for a formal occupational skills assessment if their vocational majors belong to the 62 focal occupations that are regulated by national occupational standards for different competency levels and have been promulgated for corresponding examinations.[65] These examinations are conducted at 36 skills assessment centers, which are mostly located in universities and vocational colleges and certified for operation by the GDVT. The assessment consists of a set of multiple-choice questions to test the understanding of essential knowledge and a practical skills test to evaluate the critical skills required for a certain level of occupational task performance as specified in Viet Nam's National Occupational Skills Framework.

---

[65] By 2015, a total of 83 occupations had National Occupational Skills Examinations compiled. Of these, 21 occupations have not yet been appraised for promulgation (Cf. MOLISA and NIVT 2017).

180. The new TVET law mandates vocational teachers "to participate in internship in enterprise in order to update (or) improve professional skills, and approach new technology as regulated."[66] Yet, MOLISA's recent regulation on qualification standards translates this prescription into rather vague specifications of "regularly self-study" and "participation in advanced training courses." Nevertheless, MOLISA has earmarked additional training budget from the National VET Target Program[67] and established further training programs for teachers to (i) improve teaching techniques focusing on quality improvement of practical training in classrooms and workshops, (ii) improve technical knowledge and practical skills of teachers, and (iii) improve English language skills. So far, about 6,000 teachers received training on these topics. Compared with this modest figure, MOLISA's plan for teacher training activities envisaged for 2017–2020 appears highly ambitious.

2. Insufficient Access to Education

181. **Too many of the possible student population are not receiving an education**. Despite the tremendous increase in the relative number of students enrolled at all educational levels (Table 2.8), too many students are still not receiving sufficient education for Viet Nam to move forward economically and socially. In SY2015/16, about 430,000 young men and woman who were of the age to be in LSE were not enrolled. At the USE level, over 1.4 million young people, representing about a third of the total age group who should be in USE, were not enrolled. Having this large number of people not obtaining a secondary education and therefore without the required competencies to be able to fully contribute to their country's development represents a significant loss to Viet Nam. The World Bank summary is that the systems provide students with an excellent foundation for success, but then fail to build on that foundation with too many students failing to graduate from high school and too few continuing on to tertiary education (World Bank and the Ministry of Planning and Investment 2016).

182. Table 2.38 shows that the gross enrollment rate for Viet Nam relative to selected competing economies at the primary and LSE levels compare well with neighboring countries and low-income and middle-income countries. Table 2.39 provides collaborative evidence that enrollment in primary education in Viet Nam has been a success story. A high gross enrollment rate can indicate an inefficiency in the system in which children over primary-school age are in primary school either because they enrolled late or have been retained. The net enrollment rate (NER) target of 95% for LSE has also not yet been achieved.

183. As shown in Table 2.38 and Table 2.39, Viet Nam's USE enrollment is behind its economic competitors. Table 2.40 shows that among the Asian participants in PISA 2012 and 2015, Viet Nam had the lowest percentage of 15-year-olds participating in school. As noted elsewhere in this report, if all 15-year-olds were included in the PISA analysis, Viet Nam's results would drop from above average to below average.

---

[66]   Government of Viet Nam, the National Assembly. Law on Vocational Education (27 November 2014), Article 55. Ha Noi.

[67]   Based on MOLISA's Decision No. 562/2016/QD-TCDN (19 December 2016) allocating Đ35 billion to provide training for vocational teachers on professional skills, pedagogical skills, foreign languages, and IT skills.

Table 2.38: Gross Enrollment Rate, 2017 and 2018

	2017			2018		
	Primary	**Lower Secondary**	**Upper Secondary**	**Primary**	**Lower Secondary**	**Upper Secondary**
Cambodia	107.83	69.34	N/A	N/A	N/A	N/A
PRC	100.85	N/A	85.06	102.05	N/A	N/A
India	N/A	86.61	N/A	N/A	N/A	N/A
Indonesia	103.45	95.16	80.09	N/A	N/A	N/A
Japan	N/A	N/A	N/A	N/A	N/A	N/A
Lao PDR	107.0	79.20	52.62	N/A	N/A	N/A
Malaysia	103.10	89.21	83.29	N/A	N/A	N/A
Korea, Rep. of	N/A	N/A	N/A	N/A	N/A	N/A
Thailand	99.60	121.50	112.32	121.50	N/A	N/A
Viet Nam	**107.92**	**98.67**	**N/A**	**N/A**	**N/A**	**N/A**

Lao PDR = Lao People's Democratic Republic, PRC = People's Republic of China, N/A = not available.
Source: UNESCO Institute for Statistics. http://data.uis.unesco.org/# (data extracted on 22 July 2019).

Table 2.39: Enrollment Rates and World Ranking, 2016

	Value	**Rank/138**
Primary education enrollment, net %	98.0	30
Secondary education enrollment, gross %	92.5	70

Source: World Economic Forum. 2016. *The Global Competitiveness Report 2016–2017*. Geneva.

Table 2.40: Enrollment of 15-Year-Olds among Asian Participants in PISA 2012 and 2015

	Total Population of 15-Year-Olds		**Total of 15-Year-Olds Enrolled**		**Percentage Enrolled**	
	2012	**2015**	**2012**	**2015**	**2012**	**2015**
Taipei,China	328,356	295,056	328,336	287783	100	98
Korea, Rep. of	687,104	620,687	672,101	639,950	98	100
Japan	1,241,786	1,201,615	1,214,756	1,175,907	98	98
Singapore	53.637	48,218	52,163	47,050	97	98
Hong Kong, China	84,200	65,100	77,864	61,630	92	95
Indonesia	4,174,217	4,534,216	3,599,844	3,182,816	86	70
Shanghai, PRC	108,056		90,796		84	
B-S-J-G (PRC)[a]		2,084,658	457,999	1,507,518		72
Macau, China	6,600	5,100	5,416	4,417	82	87
Thailand	982,080	895,513	784,897	756,917	80	85
Viet Nam	**1,717,996**	**1,803,552**	**1,091,462**	**874,859**	**64**	**49**

PISA = Programme for International Student Assessment, PRC = People's Republic of China.
[a] B-S-J-G (PRC) refers to the four provinces in the PRC: Beijing, Shanghai, Jiangsu, and Guangdong.
Sources: OECD. 2013. *PISA 2012 Results: Excellence Through Equity: Giving Every Student the Chance to Succeed (Volume II)*. Paris.; and OECD. 2016. *PISA 2015 Results: Excellence and Equity in Education (Volume I)*. Paris.

184. Table 2.41 presents the percentage of children entering first grade who eventually reach the last grade of primary school. Of all children who started grade 1, the vast majority (98.6%) reached grade 5.

**Table 2.41: Percentage of Children Entering Grade 1 of Primary School
Who Eventually Reached the Last Grade of Primary School
(Survival Rate to Last Grade of Primary School), 2014**

| | Sex | | Region | | | | | |
Total	Male	Female	Red River Delta	Northern Midland and Mountainous Area	North Central and Central Coastal Area	Central Highlands	Southeast	Mekong River Delta
98.6	99.6	97.4	100	97.8	99.3	96.8	98.5	98.0

| | Area | | Ethnicity of Household Head | |
Total	Urban	Rural	Kinh/Hoa	Ethnic Minorities
98.6	99.2	98.3	99.2	95.0

Source: General Statistics Office of Viet Nam. 2014. *Viet Nam Multiple Indicator Cluster Survey*. Ha Noi.

185. Table 2.42 indicates a 95.9% primary school completion rate and an overall transition from primary to LSE of 98.0%.

**Table 2.42: Primary School Completion and Transition Rate
from Primary to Lower Secondary School, 2014**

| | Sex | | | Region | | | | | |
	Total	Male	Female	Red River Delta	Northern Midland and Mountainous Area	North Central and Central Coastal Area	Central Highlands	Southeast	Mekong River Delta
Primary school completion	95.9	98.0	93.4	93.7	93.4	100.7	90.2	100.0	94.6
Transition to lower secondary school	98.0	98.3	97.8	100.0	98.7	97.1	94.8	97.9	98.3

| | | Area | | Ethnicity of Household Head | |
	Total	Urban	Rural	Kinh/Hoa	Ethnic Minorities
Primary school completion	95.9	99.0	94.4	97.6	87.7
Transition to lower secondary school		100.0	97.2	98.7	94.8

Source: General Statistics Office of Viet Nam. 2014. *Viet Nam Multiple Indicator Cluster Survey*. Ha Noi.

186. A large proportion (90%) of children had completed lower secondary school (Table 2.43). The effects of the different completion rates and transition rates are cumulative. That is, if students do not complete a particular level they are not part of the group to transition to or complete the next level. Table 2.44 shows the cumulative effect for 100 students who start grade 1 and successfully enter USE. Of 100 students who started in grade 1, only around 76 students successfully enter USE. Among ethnic minority students, only 46 of the original 100 students who started grade 1 will make it to USE.

Table 2.43: Lower Secondary School Completion and Transition Rate from Lower Secondary School to Upper Secondary School, 2014

		Sex		Region					
	Total	Male	Female	Red River Delta	Northern Midland and Mountainous Area	North Central and Central Coastal Area	Central Highlands	Southeast	Mekong River Delta
Lower secondary school completion	90.0	90.6	89.4	98.0	97.4	97.0	71.1	79.8	85.0
Transition to upper secondary school	89.5	88.2	90.9	93.0	86.5	85.8	93.9	97.9	85.3

		Area		Ethnicity of Household Head	
	Total	Urban	Rural	Kinh/Hoa	Ethnic Minorities
Lower secondary school completion	90.0	91.0	89.6	94.4	70.2
Transition to upper secondary school	89.5	94.7	87.6	91.8	76.7

Source: General Statistics Office of Viet Nam. 2014. *Viet Nam Multiple Indicator Cluster Survey*. Ha Noi.

Table 2.44: Number of Students Who Transition to Upper Secondary Education of 100 Students Who Start Grade 1, 2014

	Start Grade 1	Complete Primary	Transition to LSE	Complete LSE	Transition to USE
Total	**100**	**95.9**	**94.0**	**84.6**	**75.7**
Males	100	98.0	96.3	87.3	77.0
Females	100	93.4	91.3	81.7	74.2
Kinh/Hoa	100	97.6	96.3	90.9	83.5
Ethnic minorities	100	87.7	85.4	60.0	46.0

LSE = lower secondary education, USE = upper secondary education.
Source: General Statistics Office of Viet Nam. 2014. *Viet Nam Multiple Indicator Cluster Survey*. Ha Noi.

187. Table 2.45 suggests that Viet Nam has a lower percentage of student enrollment in TVET secondary education than either Indonesia or Thailand. However, it is unclear if the data integrate MOLISA and MOET statistics, but without reliable MOLISA data before 2013, determination is problematic. TVET enrollment is not meeting the subsector goals. The total TVET enrollment (MOET and MOLISA) in SY2013/14 was 6,854,000 students, which achieved only 44% of the target for 2015. College and secondary level reached 933,000 students, achieving only 44% of the target for 2015. Secondary level and vocational training for less than 3 months was 5,921,000 students, achieving only 79% of the target for 2015. Vocational training for 1,825,000 rural laborers reached only 38.8% against target to 2015.

188. Table 2.46 shows MOLISA's plan for expanding TVET institutions and an intended registration of 1.7 million by 2020. There are no data on part-time students. International experience suggests that an effective part-time student program might add an additional 5 million continuing-education

participants to this number. The recruitment of students from the MOET schools into TVET is an unresolved problem.

**Table 2.45: TVET Enrollment among Selected Members
of the Association of Southeast Asian Nations, 2009**

	TVET Enrollment as % of Total Secondary Enrollment
Lao PDR	0.6
Cambodia	2.2
Viet Nam	**6.4**
Indonesia	12.8
Thailand	16.4
Malaysia	5.9

Lao PDR = Lao People's Democratic Republic, TVET = technical and vocational education and training.
Sources: World Economic Forum. 2016. The Global Competitiveness Report 2016–2017. Geneva; World Bank. 2009. Education at a Glance: Viet Nam. http://siteresources.worldbank.org/EXTEDSTATS/ Resources/3232763-1171296190619/3445877-1172014191219/VNM.pdf; and International Labour Organization. 2010. Labor and Social Trends in ASEAN 2010: Sustaining Recovery and Development through Decent Work. Bangkok.

Table 2.46: MOLISA's Plan for TVET Expansion

	SY2015		2020 Plan	SY2010/11 Enrollment ('000s)
	Total	Private	Total	
Vocational colleges	190	47	250	97
Vocational secondary schools	280	102	400	180
Vocational training centers	997	352	900	1,468
Total	**1,467**	**501**	**1,550**	**1,745**

MOLISA = Ministry of Labour–Invalids and Social Affairs, SY = school year, TVET = technical and vocational education and training.
Source: MOLISA, General Directorate of Vocational Training. Viet Nam Vocational Education and Training Report 2015.

189. Expanding the existing TVET system in a low-demand market by students for TVET education may not effectively increase graduate numbers. Most students do not want to register in TVET institutions because they and their parents see TVET job outcomes as low status and unattractive employment options.

190. **Insufficient quantity and quality of facilities to meet demand.** As already noted, a great deal of effort has been made to increase the number of schools and to improve the quality of facilities. However, as also previously discussed, if Viet Nam is going to meet the challenge of moving forward from a low-middle-income nation it will need to increase the number of USE graduates. To increase the enrollment rate in secondary education significantly, spaces will need to be found for between 1 million and 1.5 million more students.

191. By the end of SY2014/15, 25% of secondary schools are anticipated to be accredited as meeting national standards. However, evidence suggests that many of the remaining 75% of school facilities are inadequate and out-of-date. Temporary and old classes still exist, especially in remote areas. Libraries, laboratories, classes for special purposes, and other teaching tools remain inadequate and out-of-date. School facilities are insufficient in quantity, quality, and type to meet the requirements for improving education quality. Equipment and teaching tools no longer meet requirements of experiments and practice of the current curriculum or the new curriculum to be implemented after.

192. To increase enrollments in science and technology, purpose-built classrooms will be required with supporting requisite equipment.

193. During PISA 2015, principals were asked to report on the impact of physical infrastructure and the educational materials on the school's capacity to provide instruction. As Table 2.47 shows, Viet Nam's principals think that their physical infrastructure is lacking and of poor quality relative to most other Asian economies and the OECD average. The same picture emerges in reference to the lack and quality of educational materials. Also, the number of computers per student is lower than all Asian economies except Indonesia and considerably lower than the OECD average.

Table 2.47: Shortage of Educational Materials, PISA 2015
(Results Based on School Principals' Reports)
(percentage of students in schools whose principals reported that the school's capacity to provide instruction is hindered to some extent or a lot by)

	Lack of Physical Infrastructure	Inadequate or Poor Quality of Infrastructure	Lack of Educational Materials	Inadequate or Poor Quality of Educational Materials	Number of Computers per Student
Singapore	11.4	10.5	0.0	0.0	0.97
Hong Kong, China	21.7	22.3	21.1	20.0	0.87
Macau, China	41.0	44.2	27.8	31.4	1.20
Taipei,China	35.3	25.5	14.6	11.6	0.47
Japan	69.3	57.5	65.3	56.7	0.44
B-S-J-G (PRC)[a]	41.6	35.8	44.8	43.0	0.35
Korea, Rep. of	58.1	52.7	50.3	43.5	0.37
Viet Nam	**61.2**	**52.7**	**46.8**	**41.4**	**0.26**
OECD average	36.3	34.6	33.9	29.8	0.77
Thailand	55.6	44.3	56.5	46.8	0.40
Indonesia	62.3	59.1	68.7	62.6	0.14

OECD = Organisation for Economic Co-operation and Development, PISA = Programme for International Student Assessment, PRC = People's Republic of China.
[a]B-S-J-G (PRC) refers to the four provinces in the PRC: Beijing, Shanghai, Jiangsu, and Guangdong.
Source: OECD. 2016. *PISA 2015 Results: Policies and Practices for Successful Schools (Volume II)*. Paris.

194. Outdated or insufficient training facilities appear to be a key constraint in the TVET system. Although MOLISA (2017) stated that "the facilities and equipment of vocational education institutions have been invested to meet the training requirements," sample reports of VET institutions give cause to concerns that "technical facilities and means of teaching and learning do not meet the requirements for high-quality training" and/or are not sufficient in scope to conduct decent hands-on training activities for all students enrolled in a course. Even comparatively well-equipped colleges report that they are facing "challenges in improving and innovating training programs in key technical industries due to difficulties in practice equipment."[68] In other surveys, students reported that they had to take turns when doing practice at college workshops and only worked at a machine about once or twice during five practical learning sessions. Though there were nine machines, only four or five functioned properly for one group of 6 to 10 students (Ho and Reich n. d.).

195. **Limited opportunities to reenter schooling.** As in Table 2.48, although the number of continuing education centers and the community learning centers of communes have increased,

---

[68] Cf. Proposals of 10 VET colleges applying for support through ADB's Skills and Knowledge for Inclusive Economic Growth Project.

the total number of students enrolled has declined. Table 2.49 shows that enrollment between SY2009/10 and SY2015/16 in regular LSE increased while enrollment in continuing education centers declined, and enrollment in USE schools decreased less than the decline in part-time programs. The increase in the NER in both LSE and USE may mean that fewer students are enrolling in part-time programs.

Table 2.48: Number of Continuing Education Centers and Number of Students Enrolled Part-Time, SY2009/10 to SY2015/16

Number	2009/10	2010/11	2011/12	2012/13	2013/14	2014/15	2015/16
Provincial, district continuing education centers	684	706	712	703	705	726	733
Community learning centers of communes	9,990	10,696	10,826	10,815	10,994	10,992	11,057
Part-time learners	390,465	332,174	296,617	273,518	243,466	224,431	215,550
Lower secondary	81,042	69,933	54,673	42,883	44,951	35,732	27,703
Percentage of part-time LS learners of total LS (%)	1.6	1.4	1.1	0.9	0.9	0.7	0.5
Upper secondary	309,423	262,241	241,944	230,635	198,515	188,699	187,847
Percentage of part-time US learners of total US (%)	10.7	9.3	8.8	8.6	8.1	7.8	7.7

LS = lower secondary, SY = school year, US = upper secondary.
Source: Ministry of Education and Training. 2017. *Education Statistics 2015–2016*. Ha Noi.

Table 2.49: Percentage Change in Enrollment of Regular and Part-Time Students, SY2009/10 to SY2015/16

Lower Secondary Regular	Lower Secondary Part-Time	Upper Secondary Regular	Upper Secondary Part-Time
3.4%	−65.8%	−14.5%	−39.3%

SY = school year.
Source: Ministry of Education and Training. Education Statistics 2015–2016. Ha Noi.

196. **Inequalities by household income, ethnicity, and location.** The government has continued efforts to increase access and retain in school students from vulnerable groups including the ethnic minorities, rural poor, domestic migrants, physically disabled, and females. However, the approaches have not yet been sufficiently inclusive and need to be more innovative. The government has noted that inequality in educational access and quality persists among different ethnic groups and disparate geographic regions (MPI 2013). The amount of income of the home where the child grows up, the geographic location of where the child goes to school, and whether the child belongs to an ethnic minority all affect the quality of education the child receives and the amount of access the child will have. Of course, where a student lives is also related to whether the student's family is poor or belongs to an ethnic minority. Of students living in poverty, 50% are from an ethnic minority and the majority of ethnic minority students live in remote rural areas. Poverty among ethnic minority groups is closely associated with low or limited access to opportunities for education and training.

197. **Educational inequalities by household income.** Figure 2.6 indicates the significant relations between the highest educational attainment and household socioeconomic status. It clearly shows that the lowest quintile household has a disadvantage in completing secondary education and has the highest proportion of no schooling among the five socioeconomic groups. PISA 2012 and 2015 studies found that students from the richest families have higher achievement than those from the poorest families in the same school, and this difference is statistically significant for all subjects (OECD 2016a). The results from the grade 11 NAM (Table 2.50) indicate that students who are from low socioeconomic level (level 1) have significantly lower scores than students from a high level (level 4). The difference is most pronounced in the results from the English test but are also very large in mathematics.

Figure 2.6: Highest Educational Attainment of Population Aged 5 Years and Older by Quintile of Household Socioeconomic Status, 2009

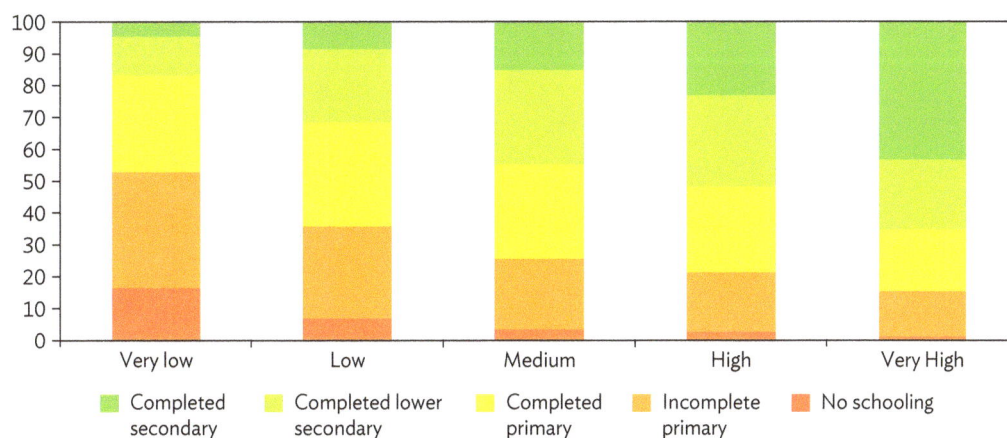

Source: Ministry of Planning and Investment, General Statistics Office of Viet Nam. 2009. Viet Nam Population and Housing Census 2009: Education in Viet Nam: An Analysis of Key Indicators. Ha Noi.

Table 2.50: Percentage of Students Meeting Standards by Socioeconomic Level, Grade 11 National Achievement Monitoring, SY2011/12

Socioeconomic Level	Mathematics	Literature	English
Level 1	28.1	32.8	5.9
Level 2	47.5	51.6	15.5
Level 3	61.7	56.8	29.0
Level 4	79.6	67.9	61.8

SY = school year.
Source: Ministry of Education and Training, Center of Education Quality Assurance. 2012. National Achievement Monitoring Grade 11 SY2011/12 Summary Report. Ha Noi.

198. Figure 2.7 shows that students who are enrolled in grade 10 have more advantage as measured by the wealth index than youth of the same age who are not in school. This indicates that poor youth tend to drop out of school sooner than more advantaged students. Figure 2.8 shows that youth who are in grade 10 tend to have higher achievement than youth of the same age who are not in school.

Figure 2.7: Youth in School Have More Advantage than Out-of-School Youth

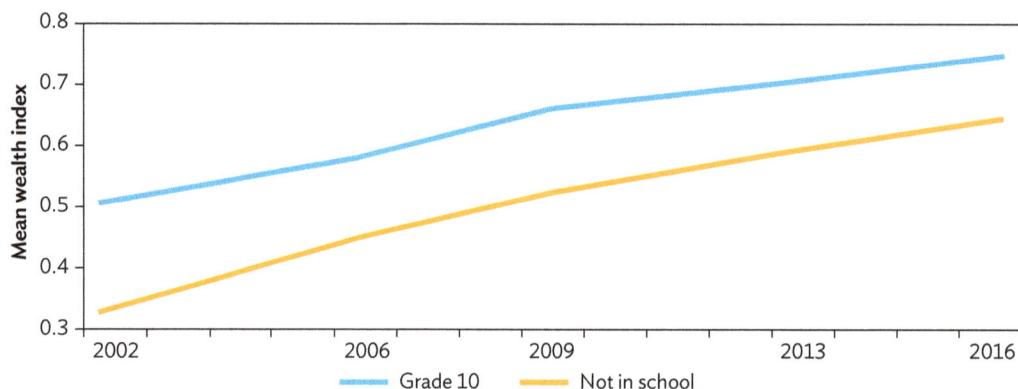

Source: Iyer, P. 2017. Thinking Outside the Box: Do Students in Vietnam Have 21st Century Skills?. *Young Lives*. https://www.younglives.org.uk/content/thinking-outside-box-do-students-vietnam-have-21st-century-skills (accessed 11 September 2017).

Figure 2.8: Mathematics Achievement of Youth in School and Youth Out-of-School

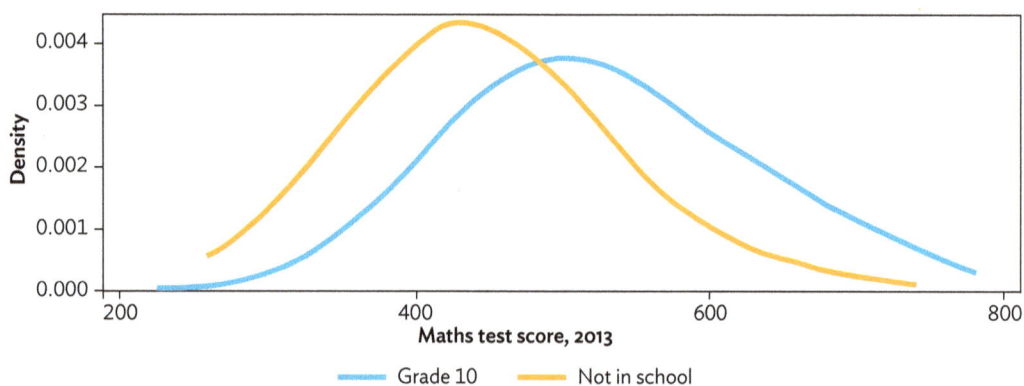

Source: Iyer, P. 2017. Thinking Outside the Box: Do Students in Vietnam Have 21st Century Skills?. *Young Lives*. https://www.younglives.org.uk/content/thinking-outside-box-do-students-vietnam-have-21st-century-skills (accessed 11 September 2017).

199. A large part of the opportunity cost of education, which increases at the LSE level, is the loss of child labor from household production. According to the National Child Labor Survey, 9.6% of children aged 5 to 17 in Viet Nam are child workers (about 1.75 million children). This is despite laws that indicate children under the age of 13 are not allowed to work and those between 13 and 15 years of age can only work in special circumstances.[69]

200. **Educational inequalities by ethnicity.** Figure 2.9 shows the variation of highest educational attainment by ethnicity. Clearly, the Kinh (ethnic majority) is better off in completing secondary education compared with the Hmong, Khmer, and Thai ethnic groups.

---

[69]   Government of Viet Nam. Labour Code. Law No. 10/2012/QH13 adopted on 18 June 2012.

Figure 2.9: Highest Educational Attainment of Population Aged 5 Years and Older by Ethnic Group, 2009

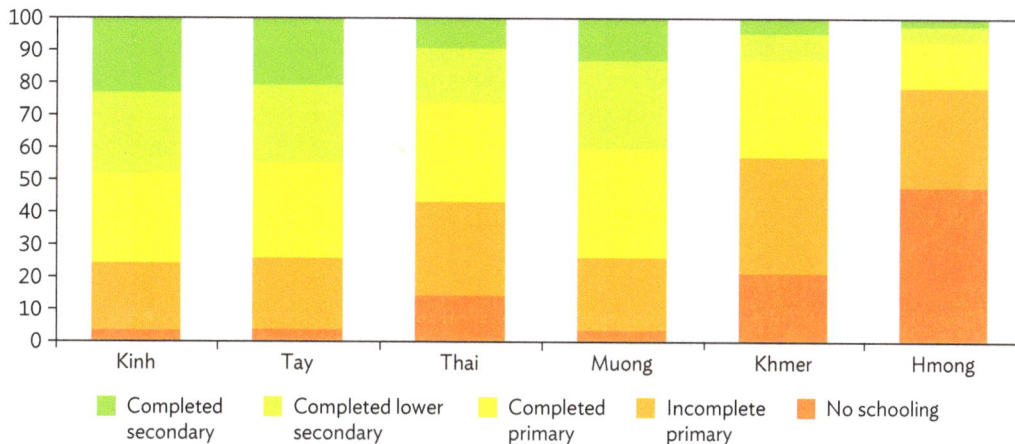

Legend: ■ Completed secondary ■ Completed lower secondary ■ Completed primary ■ Incomplete primary ■ No schooling

Source: Ministry of Planning and Investment, General Statistics Office of Viet Nam. 2009. *Viet Nam Population and Housing Census 2009: Education in Viet Nam: An Analysis of Key Indicators.* Ha Noi.

201. As was seen in Table 2.15 there has been a marked improvement in the NER for students from an ethnic minority. However, this table and Table 2.16 also show that the rate is still much lower for students from an ethnic minority particularly at the USE level where almost two-thirds of these students are not in school.

202. In addition to not being able to take advantage of access to education, students from an ethnic minority who are in school achieve considerably lower than the majority. The NAM for grade 9 administered in SY2008/09 and for grade 11 in SY2011/12 (Table 2.51) found that students from an ethnic minority scored significantly lower than the Kinh majority. Only 38.5% of grade 9 ethnic minority students achieved the acceptable standard in mathematics and only 49.3% in literature compared with the majority of the Kinh student population, where 62.2% and 69.4%, respectively, achieved the standard. For grade 11 mathematics, only 27.4% of the ethnic minority students achieved the acceptable standard compared with 58.2% for Kinh students. Iyer, Azubuike, and Rolleston (2017) also found that grade 10 students from the Kinh group outperformed students from an ethnic minority in both mathematics and English, and that the performance gap widened during the school year (Table 2.32 and Table 2.33). PISA results from 2012 and 2015 also found similar results (Table 2.25).

Table 2.51: Results for National Achievement Monitoring
(percentage meeting the acceptable standard)

	Grade 9 (SY2008/09)			Grade 11 (SY2011/12)		
	Total Population	Kinh	Other	Total Population	Kinh	Other
Math	58.1	62.2	38.5	54.9	58.2	27.4
Literature	61.5	69.4	49.3	53.5	56.3	30.0
English	57.6	59.5	46.5	24.2	25.6	12.2

SY = school year.
Source: Ministry of Education and Training. Center of Education Quality Assurance.

203. Decree No. 57 (9 May 2017) supports students from 16 ethnic minorities to proceed from lower secondary education to VET institutions at basic and intermediate level and from high schools to enter VET colleges and universities without taking entrance exams. It also regulates this group's eligibilities to receive financial support. Decree No. 86 (October 2015) regulates tuition fees and stipulates that 15 disadvantaged groups are exempted from paying fees to participate in training and education programs. Joint Circular No. 9 (30 March 2016) regulates tuition fees in public education and training institutions, including fee exemptions for students from disadvantaged areas, ethnic minorities, poor households, and people with disabilities. Decision No. 971/QD-TTg (July 2015) stipulates that also access to high-quality TVET programs should prioritize workers from poor and near-poor areas and household members from ethnic minorities that depend on agriculture farming and disabled people and fishers.

204. However, for entering TVET at elementary level an LSE qualification remains a prerequisite, and many young people among Viet Nam's disadvantaged populations are still not achieving this status. For these, the government provides the option to participate in an increasing amount of nonformal short-term courses, which are largely subsidized through a respective national target program.[70] A 2016 MOLISA report on the results of this program in the Northern Midland and Mountainous Region, Viet Nam's poorest socioeconomic region, stated that, between 2010 and 2015, 573,000 rural workers (7.6% of this region's total labor force) were trained through this program (MOLISA 2016).[71] In 2016, 9% of participants were from poor households and 0.6% were people with disabilities.

205. **Educational inequalities by geographic location.** Table 2.52 shows that the NER for rural students is lower for all levels. However, as a result of the government's effort to provide universal primary education the differences between urban and rural and among regions is minimal at this level. The differences in enrollment rates become more pronounced at the upper secondary and higher educational levels. The Red River Delta tends to be the richest region, with the highest NER for all levels of education. The Northern Midland and Mountainous, the Central Highlands, and the Mekong River have the lowest enrollment rates. Table 2.53 shows that the NER also varies considerably by province. A review of the rates for promotion, repeating a class, dropping out, and completion by province reveals a similar variation among provinces (Table 2.54 and Table 2.55). As one would expect, some provinces appear in all three tables when looking at the various rates (Soc Trang, Gia Lai, Bac Lieu, Ca Mau, and Ha Giang) but other provinces appear only on one list of the lowest 10.

Table 2.52: Net Enrollment Rate by Level of Schooling, Urban/Rural Residence, and Socioeconomic Region

Residence/Socioeconomic Region	Primary	Lower Secondary	Upper Secondary
National	96.6	85.9	64.4
Urban	97.1	89.7	74.2
Rural	96.3	84.4	60.6
Northern Midland and Mountainous	95.2	82.3	59.3
Red River Delta	97.3	92.9	81.4
North and South–Central	97.1	88.5	67.5
Central Highlands	95.8	80.5	56.1
Southeast	97.0	86.7	62.9
Mekong River Delta	96.1	79.7	49.8

Source: General Statistics Office of Viet Nam. 2013. *The 1/4/2013 Time-Point Population Change and Family Planning Survey: Major Findings.* Ha Noi. http://www.gso.gov.vn/Modules/Doc_Download.aspx?DocID=17009.

---

[70] According to MOLISA's 2015 TVET Report, about 900,000 rural workers were trained under this program in 2015, of which about 550,000 benefited from state support (DVET and NIVET 2017).

[71] MOLISA. Report Vocational Training in the Northern Midland and Mountainous Region. Unpublished.

Table 2.53: Ten Provinces with the Lowest Net Enrollment in 2015

Lower Secondary		Upper Secondary	
Province	NER Total	Province	NER Total
Soc Trang	72.6	Lai Chau	33.1
Gia Lai	74.4	Ha Giang	37.7
Bac Lieu	75.3	Ca Mau	40.7
Ca Mau	75.8	Soc Trang	42.1
Ha Giang	76.4	Bac Lieu	42.2
Ninh Thuan	77.1	Son La	42.4
Lai Chau	77.2	Gia Lai	42.5
Kien Giang	78.7	Kon Tum	43.7
Cao Bang	80.8	Dien Bien	45.5
Son La	81.4	Lao Cai	46.9

NER = net enrollment rate.
Source: General Statistics Office of Viet Nam. 2016. *The 1/4/2015 Time-Point Population Change and Family Planning Survey.* Ha Noi.

Table 2.54: Lower Secondary Promotion, Class Repeat, Dropout, and Completion Rates for 10 Lowest Provinces, SY2014/15

	Promotion	Repeat Class	Dropout	Completed
Whole Country	**97.75**	**0.84**	**1.41**	**81.70**
Bac Lieu	95.39	0.81	3.80	63.68
Kien Giang	94.01	1.19	4.80	64.06
Ca Mau	95.00	1.28	3.72	65.23
Soc Trang	93.11	1.20	5.69	65.70
Hau Giang	96.01	1.32	2.67	67.50
Ninh Thuan	96.29	1.55	2.15	68.98
Tra Vinh	95.39	1.83	2.78	69.11
Nghe An	98.82	0.39	0.78	70.95
An Giang	95.87	0.69	3.44	71.08
Gia Lai	97.55	1.28	1.17	71.92

SY = school year.
Source: Ministry of Education and Training. 2016. *Education Statistics Yearbook 2014–2015.* Ha Noi.

Table 2.55: Upper Secondary Promotion, Class Repeat, Dropout, and Completion Rates for 10 Lowest Provinces, SY2014/15

	Promotion	Repeat Class	Dropout	Completed
Whole Country	**96.59**	**0.79**	**2.62**	**78.82**
Gia Lai	96.44	1.90	1.66	54.44
Kon Tum	95.05	2.58	2.37	55.87
Ninh Thuan	94.08	2.42	3.50	59.52
Lai Chau	92.85	1.71	5.45	60.18
Ca Mau	90.11	1.46	8.42	61.82
Binh Thuan	94.07	1.38	4.55	62.70
Bac Lieu	91.92	1.74	6.34	62.75
Dak Lak	93.79	1.14	5.08	65.66
Ha Giang	93.42	0.98	5.60	65.74
Dak Nong	96.58	1.27	2.14	66.01

SY = school year.
Source: Ministry of Education and Training. 2016. *Education Statistics Yearbook 2014–2015.* Ha Noi.

206. The OECD found that 15-year-old students in Viet Nam's cities outscored their counterparts in rural areas. The NAM analysis at grades 9 and 11 found similar results. However, Iyer, Azubuike, and Rolleston (2017) found that in mathematics rural students outperformed urban students at the beginning of the year, but this gap closed by Wave 2 as urban students made more progress (Table 2.32), while results for English found urban students outperforming rural students although students in rural areas made more progress (Table 2.33).

207. Table 2.56 shows the grade 11 NAM results for SY2011/2012 by socioeconomic region, indicating a wide range of achievement among the regions with students in the Midland and Northern Mountainous region at the lowest level.

Table 2.56: Results for Grade 11 (SY2011/12) National Achievement Monitoring by Socioeconomic Region
(Percentage meeting the acceptable standard)

Socioeconomic Region	Mathematics	Literature	English
Midland and Northern Mountainous	40.1	34.5	18.8
Red River Delta	67.3	56.2	32.5
Northern and Coastal Central	54.3	58.1	20.3
Central Highlands	50.0	45.3	17.3
Southeast	60.7	58.1	36.0
Mekong River Delta	43.3	56.2	13.6
Nationwide	**54.8**	**53.5**	**24.2**

Source: Ministry of Education and Training, Center of Education Quality Assurance.

208. For people of remote areas VET institutions with boarding facilities, which are mostly located in the provincial capital cities, are generally the only option.[72] Hence, promoting access to TVET continues to play a prominent role in Viet Nam's human resources development policy framework and finds extensive support by several policy propositions on VET system development in the new TVET law and subsequent regulations. By stipulating exemptions from or reductions of tuition fees and granting other allowances for students from ethnic minorities who live in remote ("disadvantaged or severely disadvantaged") areas and/or are from poor households and for other disadvantaged groups (including disabled persons), the government stays committed to facilitate broad participation in TVET.[73]

209. Unfortunately, however, there are no clear arrangements yet on how short-term course certificates are valued in the NQF regarding the option for further advancements (pathways) toward the formal VET system. Comprehensive data disaggregating the socioeconomic background of students entering the formal TVET system and the number of students supported by state subsidies are not available.[74] Yet, there are strong indications that, despite government incentives to channel enrollments from lower secondary schools into formal intermediate TVET, Viet Nam citizens' preference for general education qualifications (USE/university) heavily challenges the attractiveness of the formal TVET

---

[72] Current national and provincial government policies to merge small VET institutions across districts into the bigger ones of capital cities to manage them more efficiently may further contribute to this constraint, rather than solving the issue.

[73] Special government programs (e.g., Programs 135 and 30a) provide financial subsidies to poor students. Half of students living in poverty are from an ethnic minority, and most ethnic minority students live in remote rural areas. Poverty among ethnic minority groups is closely associated with low or limited access to educational and training opportunities (Cf. ADB 2016d).

[74] The General Statistics Office's Household Living Standards Survey 2014 provides only general data on fee exemptions/reductions for education. According to this, the total share of people benefiting from school fee or contribution reduction or exemptions was 43.2% (GSO 2014).

system. Annually, only about 4% of lower secondary graduates proceed to vocational secondary schools and less than 2% of them decide to continue their studies at professional secondary schools (MOLISA and NIVT 2015).

210. **Migrant youth's limited access to schooling.** As noted in section II, new forms of poverty are emerging. While urban poverty has substantially decreased, rapid urbanization and the influx of immigrants from rural areas in recent years has challenged socioeconomic development in urban areas. Poor urban residents, especially domestic migrants, can suffer from a shortage of social capital, inadequate capacity to find alternative livelihoods, limited access to public services including schooling, and a lack of social integration. While clearly some out-of-school youth in urban areas are potentially eligible for LSE, not enough information is known yet about how many are out of school or their reasons for not attending school. Cameron (2012) and Jones et al. (2014) report different rates of enrollment from as low as 35% of poor migrant households, but they all reported general difficulties in accessing the public-school system because of registration issues. Brauw and Giles (2017) found in the People's Republic of China (PRC) a strong negative relationship between being a migrant youth and whether the youth enrolled in high school. They further found across counties a variation in the timing of national identity card distribution, which made it easier for rural migrants to register as temporary residents in urban destinations.

211. **Low participation rate of children with a disability.** According to the 2009 Viet Nam Population and Housing Census, almost 6.1 million or 7.8% of the population aged 5 years or older (7.1% for males and 8.5% for females), live with one or more disability in seeing, hearing, walking, or cognition; and, of these, 385,000 have severe disabilities (UNPF 2012). Table 2.57 shows the types of disability of students who would typically be in school. In 2009, of children aged 6 to 10 years with no disability the NER was 96.8%, but among children with a disability the NER was only 66.5% and only 14.2% for children with a severe disability. Table 2.58 shows that as children with a disability get older, they are more likely to either have never attended school or to have dropped out than children without a disability. In SY2013/14, Viet Nam had 56,162 students with a disability attending a primary school, which was 0.8% of all students at this level. According to the Department of Planning and Finance in 2015, only 13,572 attended LSE, which is 0.3% of the student population at this level and 1,520 or 0.1% of all students at USE. The evidence is that educational opportunity for disabled people is still very limited. Figure 2.10 shows the ratio of girls to boys in primary and secondary education and indicates a need for increased attention to gender equity among children with a disability. While the government has provided financial support programs to the disabled, access to education opportunities leading to life skills development and job opportunities is restricted.

Table 2.57: Percentage of Disability by Domain, Degree of Difficulty, Aged 5 to 15 Years, 2009

	Seeing	Hearing	Walking	Cognition	All Four Domains	Multiple Domains
At least some difficulty						
Male	0.63	0.43	0.45	0.77	1.46	0.43
Female	0.66	0.34	0.36	0.60	1.29	0.35
All people	0.64	0.39	0.41	0.69	1.38	0.39
Cannot do at all						
Male	0.04	0.08	0.11	0.16	0.23	0.09
Female	0.03	0.07	0.08	0.13	0.19	0.07
All people	0.03	0.07	0.10	0.15	0.21	0.00

Source: United Nations Population Fund. 2012. *People with Disabilities in Viet Nam: Key Findings from the 2009 Viet Nam Population and Housing Census*. Ha Noi.

Table 2.58: Percentage of Children Attending School Aged 6–17 Years, by Disability Status, 2009

		Currently Attending	Dropped Out	Never Attended
15–17 years old	Not disabled	67	30	3
	Severely disabled	4	16	80
	Disabled	12	28	60
11–14 years old	Not disabled	90	8	2
	Severely disabled	9	8	83
	Disabled	59	14	27
6–10 years old	Not disabled	97	2	1
	Severely disabled	13	3	84
	Disabled	66	4	30

Source: United Nations Population Fund. 2012. *People with Disabilities in Viet Nam: Key Findings from the 2009 Viet Nam Population and Housing Census.* Ha Noi.

Figure 2.10: Ratio of Girls to Boys in Primary and Secondary Education by Disability Status, 2009

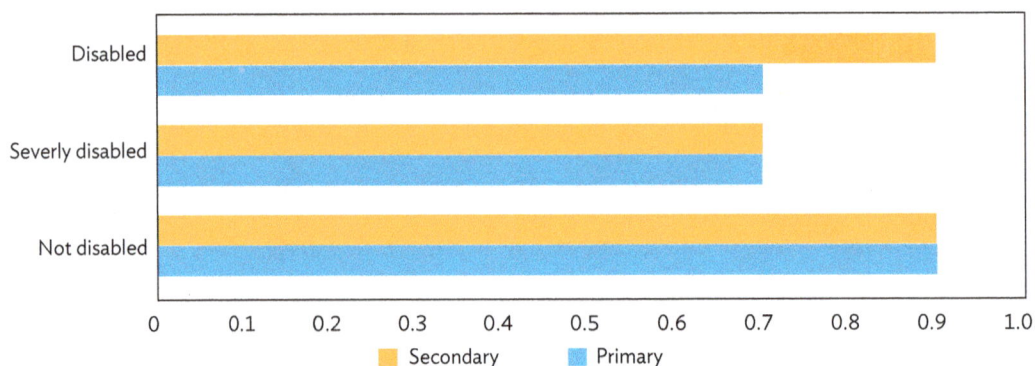

Source: United Nations Population Fund. 2012. *People with Disabilities in Viet Nam: Key Findings from the 2009 Viet Nam Population and Housing Census.* Ha Noi.

212. Viet Nam's policies for people with disabilities are highly inclusive, but there are substantial shortcomings in implementing a broad agenda (World Bank and the Ministry of Planning and Investment 2016). Foremost among the government's commitment to inclusion are the 2010 Law on Disabilities, and the United Nations Convention on the Rights of Persons with Disabilities, which Viet Nam ratified in February 2015. Protecting people with disabilities is also in the Constitution. Despite these commitments more than half of children with severe disabilities never attend school. Giving these children basic opportunities to participate in society and to engender attitudes of inclusion among others should be a major goal of the government.

213. Promotion of social participation in inclusive education has become more prevalent with the support of local and international organizations but for students with disabilities and their families, awareness of the government's requirement to provide education is limited.[75] The direct cost of education to families is one aspect that bars children with disabilities from schooling. Also, the

---

[75]   According to NCCD (2010), a a survey conducted in 2009 showed that "only 26.1% of households with disabilities wanted support to send them to school and only 6.9% of people with disabilities surveyed from ages 6 to 18 wanted to have education."

requirements of caring for a child with a disability reduce the earning capacity of the family. Other barriers include traditional teaching methods that do not address the learning needs of disabled students, low expectations for children with disabilities, rigid assessment/promotion procedures, and an emphasis on the role of special separate schools for disabled children. Currently, there is a shortage of specialized teachers and training institutions as well as appropriate teaching materials and modified school environments for disabled students.

3. Resource Management Is Ineffective and Inefficient

214. **Managers' skills are not sufficient to administer a decentralized system.** The government's stated intention is to increase decentralization through an improved financial allocation model and increased site-based decision-making.[76] In many ways, Viet Nam's education system is already decentralized in that the majority of funding for education comes from the local level (Table 2.59). While this autonomy has resulted in local ownership, it has fundamentally challenged the clarity of functional assignments, financial management, accountability, and monitoring and evaluation of the efficiency of educational expenditure programs. This has resulted in significant differences in outcomes and performance across local governments where there are critical gaps in access and quality of service provision in some districts.

Table 2.59: Public Expenditure on Education and Training, 2009 to 2013
(VND billion)

Item	2009	2010	2011	2012	2013
Government expenditure on education and training (VND billion)[a]	88,421	115,676	136,840	185,951	202,909
Central government expenditure (VND billion)[a]	7,870	14,302	14,273	23,518	25,663
Share of central government (%)	8.9	12.4	10.4	12.6	12.6
Provincial government expenditure (VND billion)[a]	80,551	100,669	122,567	162,434	177,247
Share of provincial government (%)	91.1	87.0	89.6	87.4	87.4

[a] Data for 2009–2012 were provided by the Ministry of Education and Training, Department of Finance and Planning, based on data from the Ministry of Finance. For 2013, the value is estimated based on the annual growth rate of government expenditure on education and training for 2012–2013 which is about 9.12%.
Source: Ministry of Education and Training, Department of Finance and Planning.

215. The EDS 2011–2020 indicates the need for the national education management system to be improved by decentralizing the system; strengthening cooperation between line ministries, sections, and provinces; and strengthening management capacity. In addition, an independent system needs to be built to verify educational quality and publish results in the media. The strategy calls for the enhancement of the education institutions' autonomy and accountability and for an enhanced information and communication technology (ICT) application to improve education management.

216. While MOET has provided extensive management training in the past, the planning capacity of DOETs and school principals is still generally weak particularly relative to decentralized decision-making. Two significant problems were identified in the analysis of the first two rounds of the nationwide teacher assessments in Viet Nam: (i) the capacity to self-assess using evidence of practice and to formulate professional development plans, and (ii) the capacity to set specific problems of practice and implement solutions within the local school context both individually and through collaboration with colleagues. These two elements are typically part of training for site-based management.

---

[76] Government of Viet Nam. Education Development Strategy 2011–2020 and Resolution No. 29-NQ/TW 8 on Comprehensive Innovations of Education and Training.

217. It takes time to shift educational management systems and maybe years to change the required policies, but the development of a strategy for change is the minimal requirement. In addition to extensive development of managers' skills, a detailed assessment of financial and administrative capacity and a new policy framework for decentralizing budget planning and allocation are required to ensure the sustainable delivery of primary and secondary schooling.

218. In 2015, only 22.4% of VET school managers held professional certificates for education management or vocational training management, with the lowest share (only 17.1%) recorded for managers of vocational secondary schools. This situation is all the more precarious as the current government policy strongly demands fundamental changes in the governance structure of public institutions by gradually shifting the responsibility for key administrative duties (including organizational and financial management, staff recruitment and development, effective service delivery, and quality assurance) from state agencies to institutions. MOLISA's draft reform plan envisages that by 2025 at least 20% of all TVET institutions shall be granted full autonomy status after being assessed for compliance with a comprehensive set of quality accreditation criteria and standards. However, even among 45 VET institutions invested to become high-quality schools, less than 50% of managers had such certificates (MOLISA and NIVT 2017).

219. **Decentralized governance requires a new accountability system.** Access to information, key to citizens holding the state accountable, is still lacking. The country's governance practices have neither encouraged openness and transparency nor promoted public discussion of the state's actions. Information and data are difficult to acquire.

220. Countries invest significant public resources in the provision of education, and the public and policy makers are naturally concerned about the quality of education. In recent years, the focus of the public and governments has shifted away from control over the resources and the components of the educational structure toward a focus on the outcomes of the system. There has been more interest in measuring what students have actually learned rather than the conditions that surround learning. Growing out of this moment is the idea of accountability, which is a concept of governance associated with the expectation of account giving. Accountability is the acknowledgment and assumption of responsibility for actions, decisions, and policies including the administration, governance, and implementation within the mandate and encompassing the obligation to report, explain, and be answerable for results. The OECD has reviewed the results from PISA 2009, 2012, and 2015 in more than 70 countries and found the most effective systems to be those with a decentralized administration system coupled with a public accounting for results. Decentralization by itself without accountability was found to contribute to low results on the PISA assessment. With the decentralization of powers, a new accountability model needs to be developed to ensure a focus on outcomes while at the same time, ensure that targeted resources are appropriately used.

221. Countries choose to use different forms of external assessment and the schools' own quality-assurance and self-evaluation efforts to collect data and plan for improvement. Accountability frameworks involve the annual collection, analysis, planning, and reporting on a number of different elements (for example, student achievement; dropout rates; completion rates; teacher, parent, and student perceptions; and secondary school to post-secondary transition rates) nationally and for each school and province. As with all assessments, it is good practice to collect information relating to different elements regarding school performance from several different sources. However, one of the major external assessments often involves collecting data and analyzing results from achievement tests administered to all students each year at selected grade levels. The cost of this type of accountability

system is relatively inexpensive compared with the total amount of funds expended in the education sector and relative to other inspection models.

222. Viet Nam has made a significant start on developing outcome measures of student performance at the national level by developing the NAM at grades 9 and 11 and by participating in PISA. The Upper Secondary and Professional Teachers Development Project has also developed a set of tools for measuring public perceptions about the quality of education.

223. MOET will need assistance in developing a policy framework that supports accountability and acquiring tools and skills for the annual collection, analysis, planning, and reporting on several different elements.

224. In TVET, quality assurance and system accreditation are still mainly based on input measure rather than outcomes. According to MOLISA, 25% of vocational colleges, 10% of vocational secondary schools, and 3.5% of vocational training centers have been subject to formal accreditation and recognition.[77] These accreditations were based on a set of nine quality criteria with 50 standards covering key input factors such as management, staff, pedagogy, facilities, services, and finances, and measure 150 indicators specific for each institutional level. Accreditations were to be conducted through a three-stage approach, comprising initial self-assessment, an expert-guided internal assessment and, potentially in addition, also a fully independent external assessment. The first two stages resulted in awards of sophisticated score-based quality levels, which categorize an institution's quality status either as not yet sufficient (level 1), as satisfactory but with the need of improvement (level 2), or as fully compliant to the national quality standard (level 3).

225. So far, prioritization of school accreditation on voluntary basis has apparently yielded positive results, particularly among selected colleges and secondary schools that were to become high-quality institutions. By the end of 2015, from a total of 239 applicants, 184 vocational institutions had been quality accredited at minimum level 2. Of these, 113 institutions (78 colleges and 22 secondary schools) were granted valid certificates at level 3. Less promising are the results for vocational training centers (VTCs): only 323 (11.2%) of 2,893 VTCs that were asked between 2013 and 2015 to conduct a self-evaluation actually submitted respective reports on their school quality. Apparently, none of them were certified by the GDVT, as MOLISA reported only 13 from a total of 28 VTCs that were fully accredited between 2010 and 2013.

226. MOLISA has recently revised its quality accreditation model. Essential improvements are related to measurable process standards now clearly stipulating activities for enterprise involvement in program design, implementation, student assessment, and training evaluation.

227. Apart from enhanced quality standards for all VET institutions and programs, the demand for quality accreditation has become even more ambitious by a Prime Minister Decision in May 2014 approving the High Quality Vocational School Development Project by 2020.[78] This decision stipulates a set of higher standards for institutions to be recognized as "high quality vocational schools" by introducing criteria that also largely focus on measurable outcome and output performance of vocational programs, especially for those that are based on regional and international curriculum standards.

---

[77] However, only 52.4% of these colleges were granted certificates, while this applies to 91% of institutions on which investments were made to make them high-quality TVET institutes.

[78] Prime Minister Decision No. 761/QD-TTg (May 2014) Approving The High Quality Vocational School Development Project by 2020.

228. MOET has made a very good start in collecting data about actual learning outcomes through the NAM and PISA. The OECD has indicated that PISA already provides measurement tools to this end and is committed to improving, expanding, and enriching its assessment tools (OECD 2016b). Other OECD data, such as those derived from the Survey of Adult Skills and the Teaching and Learning International Survey, can provide evidence base for monitoring education systems. In 2018, MOET participated in the Teaching and Learning Survey. However, there is no evidence that the results from NAM and PISA have been used for policy analysis or to plan for resource allocation.

229. Many development partners helped MOET develop the Education Management Information System (EMIS) mainly for the school construction purposes. However, accurate data from EMIS and the Teacher Management Information System (TMIS) are critical for effective and transparent educational planning and management. MOET continues to use the comprehensive EMIS, which was developed under one of the official development assistance (ODA) projects, and regularly updates the system for education planning. One of MOET's future challenges for the EMIS is to use the system's data strategically, not only for planning and management but also to improve teaching and learning. An integrated information technology system for managing basic education through redevelopment of EMIS (education statistics) and the Project Management Information System (human resources) and full implementation of these systems in all 63 provinces are required. The new vocational education and training management information system being rolled out by MOLISA will, in time, validate data as all TVET providers are targeted to give input.

230. **Resources devoted to education in Viet Nam**. In 2004, the National Assembly established an annual target of spending 20% of the state budget on education. As was seen in Table 2.18, Viet Nam's 2013 expenditure for education and training is 15.9% of the total government budget and about 5.7% of gross domestic product (GDP). As can be seen in Table 2.60, Viet Nam's expenditure per student is low relative to many neighboring economies. However, expenditure per year as a proportion of the GDP per capita (Table 2.61) is higher than its neighbors and, at 5.7% of GDP, compares well with some of East Asia's wealthiest nations, such as the Republic of Korea.

Table 2.60: Gross Domestic Product and Expenditure per Student among Asian Participants in PISA 2012

	GDP per Capita (in equivalent $)	Cumulative Expenditure per Students between 6 and 15 Years	Expenditure per Year as a Proportion of GDP per capita (%)
Japan	35,238	89,724	25.5
Korea, Rep. of	28,829	69,037	23.9
Singapore	57,799	85,284	14.8
Shanghai, PRC	18,805	49,006	26.1
Malaysia	15,077	16,816	11.2
Thailand	9,748	13,964	14.3
Viet Nam	**4,098**	**6,969**	**17.0**

GDP = gross domestic product, OECD = Organisation for Economic Co-operation and Development, PISA = Programme for International Student Assessment, PRC = People's Republic of China.
^a Viet Nam did not report the above 2015 information to OECD.
Source: OECD. 2013b. *PISA 2012 Results: What Students Know and Can Do – Student Performance in Mathematics, Reading and Science (Volume I)*. Paris.

Table 2.61: Government Expenditure on Education as a Percentage of Gross Domestic Product
(%)

Country	2009	2010	2011	2012	2013
Cambodia	1.66	1.54	1.51	1.56	2.02
India	3.31	3.42	3.84	3.87	3.84
Indonesia	3.52	2.81	3.19	3.41	3.36
Lao PDR	1.65	1.71	1.81	1.98	3.45
Malaysia	5.97	4.97	5.76	5.74	5.47
Korea, Rep. of	4.68			4.63	5.05
Singapore	3.03	3.11	3.08	3.12	2.92
Sri Lanka	2.05	1.72	1.81	1.50	1.62
Thailand	3.87	3.51	4.81	4.56	4.13
Viet Nam	**4.81**	**5.13**	**4.81**	**5.53**	**5.66**

Lao PDR = Lao People's Democratic Republic.
Sources: Data from UNESCO Institute for Statistics. UIS.Stat. http://data.uis.unesco.org (extracted 12 August 2018).

231. Increasing the amount of funding does not in itself ensure improved education quality. Both PISA 2012 and 2015 found that there is a relationship between the amounts of funding provided for education and the students' performance only up to a point and, beyond that level, the students' achievement did not improve even though more funds were made available. Figure 2.11 shows an increase in students' mathematical performance as funding increases up to about $50,000 but performance does not change much with increased funding after that point. Figure 2.12 shows similar results for science in 2015. It should be noted that Viet Nam achieved very high performance in mathematics and science while spending a relatively very low amount per student.

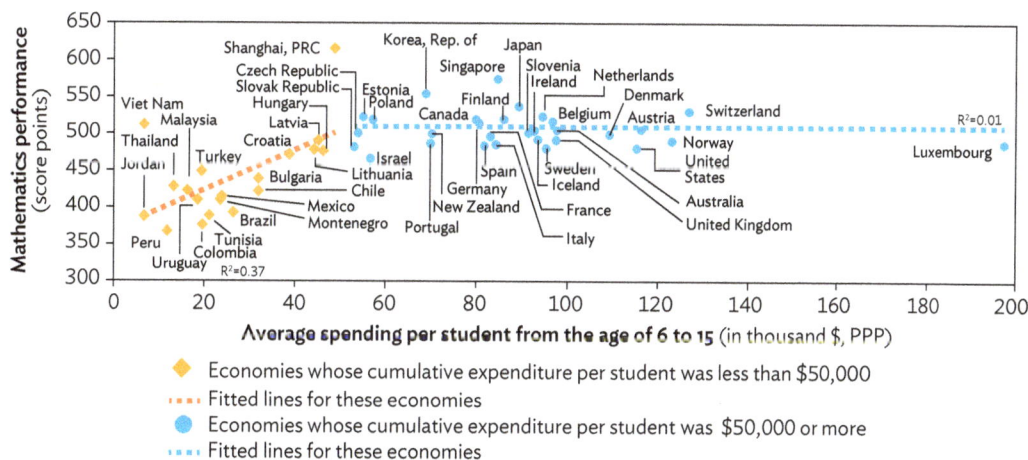

Figure 2.11 : Spending per Student for Age 6 to 15 Years and Mathematical Performance in PISA 2012

PISA = Programme for International Student Assessment, PPP = purchasing power parity, PRC = People's Republic of China.
Note: Only economies with available data are shown.
Source: OECD. 2013. *PISA 2012 Results: What Students Know and Can Do – Student Performance in Mathematics, Reading and Science (Volume I)*. Paris.

Figure 2.12: Spending per Student for Age 6 to 15 and Science Performance in PISA 2015

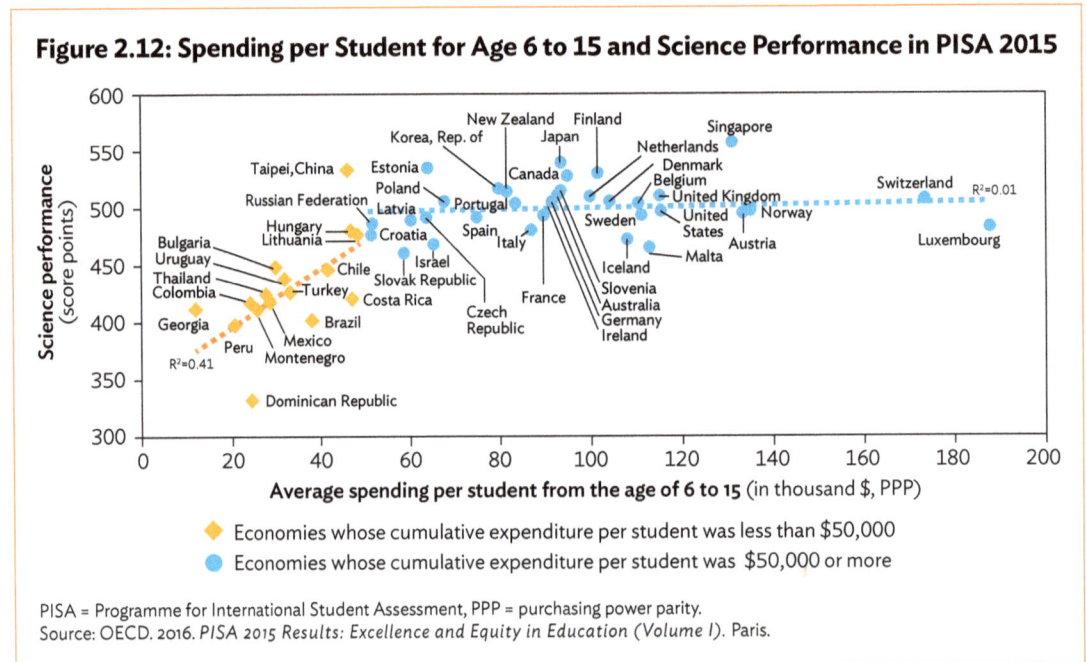

PISA = Programme for International Student Assessment, PPP = purchasing power parity.
Source: OECD. 2016. *PISA 2015 Results: Excellence and Equity in Education (Volume I)*. Paris.

232. As shown in Table 2.64, the total expenditure on education has more than doubled between 2009 and 2013 while the total number of students has increased by only about 5%. The unit cost allocated to education per student has increased even relative to inflation. Although the government has been able to increase funding for education, it may have difficulty sustaining this level of growth, which could result in being unable to continue promoting the remarkable improvement in education services quality as has been the case in the past 10 years.

233. The structure of public education expenditure suggests that there may be underinvestment in early childhood and higher education (UNDP and VASS 2016). State resources have progressively targeted high enrollment in primary schooling and lately in the lower secondary level as well. MOET planned for around 29% of the national education budget for primary education and 22% for lower secondary education, annually and throughout 1999–2014. In 2013, the actual expenditures were very close to these budget allocations (28.2% for primary and 22.1% for lower secondary). Despite these resourcing levels, demographic change suggests a decline in the number of school students, a lower rate of secondary enrollment, and weak completion rates. Expenditure on early childhood education, upper secondary education, and vocational training is relatively lower, and college-university education enrollment rates have dropped in these key subsectors. The focus on universalizing primary and lower secondary education, despite the importance of a highly educated workforce for industrialization and modernization, may help explain Viet Nam's lesser increase in mean years of schooling among comparable countries. Universal basic education is vital, but Viet Nam must aim even higher by extending preprimary and post-secondary education.

234. **Limited provision and poor quality of private schools.** Increasing the number of private education providers was a key part of the government's cost-shifting or socialization strategy. Many countries are relying on a mix of public and private education providers, as well as a mix of domestic and foreign private education providers. Worldwide experience has shown that expanded education can be achieved quickly through private education as private providers can often move faster, and sometimes more effectively to fill education supply gaps. Table 2.62 shows that between SY2008/09

and SY2015/16 the percentage of students enrolled in nonpublic schools declined significantly at the preprimary and USE levels and remained about the same at primary and LSE. The Education Law, which was amended in 2009, changed the school categories, from public, semiprivate, and public schools before the amendment to eliminating the semiprivate schools and converting them mainly to public schools after the amendment.[79]

Table 2.62: Percentage of Students Enrolled in Nonpublic Schools, SY2009/10 to SY2015/16

(%)

	2009/10	2010/11	2011/12	2012/13	2013/14	2014/15	2015/16
Primary students	0.7	0.5	0.6	0.5	0.6	0.6	0.7
LS students	0.8	0.6	0.6	0.5	0.7	0.7	0.9
US students	15.8	11.7	9.1	9.1	8.4	7.2	7.2

LS = lower secondary, SY = school year, US = upper secondary.
Source: Ministry of Education and Training. 2017. *Education Statistics 2015–2016*. Ha Noi.

235. Figure 2.13 shows that students from USE private schools in Viet Nam do not perform as well internationally as students from government schools or private schools.

Figure 2.13: Viet Nam Mean Score in Mathematics on PISA 2012, by Type of School

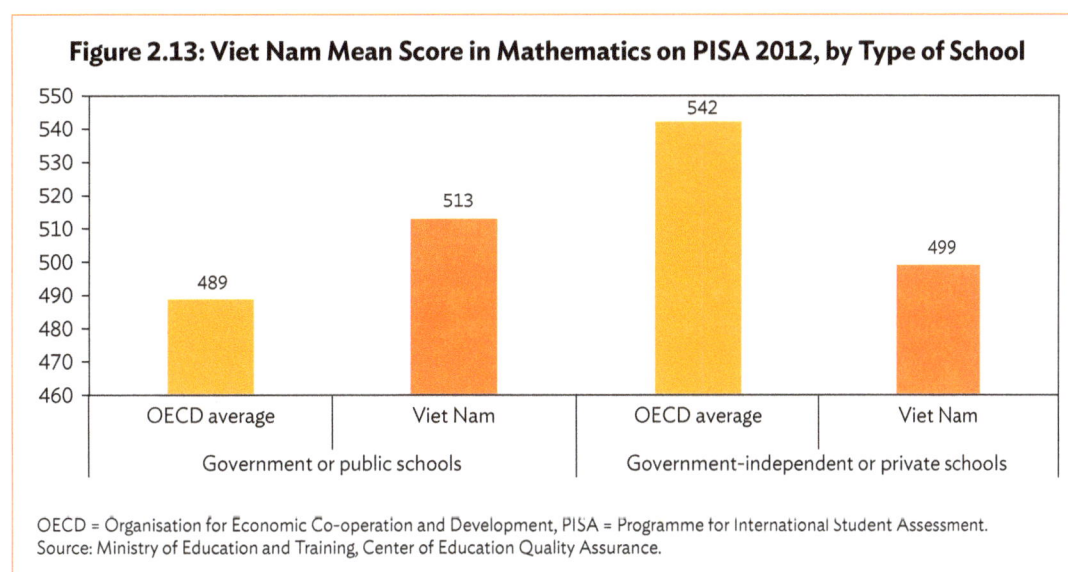

OECD = Organisation for Economic Co-operation and Development, PISA = Programme for International Student Assessment.
Source: Ministry of Education and Training, Center of Education Quality Assurance.

236. The President of ADB in a 2014 speech noted that Viet Nam needs to create an enabling business environment that encourages entrepreneurship and innovation, which requires improved governance, greater transparency and disclosure of policy making, and regulation.[80] Appropriate reforms will create opportunities for private investment, reduce the costs of doing business, and improve basic services by introducing private sector discipline and competitive market pressures. To significantly alter the mix of public and private participation and enable greater diversity and increase enrollments, the government will need to institute reforms within a strengthened, outcome-focused accountability framework.

---

[79]   Government of Viet Nam. Amending and Supplementing a Number of Articles of the Education Law No. 44/2009/QH12 issued 25 November 2009.

[80]   Public Lecture at the Foreign Trade University by Takehiko Nakao, President, Asian Development Bank, on 15 January 2014 in Viet Nam.

237. As demonstrated in the growth rate and apparent success of information and communication technology (ICT) and language schools under MOET, students can and will pay for skills training that is conducted on a flexible timetable and designed to equip them with high-demand skills to improve employability. Thus, student fees are an existing source of TVET financing and, when combined with full or partial scholarships for target groups, have proven effective in other Asian countries. Some planners assert that over time student fees can grow up to 40% of public institution revenues and still maintain TVET accessibility for those unable to pay a fee.

238. Private career schools are not burdened by being viewed as state vocational training centers below the perceived status of unemployed university and college graduates. By marketing to and attracting this group, a pressing social problem can be targeted. Although there are no statistical data, government staff and others familiar with private TVET provider operations suggest that many students who have completed college and/or university are willing to return to a nongovernment school to master employment skills.

C. ADB Support to the Education Sector

239. ADB has been a major development partner of the Government of Viet Nam in the education sector since the 1990s. As agreed with the government and other ODA agencies operating in Viet Nam, ADB focuses its support mainly on basic education, secondary education, and TVET. ADB has also extended its support, although to a smaller degree, to other subsectors, including teacher education and higher education. In the LSE and USE subsectors, ADB is the leading development partner assisting the government in improving access, quality, and relevance of secondary education, especially for disadvantaged groups and disadvantaged areas. Appendix 2 contains ADB's development strategy for the sector, Appendix 3 gives a summary of completed and ongoing ADB projects, while Appendix 4 summarizes ADB's sector strategy and results framework.

D. Analysis of Strengths, Weaknesses, Opportunities, and Threats

240. Table 2.63 outlines the strengths, weaknesses, opportunities, and threats of Viet Nam's education sector.

241. To summarize, the education sector does not provide enough school leavers with the competencies required to meet the needs of a modernizing labor market and society, because (i) the quality of graduates and school leavers is low; (ii) access to equitable and effective quality education is lacking; and (iii) resource management is ineffective and inefficient. A competent and efficient education sector will increase (i) regional and international competitiveness by improving the skills of graduates, and (ii) equity for those living in remote and economically disadvantaged areas.

Table 2.63: Education Sector – Analysis of Strengths, Weaknesses, Opportunities, and Threats

Strengths	Weaknesses
• Stakeholders (government, donor partners, nongovernment organizations, and the public) committed to and recognize the importance of the sector • Alignment of past ADB education strategies and programs with government priorities and programs • Effective ongoing coordination between ADB, donor partners, and the government • Strong comparative advantage of ADB in the secondary education subsector	• Lack of strategic framework of how various ODA projects will assist sector development • Weak institutional capacity and management in DOET, MOET, schools, and vocational education institutions • Limited capacity of education managers and teachers to implement innovative project activities • Lack of appreciation of the value of education among parents of students from an ethnic minority or with a disability • Lack of private sector involvement in determining desired competencies for employability
Opportunities	Threats
• Assist in developing strong and sustainable education systems • Assist in improving the numbers of qualified graduates for the sector • Assist in developing an accountable decentralized governance system • Promote public–private partnership in the sector • Utilize cyclone-resistant building to support climate change mitigation	• Economic fluctuations • Amount of public debt • Unsuitable facilities for competency-based learning • Delays in implementing competency-based curriculum and textbooks • Negative impact of climate change on education facilities

ADB = Asian Development Bank, DOET = Department of Education and Training, MOET = Ministry of Education and Training, ODA = official development assistance.
Source: Asian Development Bank.

III. Sector Strategy

A. Government Education Strategy, Policy, and Plans

242. The following government strategies and plans guide and define the policy framework for the long-term development of education: the Socio-Economic Development Strategy (SEDS) 2011–2020, Socio-Economic Development Plan (SEDP) 2016–2020, Education Development Strategy (EDS) 2011–2020, Resolution No. 29-NQ/TW 8 on Comprehensive Innovations of Education and Training, Resolution No. 44/NQ-CP on Radical Changes in Education and Training to Meet Requirements of Industrialization and Modernization in a Socialist-Oriented Market Economy in Course of International Integration, and Decision No. 2653/QD-BGDĐT on the Action Plan of the Education Sector for the Implementation of Resolution No. 29. Appendix 6 provides a summary of the government's education policy framework.

243. **Socio-Economic Development Strategy 2011–2020.** The strategy sets a vision (overall objectives) along with the main objectives and orientation to achieve the vision.[81] It acknowledges the need to move beyond the existing economic model, which is based on low labor cost and intensive capital investment, toward higher efficiency, productivity, and competitiveness as the core of growth.

244. **Socio-Economic Development Plan 2016–2020.** This plan sets the targets for socioeconomic development and the environment up to 2020 and provides detailed guidance for implementing the plan's three specific orientations.[82] To increase the human resources quality and enhance the science and technology potential, the plan calls for the continued innovative, fundamental, and comprehensive renovation of education and training, focusing on developing high-quality human resources by innovating the program, enhancing living skill, reducing the study load in secondary school levels, enhancing in-depth knowledge and industrial style in vocational training, and promoting creative thinking and self-study at universities. The plan wants to (i) associate education with scientific research and technology transfer; (ii) ensure the equality between public education and nonpublic education; (iii) encourage the socialized development of high-quality schools of all levels; (iv) delegate the autonomy to education and training institutions, especially university and vocational training schools; (v) pilot the transformation from public schools into education institutions managed and developed by the community and enterprises; (vi) strengthen vocational training and associate education with enterprises; (vii) emphasize the education development and vocational training development among ethnic minorities and in disadvantaged areas; (viii) complete the preferential credit policy for poor pupils or students; and (ix) encourage the formation of study encouragement funds to provide scholarship for poor pupils and students with good study results.

---

[81] Government of Viet Nam. Socio-Economic Development Strategy 2011–2020 Approved by the Eleventh Congress of Viet Nam Communist Party. Ha Noi.

[82] Government of Viet Nam. National Assembly Resolution No. 142/2016/QH13 Socio-Economic Development Plan 2016–2020. Ha Noi.

245. **The Human Resources Development Strategy 2011-2020.** The strategy aims to establish Viet Nam's human resources as a foundation for the country's sustainable development, international integration, and social stability, making them competitive with human resources in advanced countries. The strategy contains the legislative and policy-setting agenda for developing human resources management strategies for public service sectors, including education. It establishes the framework for developing and implementing the new human resources management strategy for secondary teachers.

246. **Vocational Training Development Strategy 2011-2020.** MOLISA developed this strategy based on the 2006 Law on Vocational Training.[83] This strategy lists ambitious objectives and specifies a broad array of respective "solutions" to be implemented under nine systemic reform components: (i) renovated state management of vocational education and training (VET); (ii) development of vocational teachers and managerial staff; (iii) development of occupational standards and the national vocational qualifications framework; (iv) development of respective training curriculum and instructional materials; (v) strengthening of standards for VET facilities and equipment; (vi) enhancement of quality assurance; (vii) enhancement of linkage between VET institutions, labor market, and enterprises; (viii) improved awareness about VET development; and (ix) promotion of international cooperation.

247. **Education Development Strategy 2011-2020.** This plan implements the SEDS 2011-2020 objectives[84] by developing and improving the quality of human resources, especially skilled and talented staff. It covers issues related to all educational levels from preschool to higher education and continuing education to reform the education system fundamentally and comprehensively by 2020, through standardization, modernization, socialization, and international integration.

248. The plan's eight solutions (or actions) also address issues pertaining to education management and the lack of educational equity for marginalized people: (i) innovate education management; (ii) improve the capacity of teaching and education management staff; (iii) reform context and methodology of teaching, examination, and quality assessment; (iv) increase investment resources and innovate financial mechanism for education; (v) enhance the connection between training with usage, scientific research, and technology transfer to meet society's demands; (vi) enhance support for disadvantaged regions, ethnic minorities, and social beneficiary students; (vii) develop education science; and (viii) extend and enhance international cooperation in education.

249. In addition, the plan is a time-bound action program for responsible ministries and departments, comprising an action for "Formulation, Supplementation and Development of General Framework and Education Policies" and 19 actions under "Formulation and Implementation of Plans, Programs, Projects in Education Development." Of the 20 actions, 10 deal with issues for all educational levels, 7 for higher education, 1 for tertiary education, and 1 for general education.

250. **Resolution No. 29-NQ/TW 8 on Comprehensive Innovations of Education and Training.** The resolution addresses the comprehensive renovation of the education and training system.[85] It stipulates the need for fundamental change in developing a strong and efficient education and training

---

[83] Government of Viet Nam. Prime Minister's Decision No. 630/QD-TTg (29 May 2012) Approving the Vocational Training Development Strategy during 2011–2020.

[84] Government of Viet Nam. Prime Minister's Decision No. 711/QD-TTg Approving the Education Development Strategy 2011–2020. Ha Noi.

[85] Central Committee of the Communist Party of Viet Nam. Resolution No. 29-NQ/TW 8 on Comprehensive Innovations of Education and Training. Ha Noi.

system to better meet the development, national defense, and educational needs of the people. For secondary education, it sets the following targets: intellectual, physical, and quality development of students; identification and fostering of children's aptitude and career orientation; strengthening the total education approach by prioritizing education of ideals, traditions, ethics, lifestyle, foreign language, computer skills, practical skills, and application of knowledge in real life situations; and developing children's creativity, self-learning skills, and encouraging lifelong learning.

251. **Resolution No. 44/NQ-CP on Radical Changes in Education and Training to Meet Requirements of Industrialization and Modernization in a Socialist-Oriented Market Economy in the Course of International Integration.** The resolution defines and assigns the responsibility for achieving the following tasks: [86] (i) develop awareness of the radical forthcoming changes in education and training; (ii) complete the national education system; (iii) make changes in educational programs of various levels; (iv) make changes in the forms and methods of examination and evaluation of the education and training results; (v) develop the capacity of teaching staff and education management officials; (vi) increase the involvement of the private sector in education and vocational training; (vii) change management of education and vocational training; (viii) improve the facilities and the use of information technology to education and vocational training; and (ix) proactively seek and improve international cooperation in education and vocational training.

252. **Decision No. 404/QD-TTg Approving the Project of General Education Curriculum and Textbook Reform.** The decision outlines the development of the new curriculum and the schedule for its implementation.[87] Stage I (April 2015–June 2016) covers the development, review, pilot, and issuance of the new curriculum and the relevant e-learning materials. Stage 2 (July 2016–June 2018) will compile, review, pilot, approve, and publish at least one set of new textbooks for grades 1, 6, and 10. Stage 3 (July 2018–December 2023) will be the implementation of the new curriculum and textbooks grade-by-grade for primary, lower secondary, and upper secondary levels starting in SY2018/19.

253. **Sustainable Development Goals.** Viet Nam is committed to achieving the United Nations (UN) 2030 Agenda for Sustainable Development and the SDGs (United Nations 2015). The government has established a cross-ministerial SDG task force to develop the national action plan, which identifies the 115 priority targets among 169 targets under 17 SDGs. The national action plan proposes the framework for SDG implementation and emphasizes the urgency of strengthening the government's research capacity, data collection, and analysis system, networking with knowledge institutes, and advocacy for promotion of SDGs. The Agenda for Sustainable Development has two central policy pillars for education. The first is a strong focus on monitoring and improving learning outcomes. The second pillar focuses on those who are left behind and often remain hidden.

254. **Action Plan on Gender Equality for the Education Sector for 2016–2020.** MOET is committed to achieve gender equality in the education sector through the adoption of the Action Plan on Gender Equality of the Education Sector for 2016–2020 (UNESCO Office in Ha Noi 2016). MOET's personnel department has reviewed the 2012–2015 action plan undertaken to provide a gender-responsive, results-based analysis. UNESCO and results-based management specialists have provided technical input into the first draft of the 2016–2020 action plan. The following gaps and issues were addressed: (i) gender disparity among teachers in different grades, with a concentration of

---

[86] Government of Viet Nam. Prime Minister's Resolution No. 44/NQ-CP on Radical Changes in Education and Training. Ha Noi.

[87] Ministry of Education and Training. Minister of Education Decision No. 2653/QD-BGDĐT on the Action Plan of the Education Sector for the Implementation of Resolution No. 29. Ha Noi.

female teachers in lower grades and less representation in higher educational levels; (ii) girls' levels of completion of primary and secondary school education being lower than boys' and women's literacy being lower than that of men's; (iii) the presence of gender stereotypes in textbooks and violence and bullying at schools; and (iv) the lack or inconsistency of sex-disaggregated data for analysis, planning, monitoring, and reporting.

B. Development Partner Programs

255. Viet Nam collaborates with several partners in developing its education sector. Multilateral agencies include ADB, the World Bank, the European Union, the United Nations Children's Fund (UNICEF), the United Nations Industrial Development Organization (UNIDO), and UNESCO. Major bilateral partners include Japan International Cooperation Agency (JICA), Belgian Technical Cooperation, Germany's Gesellschaft für Internationale Zusammenarbeit (GIZ), the Department for International Development of the United Kingdom, Australia's Department of Foreign Affairs and Trade (DFAT), United States Agency for International Development (USAID), and the Government of France. Nongovernment organizations (NGOs) include the Flemish Association for Development Cooperation and Technical Assistance (VVOB) of Belgium, Plan International, Oxford Committee for Famine Relief (OXFAM) of Great Britain, and Handicap International. Appendix 5 lists the major recent and current projects funded by these development partners.

256. **Partners in preschool education.** UNICEF had a project which focused on the early years of a child's life from age 0 to 6 years. The early years are considered the most important period for formation of values, self-concept, and socialization into future roles, including gender roles. UNICEF's project, which focused on the early years, from age 0 to 6, resulted in (i) enhanced psychosocial development and school readiness of children entering primary schools; (ii) preschool education for ethnic minority children in their mother tongue; (iii) strengthened policy and legal framework, advocacy, funding, and coordination; and (iv) support for families and communities in their roles as young children's primary caregivers and first educators.

257. **Active partners in primary education.** To support the government's policies to achieve the Millennium Development Goals (MDGs), including universal primary education, many development partners and NGOs joined forces to contribute to the diverse portfolio of assistance requested by the government. The Belgian Technical Cooperation, the European Union, UNESCO, UNICEF, and the World Bank funded projects to provide equitable access to quality education. UNICEF-supported activities addressed issues relating to mother tongue and bilingual education, gender equality in the curriculum, teaching–learning process and students' assessment, ethnic minority girls' transition to lower secondary education, education sub-laws, inclusive education, child participation, HIV/AIDS prevention in primary schools, and monitoring and evaluation. UNESCO's activities included sector-wide education policy and planning, literacy and lifelong learning, education for sustainable development, teacher education, and climate change and disaster risk reduction. The World Bank has two projects that impact both primary and secondary education—the Renovation of General Education Project and the Enhancing Teacher Education Project are described below.

258. **Active partners in secondary education.** ADB has been Viet Nam's major development partner in its education sector since the 1990s. As agreed with the government and with other ODAs operating in Viet Nam, ADB support focuses mainly on secondary education. ADB projects have helped

Viet Nam achieve high and sustainable economic growth by improving the quality of secondary education, thereby improving the knowledge and skills of future employees. ADB has developed a strong partnership with MOET and has committed to support secondary education, particularly in subsector policy reform and inclusive secondary education for disadvantaged groups, such as ethnic minorities and poor or near-poor groups. Through the Secondary Education Sector Development Program and Second Secondary Education Sector Development Program, ADB supported the development of science, technology, engineering, and mathematics (STEM) education; career and vocational orientation program; and teachers' standards at secondary education. These programs are closely linked with the World Bank's two recently approved projects that will impact secondary education. First, the Renovation of General Education Project is designed to raise student learning outcomes by (i) revising and piloting the curriculum using a competency-based approach; and (ii) improving the effectiveness of instruction by creating and disseminating textbooks aligned with the revised curriculum. Second, the Viet Nam Enhancing Teacher Education Program is designed to build capacity to assess and improve teachers' effectiveness through a quality professional development program delivered in schools. The project will support various teacher training institutions to complete the first phase of the government's plans to establish the Viet Nam Teacher Education Network. UNICEF's Adolescent Development and Participation project addressed the access to and opportunities for quality lower secondary education, opening the way for an adolescent-friendly learning environment. The special focus on equity and inclusion issues ensures that vulnerable groups of adolescents are reached, especially disabled young people, young people affected by HIV/AIDS, and ethnic minority girls.

259. **Active partners in technical and vocational education.** Under the government's Socio-Economic Development Strategy (SEDS) 2011–2020, technical and vocational education and training (TVET) has gained recognition and received a boost from the government's plan to develop a skilled workforce for the economy. Several development partners have provided support to this subsector, including ADB, GIZ, UNIDO, the Nordic Development Fund, the British Council, and some NGOs. German development cooperation has provided both financial (KfW) and technical support (GIZ). ADB has financed two TVET projects: (i) the Vocational Technical Project, cofinanced by the Nordic Development Fund, the French Development Agency (Agence Française de Développement), and a grant from JICA; and (ii) the Skills Enhancement Project, 2010–2015, financed solely by ADB to support Viet Nam's efforts to increase its competitiveness in regional and global markets. UNIDO provided technical assistance to benchmark Viet Nam's training system for industrial manufacturing skills against international and regional competitors, identify transferable best practices, and elaborate a strategic blueprint and strategy for reforming the industrial skills training system in line with Viet Nam's industrial development strategy.

260. **Active partners in higher education.** The World Bank has been the leading development partner in higher education. It has funded five projects in the subsector. ADB has been providing funding to the University of Science and Technology of the Ha Noi Development Project. The two major bilateral partners in higher education are the governments of Japan and France. Japan has supported the capacity building of technical universities under the Higher Education Development Support for ICT Project. It also supports the ASEAN University Network/Southeast Asia Engineering Education Development Network and the Strengthening of Tay Bac University for Sustainable Rural Development. France provides major support to Hanoi Technical University. USAID helps technical universities and vocational colleges transform engineering education into active project-based programs.

261. **Institutional arrangements and processes for development coordination.** To maximize the impact of their contributions, development partners have adopted a strategic approach within a general framework to focus on various educational levels or different geographic areas. The Education Sector Group, comprising MOET, multilateral and bilateral development partners, and NGO representatives, coordinates their activities and ensures aid effectiveness, minimizes or avoids duplication, improves cooperation, and reduces transaction costs. The group has helped enhance working relations, align education improvement efforts, provide consolidated comments on government education policies, and share information during regular meetings about education projects financed by group members.

262. **Achievements and issues.** ODA for the education sector represents about 5.5%–6.0% of Viet Nam's total public expenditure. In 2013, all 23 development partners in the education sector mapped out their education programs and projects, which helped the government and its partners to rationalize and align their priorities and resources to ensure support for education in the next cycle of development planning. The education system remains strong but inequalities in quality and access remain, especially in hard-to-reach areas, for ethnic minority children, and for children with disabilities. Emphasis on 21st century skills, such as critical thinking and ICT, is also needed. However, it is necessary to establish each project's relevance to the government's policies and plans for the sector.

263. As the major supporter for secondary education in Viet Nam, which is expanding especially in disadvantaged and less-developed areas, ADB's main challenge is to develop a coherent framework and strategy to address disparities and improve the quality of secondary education, especially in disadvantaged areas, and support the smooth transition from lower to upper secondary education.

264. Viet Nam is committed to achieving the SDGs by 2030 and is incorporating the goals into development planning and budget processes (UNDP 2015). Many development partners will withdraw in the coming years as bilateral donors, although they will continue to provide assistance through multilateral channels and/or through global programs. The Netherlands ended its bilateral support in 2012. Sweden ended its bilateral assistance in 2013, Denmark in 2015, the Department for International Development of the United Kingdom in 2016, and Finland in 2017/2018. As ODA resources diminish, Viet Nam will need to explore other innovative financing options, increase domestic resources mobilization, use existing ODA and public financing more strategically, and leverage other sources of financing. Viet Nam has already attempted to reduce its level of aid dependency in recent years, but the reduction in donor support has had clear impacts on some specific sectors.

IV. Recommendations

A. Improve the Quality of Secondary Education

265. Over the past 20 years, the Government of Viet Nam and its development partners have exerted a good deal of effort to increase the net enrollment rate (NER) at the primary and secondary levels. Evidence from the Programme for International Student Assessment (PISA) suggests that although Viet Nam's students are competitive internationally, their participation rates are low and they do not achieve well on the higher-level skills. The national achievement monitoring (NAM) results for grades 9 and 11 show that almost half of the students are not meeting national standards. In the PISA and NAM scores, there are very large gaps between urban and rural/remote areas, poor and wealthy, and ethnic minority and majority students. The TVET curriculum does not appear to be aligned with workplace expectations.

266. **Improvements to curriculum.** To cope with today's challenges, individuals' abilities to tackle complex mental tasks need to be developed, well beyond the basic reproduction of accumulated knowledge. To adjust to this new reality most countries around the world have adopted or are adopting a competency-based curriculum. At the center of the framework of key competencies is the ability of individuals to think for themselves as an expression of moral and intellectual maturity, and to take responsibility for their learning and for their actions (OECD 2016a).

267. A key competency is the ability to think reflectively which demands relatively complex mental processes. For example, having applied themselves to mastering a particular mental technique, reflectiveness allows individuals to then think about this technique, assimilate it, relate it to other aspects of their experiences, and to change or adapt to it. Reflectiveness implies the use of metacognitive skills (thinking about thinking), creative abilities, and taking a critical stance. It is not only about how individuals think, but also about how they construct experience more generally, including their thoughts, feelings, and social relations. This requires individuals to reach a level of social maturity that allows them to distance themselves from social pressures, take different perspectives, make independent judgments, and take responsibility for their actions (OECD 2016a).

268. Accordingly, the Ministry of Education and Training (MOET) has recognized the need to revise the curriculum and has committed to apply a new competency-based general education curriculum for grades 6 in SY2021/22, grade 7 in SY2022/23, grade 8 in SY2023/24, grade 9 in SY2024/25, grade 10 in SY2022/23, grade 11 in SY2023/24, and grade 12 in SY2024/25. To develop a learner's competencies, the new general education curriculum involves differentiated and integrated teaching, active learning, and education evaluation reform (Nguyen 2017).

269. The extent to which the new curriculum includes and emphasizes science, technology, engineering, and mathematics (STEM) education is unclear at this time, but as discussed in section II.B, the need for this type of emphasis is acute. STEM can be considered part of the curriculum, but it can also be thought of as a learning strategy of the already defined curriculum, which was the approach taken in the Second Secondary Education Sector Development Program—a development which MOET is encouraged to continue.

270. As noted in section II.B, Viet Nam's school system excels at accomplishing straightforward tasks but faces new challenges in developing cognitive and complex problem-solving skills. Key to making the successful change to a competency-based educational system will be how the curriculum documents are written, how the learning materials are developed, and how teachers are trained to implement the new curriculum. Also, as previously discussed, this is not the first time that MOET has tried to reform the curriculum and teaching practice. Despite having spent millions of dollars on training thousands of teachers over 15 years, teachers continue to teach frontally with limited direct interaction with students and no use of active learning methodologies.

271. During an examination of lessons from high-performing countries, the Organisation for Economic Co-operation and Development (OECD) found that a competency-based curriculum was one element of these countries' systems. Figure 4.1 summarizes the findings from the 2015 PISA showing the shift from the old system to what is termed "enabling systems" in the areas of learner perceptions; curriculum, instruction, and assessment; teacher quality; work organization (centralized compared with decentralized); and accountability.

272. In the classic bureaucratic system, instruction is teacher centered and delivery is consistent with a work organization that is directed from a central organization. The teacher standing at the front of the classroom telling students what they are to learn is consistent with a management model that externally directs and supervises the teacher. However, a system that is attempting to deliver a competency-based curriculum, which calls for students to master complex ways of thinking, may need a professional development system, a teacher assessment system, and a management system that has highly professional teachers working in a collegial manner. If teachers are being directed in what to do and how to do it, they may find it difficult to understand and model the learning environment required for their students to acquire complex competencies.

273. **Improvements to pedagogy.** A major challenge in successfully implementing the new competency-based curriculum will be in changing teaching and learning practices. Changing teacher behavior is difficult, as most teachers tend to teach the way they were taught in school, and during their pre-service and in-service education. However, teachers must use teaching techniques that encourage interdependence and collective problem-solving. Teachers themselves must be exposed during their training and subsequent in-service support programs to thought-provoking, student-centered teaching.

274. Table 4.1 outlines the reconceptualization of school practices to respond to current realities of the competencies graduates required to live and work in knowledge societies.

Figure 4.1: Findings from 2015 PISA

Lessons from high-performing countries

The old bureaucratic system	Student inclusion	The modern enabling system
Some students learn at high levels		All students need to learn at high levels
	Curriculum, instruction, and assessment	
Routine cognitive skills, rote learning		Learning to learn, complex ways of thinking, ways of working
	Teacher quality	
Few years more than secondary		High-level professional knowledge workers
	Work organization	
"Tayloristic", hierarchical		Flat, collegial
	Accountability	
Primarily to authorities		Primarily to peers and stakeholders

Source: OECD. 2016. *PISA 2015 Results: Excellence and Equity in Education (Volume I)*. Paris.

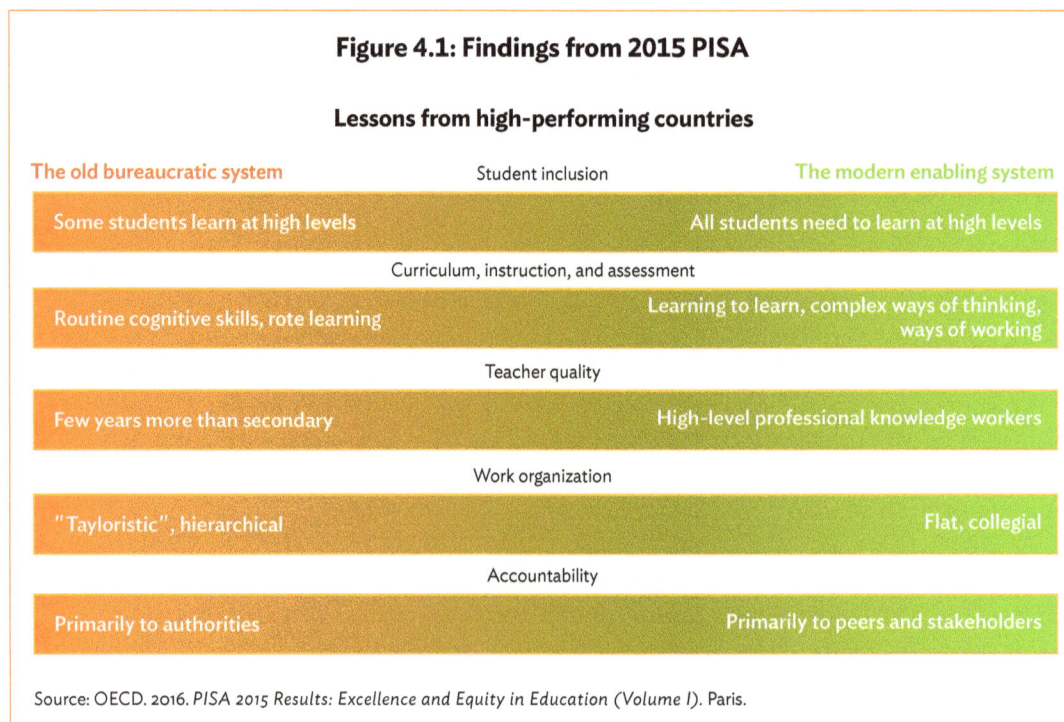

Table 4.1: A Shift in Instructional Emphasis

	Traditional Education Learning of Information	Acquiring of Competencies
Subject matter	Knowledge exists as basically universal, agreed-upon facts. Curriculum is prescribed by a list of topics to be covered.	Knowledge is continually being created through inquiry-based discovery learning. Curriculum is prescribed to be a balance of learning basic concepts, subject skills (e.g., solving a mathematical formula, writing a paragraph), and developing strategies for applying learning to everyday situations (e.g., problem-solving, critical thinking, following through the processes of science, arguing points of view).
View of students	Receivers of knowledge.	Are inquirers and co-creators of knowledge.
Role of teacher	Deliver the curriculum. Pace instruction according to a predetermined series of teaching events.	Act as a guide for locating information, be a co-inquirer with students and mentor the development of application skills. Pace instruction according to learning events.
School milieu	The milieu and the local environment are not significant considerations in curriculum documents.	The local community and the school are considered to be highly relevant and strategies for getting input from community members are given high priority.

Source: Carson, T. R. 2009. *Implementing the New Curriculum in China: Re-thinking Curriculum Change from the Place of the Teacher*. Canada: University of Alberta.

275. Viet Nam's model for professional development of teachers consists of requiring teachers to attend a series of workshop sessions each year, usually during the summer months. Teachers are provided a list of topics which may or may not be related. MOET dictates compulsory content for in-service to meet the requirements each school year of about 30 periods (each period is 45 minutes) and the respective DOETs define compulsory content to meet the requirements for developing local education for each school year for another 30 periods. In addition, teachers are expected to complete optional content for self-study for MOET-regulated continuing professional development which is about 60 periods with 41 topics for USE.[88] The sessions generally consist of someone delivering a lecture to a large hall full of around 100 or more teachers.

276. Most development partner projects have an in-service component to instruct teachers on how to implement a new strategy or system. Due to the large number of teachers in Viet Nam, most development projects use a variation of a "train the trainer" or "cascade" model of training in which project staff trains key members of MOET, DOETs, and bureaus of education and training offices in the hope that these people will be able to in turn train teachers. The cascade model, a mechanism delivering training messages from trainers at the central level to trainees at the local level through several layers, is largely used for in-service training, as it can train teachers quickly and economically. This model has been used in many developing countries due to its low cost, but it is often criticized for its ineffectiveness, because the message is often distorted through the long-distance one-way process, making hardly any change in the classroom.

277. **Improvement to teacher assessment.** Frequently, a distinction is made between evaluation for administrative purposes and evaluation that stimulates continuing professional development (CPD). Clearly, these two purposes can be closely related but there are important differences to be realized. Evaluation for administrative purposes has strong ties to job security, promotional opportunities, and financial compensation. In brief, a "low" or "poor" evaluation can result in negative consequences. Often, with good reason, those being evaluated are primarily concerned with their ranking and how to most expeditiously raise their standing.

278. In Viet Nam, the implementation of the teacher standards as a tool for "stimulating professional growth" caused some initial uncertainty. The major confusion seemed to come from misunderstandings that determining teacher rankings by evaluating evidence in light of the teacher standards is closely related to "evaluation for administrative purposes." That is, there could be negative consequences for teachers and principals who are attempting to evaluate evidence honestly. With several years of experience since implementing teacher assessment based on standards in SY2011/12, some of this uncertainty has been resolved. The standards have been revised to better reflect the teacher competencies required to implement the new curriculum and are being implemented under the Second Secondary Education Sector Development Program.

279. Evaluation to establish reference points for formulating professional growth plans requires a major shift in thinking. It requires those involved to think about the context within which instruction is taking place and how a teacher interacts with it. It requires careful consideration of the intended curriculum, the nature of the students, and the school milieu. Qualitative judgments need to be

---

[88] Minister of Education and Training, Circular No. 30/2011/TT-BGDĐT.

made by examining evidence of practice for indicators that desired outcomes are being achieved and for indications that the situation needs improvement. Priority is placed on "growth," which requires teachers to assess their competencies at a particular point in time within their own teaching situation, and then plan to develop their abilities to more productively work in that situation over a period of time. The measure of success is a consideration of how much growth has taken place over that period of time. From this viewpoint, a teacher could have a "good" administrative ranking, but may demonstrate little professional growth from one point in time to another, whereas a beginning or struggling teacher may demonstrate a significant amount of growth during a similar time period.

280. The challenge to establishing self-initiated professional growth strategies for improving the quality of instruction is to break strongly held understanding that teacher evaluations are one-time events and are completed without due regard to the context within which teachers work. The more productive view is to "create a culture of change" wherein all constituents in a school system are continually working on plans for growth—individually and collectively. The concept of creating a culture of change as a central pillar of reform was developed extensively by internationally renowned educator, Michael Fullan (Fullan 2001).

281. In Viet Nam, teachers' performance is evaluated relative to the 25 criteria that define the six teacher standards. Circular No. 30/2009/TT-BGDDT (22 October 2009) establishes the annual teacher assessment, while Circular No. 660/BGDDT-MGCBQ:GD provides the guidelines for collecting and assessing evidence. The annual assessment consists of a teacher's self-evaluation coupled with an external assessment usually done by the school principal using subjective criteria. One issue of this system is that there is little common understanding of what constitutes performance at a given level.

282. During the teacher assessment process, the use of a rubric to assess starting points and set targets for growth was not clearly explained. Part of the problem seems to stem from the "labeling" of the four proficiency levels in the rubric: poor, fair, good, and excellent. These terms lead to "value" judgments as opposed to "evaluative" considerations based on clearly setout criteria. Few teachers consider themselves to be poor or fair and teachers who have worked through the assessment process report that they are reluctant to designate others as poor or fair.[89]

283. A significant amount of work is needed to help teachers and principals understand the method of conducting criterion-referenced assessments using rubrics to categorize degrees or levels of proficiency in performing professional activities. Australia's terms of graduate, competent, highly accomplished, and leader more accurately label degrees of proficiency. They lend themselves more easily to articulating indicators of performance levels with which teachers can identify (Table 4.2).

---

[89]   The International Consultant (2012) provides detailed feedback from the 2011 teacher assessments.

Table 4.2: Example of Teacher Standards in Australia

Standard 2: Know the content and how to teach it. Criteria 2.3: Content selection and organization			
Level	**Proficiency**	**Description of Proficiency**	**Indicators**
1	Graduate	Has theoretical knowledge but little practice	Organizes content into effective learning and teaching sequence
2	Proficient	Has practical experience implementing curriculum	Organizes content into coherent, well-sequenced learning and teaching programs
3	Highly accomplished	Has confidence in using innovative classroom techniques	Exhibits innovative practice in the selection and organization of content and delivery of learning and teaching programs
4	Leader	Provides leadership in collaborating with others on innovative techniques	Leads initiatives that utilize comprehensive content knowledge to improve the selection and sequencing of content into coherently organized learning and teaching programs

Source: Australian Institute for Teaching and School Leadership. www.aitsl.edu.au.

284. A newly graduated teacher can be expected to know the basic theories but will have limited experience in putting them into practice. A proficient teacher follows through with implementing prescribed teaching. A highly accomplished teacher is competent in creatively adapting and modifying externally provided materials to more effectively meet the needs of individual and groups of students. A leader is clearly a teacher who collaborates with colleagues to support overall school and departmental improvement goals. Evidence of competency within each level will be different.

285. One way to improve on this system would be to have each teacher develop a teaching portfolio, which is a collection of items of evidence, in either hard copy or soft copy form (Table 4.3). They should be collected and maintained over time so that comparisons can be made to note improvements and professional growth. Central to implementing processes for stimulating professional growth is that teachers will take the responsibility for gathering evidence that reflects their competencies in light of the 25 criteria. The gathering of this evidence is to be an ongoing process from one school year to the next. Items of evidence vary greatly and the same item may be used to evaluate a number of competencies pertaining to one or more standards.

286. Evaluation for stimulating professional growth progresses from the teacher's assessment to the development of their profession growth plan. The teacher's individual plan should be related to the school's overall plan for improvement. Many individual professional development efforts have been doomed to failure because the goals and strategies for achieving them are too ambitious. Teachers and mentors alike can quickly be overcome with too much input and time constraints for experimenting with change. Table 4.4 outlines the process for developing a teacher's CPD plan.

Table 4.3: Examples of Evidence for a Teaching Portfolio

Local School Plan – Many schools develop annual school plans that document local community initiatives, the school culture, and particular student characteristics. School plans include strategies for improving the overall performance of students and for developing local school staff activities. A teacher could include in his portfolio that part of the school plan in which he or she will be involved or provide leadership.

Subject Department Plans – Departments within each school develop plans to implement new curriculum and teaching methodologies. These plans can also include mentoring activities that involve experimenting with new techniques and assessing their effectiveness in improving student outcomes either for individual or groups of students. A teacher could include in her or his portfolio documents of planning for introducing experimental techniques, reflections on productive aspects of methods tried, and examples of student work that shows evidence of improved achievement of learning outcomes.

Teacher Practice – Individual teachers should be encouraged to include two different types of evidence in their portfolios: (i) items that demonstrate a teacher's ability to plan and conduct teaching—lesson plans, learning materials, assessment instruments, and student records; and (ii) items that demonstrate student achievement—samples of exemplary work, photographs of project work and bulletin boards, letters from parents, and student self-assessments. Evidence of student achievements provides a basis upon which to measure a teacher's successes and benchmarks for interpreting whether efforts to improve teaching methods are working.

Source: ADB. 2013. *Teacher Assessment for Stimulating Professional Growth*. Consultant's report (Secondary Education Sector Development Program). Ha Noi.

Table 4.4: Process for the Teacher Continuing Professional Development Plan

Step 1: Focus on a priority area of interest or concern
At the conclusion of the annual assessment process, a teacher (individually or in collaboration with a mentor) should select a few areas within which he/she intends to enhance his/her competency. This consideration should include areas of particular interest as well as perceived areas of weakness. Professional growth is more likely to take place and be self-motivating if a teacher is supported in pursuing areas of personal interest. Ideally, the areas of interest should be related to areas the school has identified in its improvement plan.

Step 2: Limit the scope
Select a small number of priority areas of interest or concern.

Step 3: Consider strategies
Consider what specific strategies could be used to address each priority area. Reflect on how realistic it will be to implement the strategies. This step is often overlooked in planning for change. For example, a goal may be to earn a master's degree in physics but this is unrealistic since the teacher is working in an area that is remote from an institution that offers such a program. On the other hand, a goal may be to work with a colleague to explore the internet to locate and implement innovative learning materials in physics.

Once specific strategies are considered for each priority, one area should be chosen for which the teacher is satisfied that the strategies for change are reasonable and for which he or she will receive support from lead teachers and principals.

Step 4: Develop the plan
- Clearly state the goals for the plan and the strategies to be used.
- Identify the items of evidence that were used during the assessment to designate a starting point from which improvements will be planned.
- Outline the specific steps that will be taken to learn and incorporate higher levels of competency.
- Identify indicators (items of evidence) that will provide measures of enhanced proficiencies.
- Identify what support will be needed from colleagues, lead teachers, and principals to effectively implement the plan.

Source: ADB. 2013. *Teacher Assessment for Stimulating Professional Growth*. Consultant's report (Secondary Education Sector Development Program). Ha Noi.

287. Part of the strategies would be to consider what form of CPD would be required, which could include working with a mentor/coach, attending specific workshops to collect information on teaching strategies, or undertaking specific research. In this system, the teacher and the school determine which CPD activities will be undertaken.

B. Increase Access to Upper Secondary Education

288. In 2016, the NER for lower secondary education (LSE) was 92.3%, approaching the government's 2020 target of 95%. Efforts are still needed to encourage disadvantaged youth from poor families, including ethnic minorities and youth with a disability, to attend and complete LSE. However, the NER in 2016 of 63.0% for upper secondary education (USE) is a long way from the government's target of 80% of youths within the age range for obtaining USE or equivalent level by 2020. Current strategies have resulted in some improvement to the NER in USE, but more radical strategies and policies may be required to meet the government's stated objective for USE and to supply the numbers of well-educated USE graduates required by the emerging job market.

289. **Entrance examinations for upper secondary education.** Admission to upper secondary school is typically selective in Viet Nam (Bodewig et al. 2014). Students who successfully complete LSE are awarded the Lower Secondary Education Graduation Diploma. However, USE is offered mostly only to students who have earned the Lower Secondary School Diploma and passed an entrance examination (WENR 2012).

Table 4.5: Criteria for Admission to Grade 10, by Province

	Selective Schools				Nonselective Schools			
	Entrance exam		Entrance exam plus other criteria		All students who apply gain entry		Other criteria for admission	
Province	N	%	N	%	N	%	N	%
Ben Tre	7	78	0	0	2	22	0	0
Da Nang	7	78	1	11	0	0	1	11
Hun Yen	5	56	2	22	2	22	04	0
Lao Cai	2	17	3	25	3	25	4	33
Phu Yen	5	38	2	15	2	15	4	31
Total	26	50	8	15	9	17	9	17

Source: Iyer, P., O. B. Azubuike, and C. Rolleston. 2017. *Young Lives School Survey, 2016–17: Evidence from Vietnam.* Oxford: Young Lives, Oxford Department of International Development, University of Oxford.

290. Each school that requires an entrance examination develops its own examination. In some cases, a provincial or city exam may be needed. High schools for the gifted are very competitive, with admission exams passed by only 1% to 2% of test takers. The various entrance examinations vary in level of difficulty, with the examination being more difficult depending on how desirable the particular school is thought to be. Parents are aware of which are the most desirable schools.

291. In a situation where only a few spaces are available and the desire is to reduce the number of students entering USE, the selective process may be desirable. However, if the intent is to increase the number of students entering and graduating from USE, then the entrance examination only serves as a roadblock for students to progress from LSE to USE.

292. **Increase relevance of upper secondary education to TVET, higher education and employment.** The main purpose for most students and parents to attend USE is to prepare for entry to university. But USE has little relevance for students who are not interested in or who could not afford to attend university. However, LSE graduates do not yet possess the skills required to successfully enter an increasingly sophisticated workforce. USE graduates must be adequately prepared for the next stage of their lives, whether that is TVET, higher education, or the workplace. Therefore, USE must lay the foundation for an individual's orientation toward lifelong learning. In a rapidly progressing society, the content of all formal learning, even at advanced skill and higher educational levels, has built-in obsolescence. An individual must be equipped to know how to continue learning and adapting to the changing and increasingly complex demands of society and the workplace.

293. MOET is introducing a new competency-based curriculum for basic education in part to address the issue of becoming more relevant to the student and to better prepare them to become productive members of the workforce and society at large.

294. **Increase the relevance of technical and vocational education and training to secondary education**. Students and parents, employers, and public authorities perceive TVET's role and importance to be inadequate to society and the economy (ADB 2018). Its reputation compared with other subsectors providing general and higher education qualifications is still low.

295. Under the Second Secondary Education Sector Development Program, vocational and career orientation is being introduced to LSE and USE schools. This initiative should increase the awareness of career options including TVET-related careers. However, for students and parents to consider TVET as an available option, they will need to see graduates from TVET programs both at the secondary and post-secondary level who are able to find skilled careers that match their TVET training and offer attractive salaries. This will entail a major shift in the current TVET programs so that they are more aligned with the needs of the workplace.

296. Targets, objectives, and solutions that can be associated with the strong commitment of the Ministry of Labour–Invalids and Social Affairs (MOLISA) to overcome prevailing shortcomings of the country's TVET system and accelerate its progress, both (i) in producing graduates with the skills required by industry and demanded on the labor market, and (ii) in enabling students to acquire such skills through effective training programs and methods, are manifold and addressed in several components of MOLISA's Project Plan on Renovation and Improvement of the Quality of TVET until 2020 with an Orientation to 2030 (ADB 2018).

297. Key interventions focus on upholding, updating, and refining the considerable accomplishments during recent years in the fields of the (i) national qualification framework; (ii) development of occupational skills and training quality standards; and (iii) rigorous standardization of core input factors for an advanced skills supply system such as the vocational education and training (VET) qualifications of teachers and school managers, competency-based curriculum design and practice-oriented training delivery methods, as well as work regimes specifying teacher duties, minimum workloads, and maximum class sizes. These and other standards, norms, and regulations largely comply with the recommendations of ADB's earlier TVET assessment and other expert reports and have built a good and necessary basis for further activities toward the nationwide implementation of this innovative but complex reform process framework.

298. **Cash incentives for attendance.** Conditional cash transfers (CCTs) are programs that transfer cash, generally to poor households, on the condition that those households make prespecified investments in the human capital of their children. CCTs are one of the most prevalent social assistance programs in low- and middle-income countries (Saavedra 2016). Gentilini, Honorati, and Yemtsov (2014) report that over 50 countries worldwide operate CCTs, more than twice the number in 2008.

299. Table 4.5 indicates the criteria for Admission to Grade 10 by provinces.

300. Overall, it would seem that Viet Nam could realize a NER gain of around 9%–10% in USE through a carefully designed CCT program that will encourage the students from the poorest families (including students from ethnic minority families) to attend USE particularly if the conditions were tied to a large payment for either enrolling in the next grade or graduation. Any CCT program should be available to students enrolled in regular USE, TVET, or equivalency programs.

301. **Improve the quantity and quality of facilities.** As noted in section II.B, if Viet Nam is going to move forward from a low-middle-income nation, it will need to increase the number of graduates from USE. If the NER in USE is to increase from the current SY2015/16 rate of 63.0% to the government's target of 80.0%, spaces will need to be found for about 655,000 more students. To fully address the needs of the workplace, more well-trained potential employees may be required beyond the government's target, which will require even more spaces.

302. As also reported in section II.B, the evidence for accreditation of schools is positive in that national standards have been established and this reinforces the ongoing push in Viet Nam to invest public funds to improving minimum school quality inputs. However, as reported at the end of SY2014/15, only 25% of secondary schools meet national standards. Also, as can be seen in Table 4.6, the percentage of funds allocated to capital expenditure between 2010 and 2015 declined at both the LSE and USE levels; this trend could be expected since the total number of secondary students was declining over this same period. Although there is little need for additional spaces to accommodate LSE students, the quality of facilities still requires upgrading, while at the USE level both upgrading of facilities and building of additional classrooms are needed. Development partners have been a major source of funding for capital improvements but as earlier noted this funding source will be declining in the coming years. Thus, facilities will need to be able to allow for the implementation of the new competency-based curriculum where active student-centered learning is encouraged.

303. MOET will need to find alternative means to fund capital improvements and find alternative strategies to more effectively and innovatively provide the required learning environment.

304. One innovative way to increase infrastructure is through public–private partnerships (PPPs). PPPs have emerged as a modality that can contribute to improving the cost efficiency of education delivery. In successful PPPs, the roles of partners are clearly stated, and performance targets are clearly defined and effectively and efficiently monitored. The private partner in a PPP may be a nongovernment organization or a for-profit enterprise. PPPs can expand education infrastructure and generate benefits in education service delivery, information and communication technology (ICT) utilization, skills training, and sustainable financing. Innovative service delivery initiative that may draw PPP support include output-based aid, voucher schemes, school and education institution management initiatives, and service-delivery contracting initiatives.

Table 4.6: Trends in the Expenditure for Secondary Education in Viet Nam, 2010–2015

Item	2010	2011	2012	2013	2014	2015
Lower Secondary						
Total government expenditure on LSE (VND billion)	26,336	30,489	41,799	44,804	48,796	50,376
Total capital expenditure (VND billion)	6,764	7,677	8,728	7,860	6,652	7,268
Total recurrent cost (VND billion)	19,572	22,812	33,071	36,944	42,144	43,108
Percentage of capital expenditure of total	25.7%	25.2%	20.9%	17.5%	13.6%	14.4%
Upper Secondary						
Total government expenditure on USE (VND billion)	13,593	15,421	19,772	21,093	28,610	29,637
Total capital expenditure (VND billion)	4,485	4,488	5,072	5,139	5,111	5,617
Total recurrent cost (VND billion)	9,108	10,933	14,700	15,954	23,499	24,020
Percentage of capital expenditure of total	33.0%	29.1%	25.7%	24.4%	17.9%	19.0%

LSE = lower secondary education, USE = upper secondary education.
Notes:
Capital expenditure includes new goods and civil works and rehabilitation.
Recurrent expenditure includes wages and benefits, subsidies, and services payment.
Source: Data were provided by the Department of Finance and Planning and the Ministry of Education and Training, based on data from the Ministry of Finance.

305. To achieve the required learning outcomes using PPPs, governments will need to formulate better policies, regulations, and monitorable performance targets to foster accountable PPPs in the education sector. This will involve, among other things, making the regulatory environment more facilitative of market-based mechanisms in the education sector.

306. The Pantawid Pamilyang Pilipino Program in the Philippines includes a very large PPP to rapidly increase the number of classrooms at the upper secondary level. The program involves a CCT program to make attendance at school attractive to students and a PPP to provide the spaces required.

307. Given the limited revenues available for sustained financing, many governments have developed policies that focus on diversifying TVET funding sources by stimulating more private investments from both private households as well as employers, improving the targeting of public spending, and increasing the income of training institutions through productive activities. Liberalizing the training market shall trigger a structural transformation of a supply-driven system into a demand-driven one.

308. In remote areas, MOET's favored strategy is to provide boarding or semi-boarding schools whereby students come to a central point to receive schooling. In Africa and the South Pacific, shipping containers are converted into classrooms or classrooms are prefabricated. A classroom can be delivered by helicopter to any remote location and equipped with solar energy panels and a rainwater-collecting system to make the structure self-sufficient. Each structure takes about 8 weeks to complete and has become very efficient in terms of material versus covered square meter. Having a school or classroom in remote communities would enable students to stay in their community, making it a more cost-effective option than building larger structures. Also, the school could serve as a resource for adult learning in the community.

309. As most areas of Viet Nam, including remote areas, are covered by 4G, instruction can be provided via ICT from a remote location. Teachers from ethnic minority backgrounds could serve several communities from one central location. At the local level a local liaison or outreach person is all that is needed to ensure that students attend school and to assist with any technical issues.

310. Appreciation for ICT's potential to enhance learning and improve the delivery of educational content has begun to be appreciated only recently. In ADB-supported ICT projects, students were more interested and motivated, absenteeism was reduced, standardized test scores were higher, collaboration and teamwork was enhanced, and communication and computational skills improved.

C. Improve Management of Schools

311. **Decentralization and accountability**. A country must carefully consider the structure of the educational management system when examining ways to implement a new concept such as a competency-based curriculum, because the structure and the culture it creates have an impact on all aspects of the system. To understand this and Viet Nam's current structure, Table 4.7 provides a brief summary of four management models: the classic, central control, close-to-school support, and site-based management. The models are useful for gaining insight into how shifting the locus of control among various levels of government can drive the management process.

312. Across the world, the classical model is the most frequently seen educational management system. Viet Nam's system shares many of the model's characteristics. In this model, most of the management responsibilities are under the aegis of some central agency, often a national ministry of education. The central government develops new strategies. The central governing body is responsible for implementing the new initiative. The role of other levels of the system would be to follow the implementation instructions. Central supervision controls and provides support in pedagogical and administrative areas. Although the central agency may be responsible for inspecting every school and teacher, all echelons of administration have both supervisory and support responsibilities for promoting quality education.

313. Site-based management, defined as the decentralization of decision-making authority to the school site, is one of the more popular strategies that came out of the 1980s school reform movement in the United States (Oswald 1995). The decentralization of decision-making has been one of the topics debated in the broad discussion on appropriate change strategies concerning school improvement, teacher development, and pupil learning for the past several decades (Skilbeck 1984, Marsh 1992, Fullan 2001, Hopkins 2001, Hargreaves 2007). The call for decentralization has been a result of the central agencies' failure to design, plan, and implement new school curricula. Decentralization is where decision-making authority is passed down to lower organizational levels, requiring principals and teachers to participate in a more central way in determining school goals and policies and to exercise their professional judgment about the content of curriculum and means of instruction (Robbins 1994). Site-based management was expected to improve schools through decentralization of administration, participation by staff, parents, and the community in the administration of the school, making schools more effective (Phillips 1997).

Table 4.7: Roles and Responsibilities under the Four Models of Educational Management

Level	Classical Model	Central Control Model	Close-to-School Support Model	Site-Based Management Model
Central Agency or Ministry of Education	Responsible for policies; planning; teacher training, recruitment, salaries, and placement; and curriculum and learning resources, allocation of funds, and system control and monitoring.	Responsible for policies, planning, teacher training, curriculum and learning resources, allocation of funds, and system control and monitoring. Inspection of all schools every 3 to 5 years and informing the public of findings.	Small team in charge of development of supervision policies. Annual national planning.	A limited resource allocation is determined at this level. Planning is for the overall system but often with a means to influence local planning. There is no external direct school supervision. Accountability systems, using outcome indicators, are established to monitor the implementation of regional plans.
Regional supervision office accountable to the central ministry; could be appointed by the central ministry	Control of the development of education in the region. Responsible for supervising several schools. Responsible for conveying implementation strategies to schools. Provide advice and resources to schools.	Control of the development of education in the region. Responsible for supervising several schools. Responsible for conveying implementation strategies to schools.	In charge of identifying schools that are most in need, planning interventions for these schools, and offering them intensive and development-oriented supervision. Controlling the finances of all schools.	No specific supervision officers. Responsible for regional planning. Monitoring schools through review of schools' outcome indicators.
School level principal or head teacher and teachers	Implement circulars and directives. Informal supervision of teachers.	Implement circulars and directives. Planning to "pass" an inspection. Regular supervision of school and teachers.	Informal supervision of teachers.	Schools are responsible for major planning and decision-making, often including the setting and administration of budgets. Regular supervision of teachers and planning for professional staff development. Involved in school self-evaluation and development of school improvement plans.

Source: ADB. 2013. *International Trends in Decentralization of Secondary Education Management.* Consultant's report (Secondary Education Sector Development Program). Ha Noi.

314. Several countries that are moving to competency-based curriculum also use the site-based management system. This does not mean that site-based management system must be used but there seems to be a connection between the management system and competency-based curriculum. In Canada, Australia, and the United States, systems that are implementing competency-based curricula also use site-based management systems. In Malaysia and Sri Lanka, systems that have indicated interest in the competency-based curriculum have also expressed interest in shifting to site-based management.

315. The site-based management model is predicated on the idea that teachers and the local community can be the best managers of the school's quality and operation since they are most familiar with the local context and issues and are most directly responsible for the actual learning within the school. In this model, public trust in the professionalism of teachers and local administrators as well as parents' interest in education is necessary. In addition, the teaching staff is respected as having the skills and professional conscience to participate in self- and in peer-evaluation.

316. In its pure form, all decisions affecting the schools (planning, funding, facilities, curriculum, learning resources, teacher qualifications and recruitment, teacher training, student admission criteria, pedagogy, and monitoring and supervision) are under the control of the school and the parents the school serves. The best example of site-based managed schools are private schools where all these decisions are made by the school and whatever governing board the school has established. With private schools the role of the state tends to be extremely limited.

317. However, in public education where funding is provided by the state, governments tend to have maintained some control over school decision-making. In this model, there is no formal supervision of schools organized by the Ministry of Education. Within this structure schools have the autonomy to make decisions about how education is delivered, and with it, the usual accompanying accountability that provides information to the local community and also to the ministry. The model uses a system of outcome indicators and focuses on whether students have acquired the required competencies and whether the parents and the public are satisfied with the system instead of on inputs to the system (teaching methods, school organization, and teacher numbers or qualifications). Student assessment results are often considered critical to an accountability system, but other indicators are also frequently used.

318. The findings from the 2015 Programme for International Student Assessment (PISA) relative to autonomy and accountability indicate that students tend to perform better in countries where schools have greater autonomy over what is taught and how students are assessed (OECD 2016a). Further, in countries where schools are held to account for their results and where schools enjoy greater autonomy in resource allocation, students tend to do better than those in schools with less autonomy. Also, this study found that in countries that use standards-based external examinations, students tend to do better overall.

319. By participating in PISA 2012, 2015, and 2018, Viet Nam has made a great start in collecting data which policy makers can use to adjust the system. Results from PISA 2021 and 2024 will be an important gauge to assess the implementation of the new competency-based curriculum. However, there is little evidence to show that the policy makers have used the PISA results effectively. MOET needs to take advantage of OECD expertise to conduct a critical analysis of the secondary education system.

320. The national achievement monitoring (NAM) system is an effective tool for judging the quality of the secondary education system at the national level. For these tests to be more effective, they need to be administered yearly and results should be reportable at the provincial and school levels. These results would be critical for holding provinces and schools accountable.

321. With the existing capacity of managers at all levels, a decentralized site-based system would be extremely difficult to implement and will require extensive upgrading of their management skills.

322. The situation in TVET is similar to secondary education (ADB 2018). The capacity of state management agencies at all levels is limited; the contingent of state management officials in charge of vocational education is inadequate, unprofessional, and partially unqualified, especially at the local level. The application of information technology in VET management and training has not met the requirements. Scientific research activities in vocational education have not paid due attention to investment needs.

323. Quality assurance conditions at VET institutions are weak and do not effectively contribute to the improvement of training quality (training programs are not matching practical conditions of production, business, and services; the number of teachers are inadequate and most are short of professional and pedagogical skills; universities have trained teachers only in some occupations/disciplines; the capacity of vocational teacher training facilities in some colleges have not met the requirements for improving pedagogical and professional skills; training facilities and equipment have not met the requirements of training programs and are often outdated compared with the technology applied in the industry).

324. So far, independent VET quality accreditation centers have not been established. National vocational skill standards have been promulgated late, and many key occupations do not have national vocational skill standards. The organization for assessing and granting vocational skills certificates is still in a pilot period and not yet widely implemented.

Appendix 1: Secondary Education Sector Problem Tree

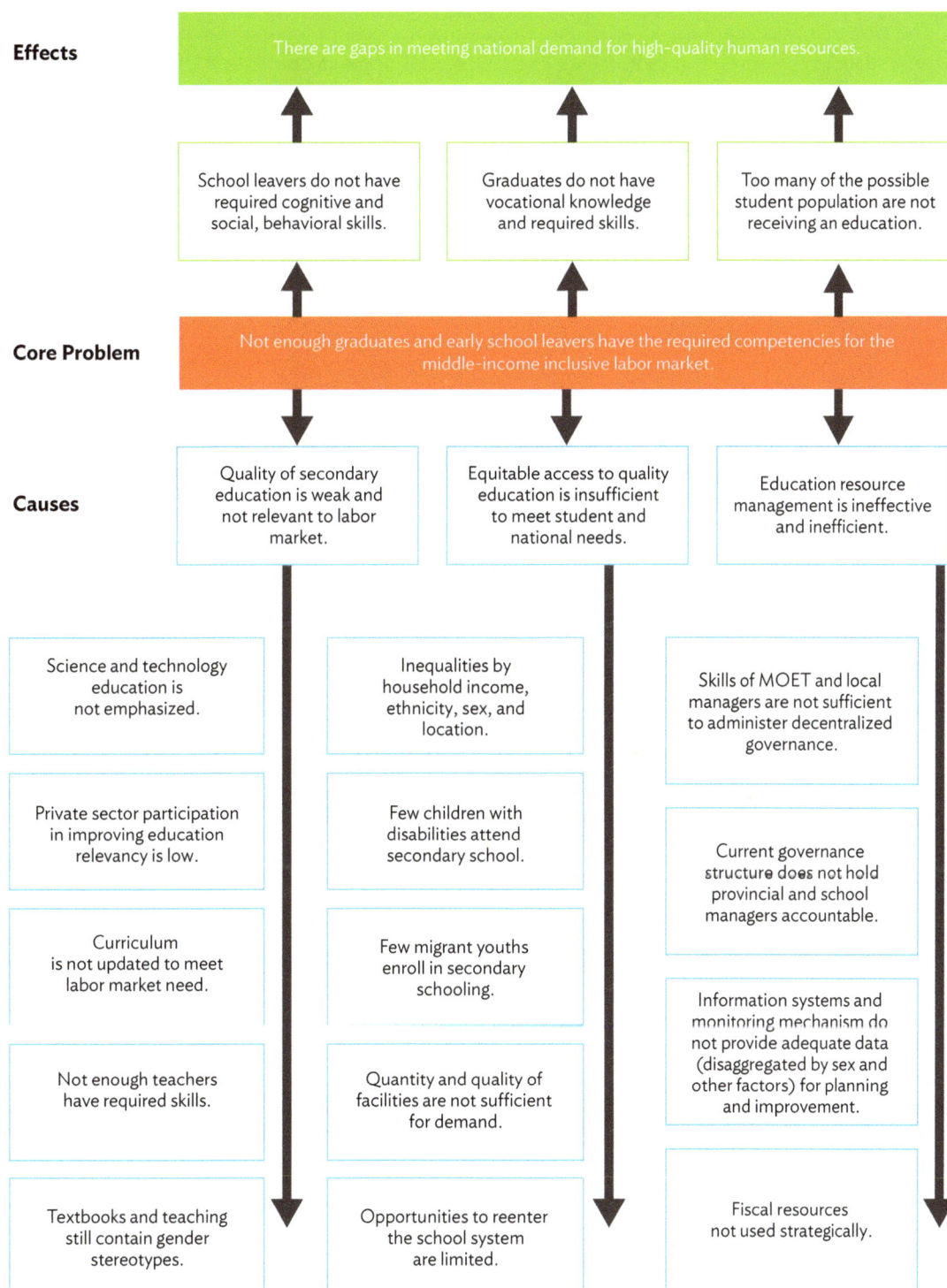

Effects

There are gaps in meeting national demand for high-quality human resources.

| School leavers do not have required cognitive and social, behavioral skills. | Graduates do not have vocational knowledge and required skills. | Too many of the possible student population are not receiving an education. |

Core Problem

Not enough graduates and early school leavers have the required competencies for the middle-income inclusive labor market.

Causes

| Quality of secondary education is weak and not relevant to labor market. | Equitable access to quality education is insufficient to meet student and national needs. | Education resource management is ineffective and inefficient. |

| Science and technology education is not emphasized. | Inequalities by household income, ethnicity, sex, and location. | Skills of MOET and local managers are not sufficient to administer decentralized governance. |

| Private sector participation in improving education relevancy is low. | Few children with disabilities attend secondary school. | Current governance structure does not hold provincial and school managers accountable. |

| Curriculum is not updated to meet labor market need. | Few migrant youths enroll in secondary schooling. | Information systems and monitoring mechanism do not provide adequate data (disaggregated by sex and other factors) for planning and improvement. |

| Not enough teachers have required skills. | Quantity and quality of facilities are not sufficient for demand. | |

| Textbooks and teaching still contain gender stereotypes. | Opportunities to reenter the school system are limited. | Fiscal resources not used strategically. |

MOET = Ministry of Education and Training.
Source: Asian Development Bank.

Appendix 2: ADB's Sector Development Strategy – Past, Present, and Future

1. The Asian Development Bank (ADB) has been a major development partner of the Government of Viet Nam in the education sector since the 1990s. This appendix outlines ADB's completed and current projects, the lessons learned from these projects, and the future approach for the sector.

A. COMPLETED PROJECTS

2. Since 2006, seven ADB loan-funded projects in secondary education have been completed. Their key achievements and contribution, based on project completion reports, are summarized below and in Figure A2.1.

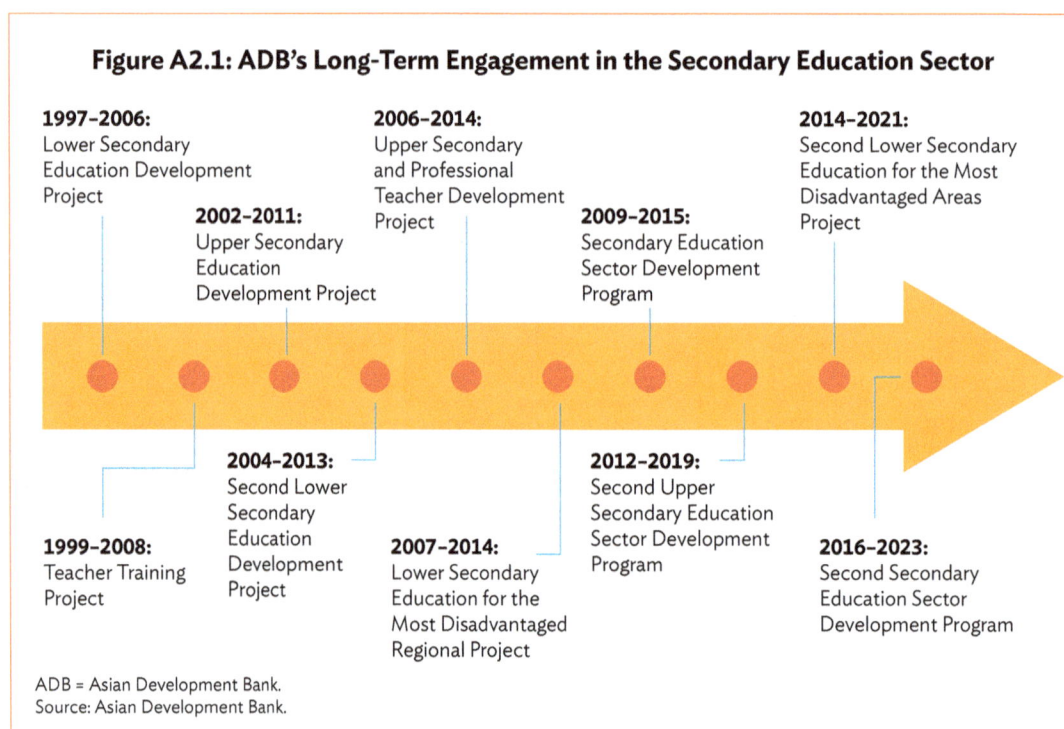

Figure A2.1: ADB's Long-Term Engagement in the Secondary Education Sector

1997–2006: Lower Secondary Education Development Project

2002–2011: Upper Secondary Education Development Project

2006–2014: Upper Secondary and Professional Teacher Development Project

2009–2015: Secondary Education Sector Development Program

2014–2021: Second Lower Secondary Education for the Most Disadvantaged Areas Project

1999–2008: Teacher Training Project

2004–2013: Second Lower Secondary Education Development Project

2007–2014: Lower Secondary Education for the Most Disadvantaged Regional Project

2012–2019: Second Upper Secondary Education Sector Development Program

2016–2023: Second Secondary Education Sector Development Program

ADB = Asian Development Bank.
Source: Asian Development Bank.

3. **Lower Secondary Education Development Project** ($50 million, 1997–2006). This project aimed to assist the government in developing lower secondary education (LSE) through (i) improved quality of LSE, (ii) increased access to LSE, and (iii) institutional development for LSE (ADB 2007a). Overall, the project was effective in improving the quality and equity of LSE. The increase in the number of fully furnished classrooms enhanced access to schooling facilities and eliminated triple shifts in poor areas. The enrollment rate increased from 77% in SY1998/99 to 89% in SY2003/04. The project's target of reducing the gap in enrollment rate by 15% was achieved, the dropout rate reduced by 35%, the repetition rate decreased by 60%, the completion rate increased by 16%, on-schedule graduation rate increased by 20%, and student–teacher ratios decreased due to the increased number of teachers in project schools. By the end of the project, 31 out of 64 provinces of Viet Nam had achieved universal LSE.

4. **Teacher Training Project** ($25 million, 1999–2008). The overall objective of this project was to assist the government in improving the quality and efficiency of LSE by providing a sufficient number of qualified teachers (ADB 2008). The project equipped new lower secondary teachers with the knowledge and skills needed for the modern curriculum, active-learning teaching methods, and revised textbooks and instructional materials. By the end of the project, the net enrollment rate for LSE increased from 49% in SY1997/1998 to 81% in SY2005/06; the percentage of qualified LSE teachers increased from 84% to 96% and the LSE student/teacher ratio reduced from 29:1 to 21:1; and the LSE dropout rate decreased from 8% to 1%.

5. **Upper Secondary Education Development Project** ($55 million, 2002–2011). The project aimed to help the government expand quality upper secondary education (USE) by supporting quality improvement in USE; improving access, equity, and USE participation in disadvantaged provinces; and strengthening management (ADB 2013b). It implemented new upper secondary curricula, textbooks, learning materials, teaching methods, and support systems in schools in 22 project provinces; supplied technical centers for career orientation with materials and equipment; upgraded four demonstration schools attached to teacher training universities; supplied computers, libraries, teaching materials, and science equipment to ethnic minority boarding schools and 128 model schools; developed a new model for a technical upper secondary school to offer vocational courses; provided equipment to three schools to support the new curricula and to demonstrate the effective use of learning materials in support of student-centered learning; and provided in-country and overseas training to teachers and education managers. By project completion, 2,441 schoolrooms had been constructed and provided with furniture, equipment, and sanitation facilities. The project examined different approaches to defining policies on the financing of education, decentralizing education management, and developing a student-based education management information system to help identify and support vulnerable groups in rural areas.

6. **Second Lower Secondary Education Development Project** ($55 million, 2004–2013). A follow-up to the Lower Secondary Education Development Project, this project was designed to support the government in universal quality LSE by 2010 (ADB 2013a). The project provided in-service training that covered student-centered teaching methods including the use of information and communication technology (ICT) in classrooms; improvements in the assessment of student learning, vocational orientation, and continuing education; investment in the infrastructure of lower secondary schools, particularly for disadvantaged and ethnic minority students; introduction of fundamental school quality levels; and in-service training on planning and management. The project was rated only *partly successful* due to the poor performance of the executing agency.

7. **Upper Secondary and Professional Teacher Development Project** ($34 million, 2006–2014). The project was designed to support the government's goals to improve the quality of secondary education through support for teacher education for upper secondary and professional secondary education (MOET 2013). Its specific outcomes were to (i) improve quality of upper secondary and professional secondary pre-service and in-service teacher training; (ii) expand access for ethnic minorities, particularly women, to upper secondary and professional secondary teacher development; (iii) strengthen capacity for planning, management, and delivery of teacher training at upper secondary and professional secondary levels; and (iv) improve facilities to strengthen instructional capability in teacher training institutes.

8. **Lower Secondary Education for the Most Disadvantaged Regions Project** ($50 million, 2007–2014). The project improved access to more equitable learning opportunities for disadvantaged

groups and strengthened social and economic inclusion through universal secondary education (ADB 2007b). It improved the net enrollment rate (NER) in LSE in the 103 target districts by (i) building schools, classrooms, semi-boarding facilities, and teacher housing in remote areas; (ii) providing in-service and pre-service teacher training to meet the needs of ethnic minorities and girls; (iii) developing instructional materials, including bilingual materials in the Vietnamese and ethnic minority languages and materials for ICT training and for the ethnic minority education management information system (EMIS); (iv) providing targeted scholarships; and (v) pilot testing innovative initiatives, including school feeding and awareness-raising programs to promote secondary education among the hardest-to-reach groups.

9. **Secondary Education Sector Development Program** ($60 million, 2009–2015). Closed in December 2015, this project improved the learning outcomes of secondary students through the effective and accountable management of secondary education, improving quality to enhance international competitiveness, and providing better access and equity for disadvantaged groups. The project (i) updated the Secondary Education Sector Master Plan, 2011–2020; (ii) developed new national standards and established a national accreditation board for secondary schools; (iii) introduced a new human resources management strategy for secondary teachers; (iv) strengthened ICT in secondary education; (v) upgraded and accredited secondary education teachers; (vi) developed the national achievement monitoring system and participated in the Programme for International Student Assessment; (vii) introduced a system for the periodic upgrading of the secondary curriculum; (viii) upgraded the foreign language training; (ix) supported gifted students; (x) expanded continuing education; (xi) expanded integrated education for disabled students; (xii) ensured equitable treatment for girls or females and ethnic minorities; and (xiii) pilot tested the Conditional Cash Transfer program.

B. ONGOING PORTFOLIO

10. As the lead donor in the secondary education sector, ADB has a current project portfolio valued at about $270 million.

11. **Second Upper Secondary Education Development Project** ($90 million, 2012–2019). This project is the continuation of the first Upper Secondary Education Development Project, which was successfully completed in 2011. The project promotes the ongoing reform of upper secondary education (USE) through the upgrading of teaching and learning to international standards, improving student access and retention, and strengthening school management for USE. A national project with investments to improve access to selected disadvantaged provinces provides textbooks and instructional materials based on the new USE curriculum; improves the academic environment for gifted USE students; supports continuing education centers to improve in-service teacher training; improves the quality of foreign language training and education; and establishes centers for pedagogical excellence. To increase access and retention of disadvantaged groups, the project develops new facilities at existing upper secondary schools in target provinces; provides support for ethnic minority boarding schools; pilots an inclusive education program for students with special needs; and provides capacity development of private sector schooling. To strengthen planning and management, the project will develop the capacity of USE managers, provide block grants to support local government, support pilot research studies in USE, and support research and training capacity for education management.

12. **Second Lower Secondary Education for the Most Disadvantaged Areas Project** ($80 million, 2014–2021). The project is the continuation of the Lower Secondary Education for the Most Disadvantaged Regions Project, which was successfully completed on 31 December 2014. The project was designed to reduce disparities in socioeconomic development between regions and ethnic groups. Its outcome will be more equitable access and retention of ethnic minorities, girls, and disadvantaged children in lower secondary schools in the Northern Midland and Mountainous areas, Central Highlands, Mekong River Delta, and north central and central coastal areas, which are frequently affected by typhoons. To increase access to LSE, necessary facilities will be provided. To improve the quality and relevance of LSE, the project will develop new regional competency-based textbooks to address the needs in disadvantaged areas. New school clusters will be established to help improve the quality of LSE in poor isolated lower secondary schools by networking them using ICT within school clusters.

13. **Second Secondary Education Sector Development Program** ($100 million, 2017–2023). The program consists of two loans: (i) a policy-based loan for $50 million, and (ii) a project loan of $50 million (ADB 2016c). The program builds upon the education reforms supported by the Secondary Education Sector Development Program. It introduces new features to improve the quality and relevance of secondary education, increase equitable access for disadvantaged adolescents, and strengthen education governance.[1] These features include (i) pedagogically innovative school models; (ii) upgrading teacher standards; (iii) strengthening science, technology, engineering, and mathematics education; (iv) providing locally tailored vocational guidance; (v) targeting support to emerging disadvantaged groups; and (vi) strengthening local decision-making.

14. **Future direction for ADB support to the education sector.** ADB has provided extensive support to MOET to implement a series of education policy reforms with an emphasis on secondary education. The Secondary Education Sector Development Program and the Second Secondary Education Sector Development Program have been major contributors to the development and implementation of the education policy reform agenda in Viet Nam. Future ADB support will focus on improving labor productivity and linking skills and education to labor market demand at post-secondary level. ADB support could also be considered for increasing opportunities for public–private partnership in education and technical and vocational education and training, and linking innovation, research, and development to industry demand.

C. LESSONS LEARNED AND BETTER PRACTICES

15. **Long-term vision for change.** Project-driven and project-based activities have not been successful in eliminating persistent weaknesses in equity, quality, systemic accountability, and institutional capacity. A comprehensive and dedicated plan for institutional and human resources development should be developed to carry out and sustain educational reforms in a dynamic socioeconomic environment to meet the country's new and emerging challenges. Educational reform requires strong government ownership and commitment in implementing the policy changes required and providing input to support the reform. Also required is the cooperation of the project beneficiaries. Due to the workload of the officers of the relevant MOET departments, it is sometimes a challenge to encourage them to prioritize the development of policies and obtain recommendations and approvals in a timely manner. An understanding of how each project fits into the government's larger change initiatives can help all those involved in the project to appreciate the project's value.

---

[1] ADB provided project preparatory technical assistance for the Second Secondary Education Sector Development Program.

16. **Focus on results.** The outcomes and outputs need to be specific, measurable, achievable, and relevant with time-bound indicators that focus on the quality, not just the quantity of the outputs. The design of capacity-building activities needs to be structured with a model defining how competencies will be developed and including pre- and post-training assessments to measure the impact of training and implementation. Without a structure, the measure of success of capacity-building activities is often reduced to counting the number of persons trained. It is important for the project management unit (PMU) staff to closely monitor the project's success using the design and monitoring framework and to request modifications to the design and monitoring framework that correspond with agreed changes in project scope.

17. **Need to examine different professional development models.** Viet Nam's present system for implementing change involves a top–down approach. Large workshops are conducted to disseminate information, using a cascading approach (train-the-trainer), so that new directions are passed down through the departments of education and training and the bureaus of education and training to local schools. However, the effectiveness of this approach has been questioned in several studies because the information often being passed along does not, by its nature, take into consideration the conditions in local schools nor does it ensure school-wide support for change initiatives. Internationally, implementation of reforms is now considered to be most effective if schools are held responsible and accountable for planning that takes into account local contexts and for committing to actions that support national goals.

18. **Geographic targeting.** In some previous ADB projects where targeted assistance was to be provided to disadvantaged areas, the government identified disadvantaged areas at the province level and with a very broad geographic spread, covering almost one-third of Viet Nam's provinces. The assistance, as a result, was spread too thinly. More recent projects have experienced greater success at reducing intra-provincial poverty through targeted identification at the districts and schools on the basis of an integrated assessment of education, socioeconomic, and poverty indicators. Also expanding the definition of disadvantaged area from three ethnic minority regions with high income-poverty rates to include the typhoon-affected areas, which are equally poor and vulnerable, has been a positive improvement.

19. **Staffing of project management units.** Project implementation requires that the government's policies and direction must be reconciled with the requirements of the sponsor. This reconciliation requires that the timeline for a project be long enough for the planning and approval of activities and discharge of the counterpart fund. It also requires that the PMU staff understand both the requirements of the government and ADB. If the recruited PMU staff does not possess knowledge of project management and ADB requirements, then training must be arranged early in the project implementation. Projects can avoid some implementation difficulties if the project managers and the PMUs are appointed early enough so they can assist with the design of project details.

20. **Implementation delay.** Several ADB education projects have had a late start-up because of delay in the declaration of loan effectiveness or the signing of the technical assistance letter. With more harmonized procedures for project administration, the performance of many projects has gradually improved. Close consultation and communication with the government office, the Ministry of Planning and Investment, the Ministry of Finance, and the State Bank of Viet Nam has helped develop the executing agencies' ownership and commitment to smooth implementation. However, delays are still caused by such factors as the slow and complex approval of procurement plans and the few staff in the State Treasury assigned to the education sector. There still is a need to closely monitor

advanced contract action to recruit start-up consultants before project effectiveness. To ensure timely, good-quality implementation, close monitoring and intensive support from the government and ADB are needed.

21. **Project design**. Successful project implementation requires that the project design be feasible with realistic outcomes and outputs that will meet the needs of the borrower. The feasibility study report prepared by MOET, which is the official appraisal document for the government, needs to be consistent with the report and recommendation of the President. As government agencies, including the state treasury, preferred to use the feasibility study report in reviewing and processing documents submitted by the PMU, any inconsistencies hindered timely implementation. Technical assistance consultants should work out issues with the government before submitting any report to avoid such discrepancies. When ADB and the government have had to modify the initial design, the necessary clarification contributes to the initial slow implementation of projects.

22. **Timely recruitment of consultant services.** In designing the consultant services package, it is critical to ensure that the package contains sufficient technically qualified loan implementation consultants to assist with carrying out project activities. It is important that the national and international consultants be recruited as soon as possible and the process of identifying and assigning these consultants be well planned. The timing of external consulting support needs to match with project timelines. Delays in consultant recruitment result in delayed implementation of the entire project. Advance actions and project readiness filters should be applied to minimize start-up delays. The PMU needs to cooperate closely with third party vendors to ensure that the consultants selected have the desired qualifications and are suitable for the project. Consultants not only need to process the required knowledge but must have the skills needed to influence teachers and staff of the beneficiary institutions.

23. **Using market prices for civil works** Escalation of civil works costs has been a major delaying factor in numerous ADB-funded projects in Viet Nam. Positive outcomes in terms of cost and quality are associated with using market prices in cost estimates for civil works and involving local communities in the management of works.

D. ADB SUPPORT FOR SECTOR-RELATED PROGRAMS

1. Strategy 2030

24. Strategy 2030 is ADB's overarching corporate strategy, which aims to make ADB operations respond effectively to the region's changing needs. ADB will continue its efforts to eradicate extreme poverty and expand its vision to achieve a prosperous, inclusive, resilient, and sustainable Asia and the Pacific. The strategy has seven operational priorities (addressing remaining poverty and reducing inequalities; accelerating progress in gender equity, tackling climate change, building climate and disaster resilience, and enhancing environmental sustainability; making cities more livable; promoting rural development and food security; strengthening governance and institutional capacity; and fostering regional cooperation and integration. Improving education and training is one of key areas for the first operation priority: addressing remaining poverty and reducing inequalities. ADB will continue to support education as a basic need of people (ADB 2019).

2. The Country Partnership Strategy for Viet Nam, 2016–2020

25. The country partnership strategy will support investments and policy reforms that promote more inclusive and environmentally sustainable economic growth (ADB 2016a). To achieve this, ADB's strategic framework will be based on three pillars: (i) promoting job creation and competitiveness, (ii) increasing the inclusiveness of infrastructure and service delivery, and (iii) improving environmental sustainability and climate change response.

26. ADB will seek to refine and focus its support within each operational sector, targeting larger but fewer investments in a few subsectors. This approach aims to make resource use more efficient, and will be supported by strengthened staff capacity and increased experience in the targeted subsectors.

27. **Pillar 1: Promoting job creation and competitiveness.** ADB will help the government deepen ongoing market-based economic reforms to create more jobs and improve the global competitiveness of the economy. This will include assistance to increase the pace and impact of structural reforms, enhance the enabling environment for private sector development, and promote improved physical connectivity to develop supply chains within Viet Nam and through external trade. Cutting across these activities will be efforts to promote a more accountable and transparent system of public expenditure and fiscal management.

28. **Pillar 2: Increasing the inclusiveness of infrastructure and service delivery.** To mitigate the risk that structural transformations will increase inequality, ADB will support the creation of more diversified economic opportunities and broaden access to these opportunities and to essential social services. This will include support for secondary education, the development of a more inclusive urbanization process, and promotion of equitable service delivery. This support will target regions that have disproportionately high numbers of poor, near-poor, and other vulnerable groups including ethnic minorities.

29. Access to services will be improved through a targeted package of interventions spanning health and education. In secondary education, ADB will develop a programmatic approach to support the development of secondary education in Viet Nam, including stronger support for policy reforms that support improvements in access and quality.

30. **Pillar 3: Improving environmental sustainability and climate change response.** To lift the sustainability of economic growth, ADB will support more effective natural resource management, invest in activities that mitigate the potentially adverse consequences of climate change, and ensure that infrastructure is properly adapted to deal with heightened climatic risks.

31. **Gender, social protection, and social safety nets.** ADB will support gender equity across all country partnership strategy pillars, with a particular focus on (i) reducing gender gaps in human capital development and access to social services (health, education, water, and electricity), while integrating gender-based violence prevention in relevant areas of ADB operations; (ii) closing gender income and productivity gaps, and reducing occupational segregation by targeting support for vocational training, female entrepreneurs, women's associations, women's access to microfinance, and women's participation in and benefits from deepening of agricultural value chains; and (iii) supporting women's leadership and gender-responsive budgeting practices.

32. **Country Operations Business Plan for Viet Nam (2017–2019).** The business plan indicates the key country development outcomes to which ADB contributes: (i) the education system meets the needs of a middle-income country and supports the development of a productive, competitive, and innovative economy; and (ii) improved conditions for job creation and employment (ADB 2016b).

3. Intersection of ADB Strategy and Government Plans

33. ADB's country partnership strategy for 2016–2020 is fully aligned with Viet Nam's Socio-Economic Development Strategy 2011–2020 and supports Viet Nam's efforts to address issues related to its recent transition to a middle-income country and to reach its goal of obtaining industrial status by 2020 (Figure A2.2).

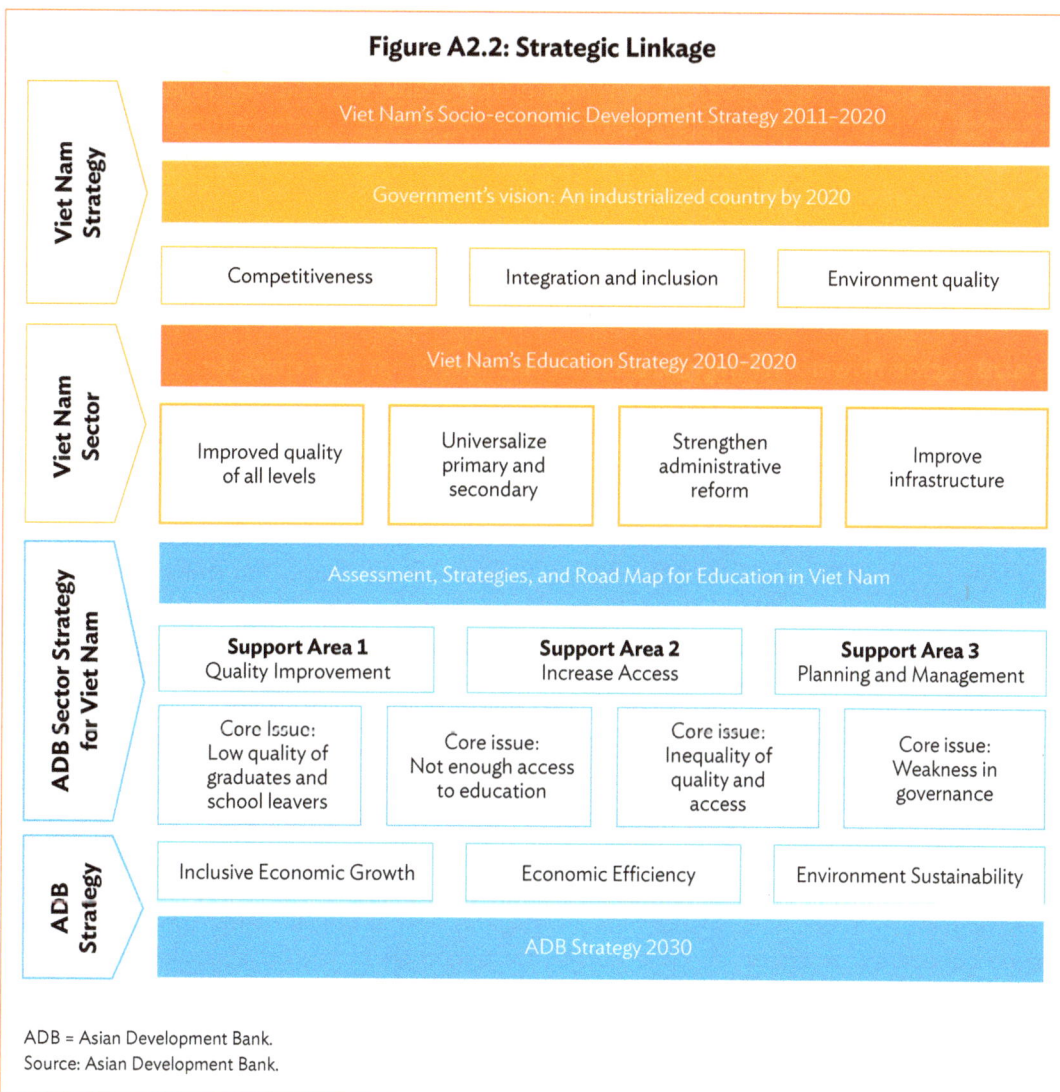

Figure A2.2: Strategic Linkage

Viet Nam Strategy

Viet Nam's Socio-economic Development Strategy 2011–2020

Government's vision: An industrialized country by 2020

- Competitiveness
- Integration and inclusion
- Environment quality

Viet Nam Sector

Viet Nam's Education Strategy 2010–2020

- Improved quality of all levels
- Universalize primary and secondary
- Strengthen administrative reform
- Improve infrastructure

ADB Sector Strategy for Viet Nam

Assessment, Strategies, and Road Map for Education in Viet Nam

- **Support Area 1** Quality Improvement
- **Support Area 2** Increase Access
- **Support Area 3** Planning and Management

- Core Issue: Low quality of graduates and school leavers
- Core issue: Not enough access to education
- Core issue: Inequality of quality and access
- Core issue: Weakness in governance

ADB Strategy

- Inclusive Economic Growth
- Economic Efficiency
- Environment Sustainability

ADB Strategy 2030

ADB = Asian Development Bank.
Source: Asian Development Bank.

34. Education projects in Viet Nam have been both national and regional in scope; and this mix is likely to continue. National focus is germane for projects targeting enhancement of quality of education outcomes to better address labor requirements, but since poverty tends to be geographic in nature, projects designed to address disadvantaged populations tend to be regional. The successful implementation of the actions proposed also relies on a significant increase in the integration of programs and services. This is a particular challenge for Viet Nam where services and programs have been disconnected from each other and from the needs of industry and commerce.

35. Of the 10 current and past educational projects in Viet Nam, all except Loan 2582/2583 for the Secondary Education Sector Development Program and Loan 3493/3494 for the Second Secondary Education Sector Development Program, have been investment or project-based lending. Both programs are sector development programs involving an investment loan and a program loan. Investment lending finances expenditures for inputs in discrete investment projects, such as works, goods, and services and allows for ADB and the government to monitor discrete investment operations. MOET is most familiar and comfortable with this loan modality. However, the government has indicated a preference for a more programmatic approach to borrowing. MOET and the government have identified a comprehensive policy reform agenda and may not want to take on new policy reforms at this time, so there may be limited interest in policy-based lending. ADB will continue to explore cofinancing opportunities with other development partners. Since the World Bank is also moving toward programmatic approaches to education sector development, there may be opportunities for ADB to cofinance with the World Bank to address the priority needs of the sector.

36. **ADB sector-forward strategy.** Viet Nam's economy is not performing efficiently compared with its neighbors and labor productivity is low. Competitiveness can be intensified by increasing productivity and reducing skills shortages, particularly in foreign direct investment industries where frequent complaints are about the lack of highly skilled labor and managers and supervisors. In addition, Viet Nam needs to improve its efficiency by moving to higher value-added and knowledge industries. At the same time, measures must be put in place to ensure that growing industrialization and the need to improve efficiency are not accompanied by widening inequality. The strong thrust toward greater competitiveness and higher added value must be accompanied by an equally strong thrust to promote social inclusiveness. The government has recognized the need for inclusive economic growth and sees improvement to education as a major tool to achieve this goal.

37. **Future direction for ADB support to education.** ADB has provided extensive support to MOET to implement a series of education policy reforms with an emphasis on secondary education. The Secondary Education Sector Development Program and its second follow-on programs have made major contributions to the development and implementation of the education policy reform agenda in Viet Nam. The proposed ADB support in the future is directed at improving labor productivity and linking skills and education to labor market demand at post-secondary level. ADB support could also be considered for increasing opportunities for public–private partnership in education and technical and vocational education and training, and linking innovation, research, and development to industry demand.

Appendix 3: Summary of Recently Completed and Ongoing Secondary Education ADB Projects in Viet Nam

No.	Project Name	$ million	Approval	Complete	Key Activities	PCR/ Performance Rating (commitment rate)
1537	Lower Secondary Education Development Project	50	16 Oct 1997	12 Jun 2006	The project assisted in developing lower secondary education (LSE) through (i) improved quality of LSE; (ii) increased access to LSE; and (iii) institutional development for LSE. By the end of the project, 31 out of 64 provinces achieved universal LSE.	Satisfactory (100%)
1718	Teacher Training Project	25	14 Dec 1999	28 Nov 2008	The project helped improve the quality and efficiency of LSE by providing a sufficient number of qualified teachers. It equipped new lower secondary teachers with the knowledge and skills needed for the modernized curriculum, active-learning teaching methods, and revised textbooks and instructional materials.	Satisfactory (85.9%)
1979	Upper Secondary Education Development	55	17 Dec 2002	6 Dec 2011	The project disseminated nationwide new curricula and textbooks; conducted pilot studies on localized school management, training in assessment, competency-based evaluation, quality assurance measures, and life skill training and career advice for poor students; provided equipment for 38 vocational orientation centers to give career advice; produced 5 upper secondary school (USS) models; and provided education management information system equipment for 64 department of education and training offices. This loan was one of the most successful projects and was introduced several times as a model case in the annual reports and Asian Development Fund brochure.	Satisfactory (116.5%)
2115	Second Lower Secondary Education Development	55	26 Nov 2004	15 Jan 2013	The project improved teacher quality; provided equipment and facilities; improved foreign language teaching and the use of information and communication technology; enhanced vocational orientation and continuing education; and upgraded school facilities in 28 disadvantaged provinces. It also developed the fundamental school quality levels.	Satisfactory (96.7%)

Continued on next page

Table continued

Continued on next page

Table continued

No.	Project Name	$ million	Approval	Complete	Key Activities	PCR/ Performance Rating (commitment rate)
3201	Second Lower Secondary Education for the Most Disadvantaged Areas	80	30 Oct 2014	30 Oct 2021	The project helps the government assist the poor and near-poor by enhancing LSE. It targets areas that have large ethnic minority populations such as the Northern Midland and Mountainous Areas, Central Highlands, Mekong River Delta, as well as the north central and central coastal areas, which are frequently affected by typhoons.	On track (effective May 2015)
3493	Second Secondary Education Sector Development (Program Loan)	50	1 Jul 2014	30 Jun 2016	This policy-based loan builds on the educational reforms supported by the Secondary Education Sector Development Plan and is designed to help the government to promote ongoing education policy and system reforms for addressing management and accountability, quality and relevance, and access and equity through 13 reform actions. All target reform actions were completed successfully in 2016.	
3494	Second Secondary Education Sector Development Program (Project Loan)	50	1 Apr 2017	31 Mar 2023	The project loan will support (i) a revised teacher assessment system, (ii) an upgraded STEM program, (iii) equipment for the model resource schools, (iv) development of vocational orientation programs, (v) a survey on the education situation of domestic migrant youth, (vi) instructional materials targeting migrant youth, (vii) professional development for teachers focused on youth with special needs, (viii) provision of adaptive learning materials for disabled students, (ix) evaluating the progress in decentralization and redefining the role and function of local education authorities, (x) developing a mechanism to promote autonomy of public institutions, (xi) PISA and TALIS participation, and (xii) scaling up of the NAM.	

INSETT = in-service teacher training; MOET = Ministry of Education and Training; NAM = National Achievement Monitoring; PCR = project/program completion report; PRESETT = pre-service teacher training; PISA = Programme for International Student Assessment; STEM = science, technology, engineering, and mathematics; TALIS = Teaching and Learning International Survey.

[a] PCR was issued in June 2015.
[b] PCR was issued in June 2016.
[c] This is the first project successfully completed without a loan extension.
[d] This program loan was successfully completed upon approval of the second tranche in November 2012 with full compliance of all reform conditions.
[e] Central Program Management Unit, Ministry of Education and Training. 2015. Project Completion Report: Secondary Education Sector Development Program (Loan No. 2582/2583-VIE [SF]). Ha Noi.
Source: Asian Development Bank.

Appendix 4: Sector Road Map and Results Framework

CPS Objectives and Related Impacts	CPS Priority Areas	Key Outcomes that Contribute to	Outcome Indicators	Ongoing ADB Interventions	Main Outputs Expected from ADB Interventions
Promoting job creation and competitiveness	Deepen structural reform	Long-term decline in productivity growth reversed and begins to increase	By 2020: • 20% increase in employees in the skilled labor force • Increased employer satisfaction with the knowledge, skills, and attitudes of employees • 80% of graduates meet job requirements • Viet Nam becoming among the 50 leading countries in terms of competitiveness	(i) Ongoing projects with approved amounts Second Upper Secondary Education (24% of funds) ($90 million) Second Lower Secondary Education for the Most Disadvantaged Areas (22% of funds) ($80 million) Second Secondary Education Sector Development Program (27% of funds) ($100 million)	(i) Planned key activity areas By 2020: • 100% of secondary curricula upgraded and instructional materials are gender- and ethnic minority-sensitive • STEM education model and vocational and career orientation programs adopted and implemented in all secondary schools, including guidance and counseling programs for teachers for ethnic minorities and vulnerable girls • Roles in and responsibilities for curriculum development and management by secondary education institutions approved (2015 baseline: Not applicable) • A 2016–2020 Action Plan on Gender Equality for the Education Sector adopted and implemented
Increasing the inclusiveness of infrastructure and service delivery	Increasing the inclusiveness of infrastructure and service delivery	Education system needs of a middle-income country met and development of a productive, competitive, and innovative economy supported	By 2020: • The results of PISA 2018 improved overall by 3 percentage points in mathematics and 2 percentage points of top performers in mathematics and reading while maintaining performance in science and overall gender parity • Student performance on NAM is improved while maintaining gender parity and better performance of ethnic minority students • School life expectancy increases from 6 to 9 years		(ii) Ongoing projects • 37,500 USS teachers complete in-country training on teaching strategies and methods (40% of participants are female) and 1,050 new USE facilities are provided in disadvantaged target provinces

Continued on next page

Table continued

CPS Objectives and Related Impacts	CPS Priority Areas	Key Outcomes that Contribute to	Outcome Indicators	Ongoing ADB Interventions	Main Outputs Expected from ADB Interventions
Increasing the inclusiveness of infrastructure and service delivery	Increasing the inclusiveness of infrastructure and service delivery	Education system needs of a middle-income country met and development of a productive, competitive, and innovative economy supported	• 80% of youngsters over 18 years of age complete secondary education or equivalent • Government expenditure on education is maintained at 20% of total government expenditure • Regional gender gaps in NER are reduced by 30% (LSE largest gap is 10.0% in 2015) • The gap in NER of students from an ethnic minority and the majority is reduced by 40% (2012 gap is 13.7% in lower secondary and 27.6% in upper secondary) • At least 80% of students with a handicap attend secondary school (12.7% in 2013)		• 660 LSE classrooms and 350 semi-boarding facilities constructed and about 24,000 LSS teachers receive training on the new textbooks • The average performance of Vietnamese students in PISA 2015 and 2018 are at or above the 2012 level • The results for NAM grade 9 and 11 are statistically improved • 90% of teachers in participating schools are using the desired learning methodologies and 70% of provincial, district, and secondary school education policy planners participate in the training programs on site-based education planning and management • 20% increase in graduates in 15 occupational training programs and 30% of them female • 90% of graduates, including 35% females, in related employment or undertaking further study

ADB = Asian Development Bank; CPS = country partnership strategy; LSE = lower secondary education; LSS = lower secondary school; NAM = national achievement monitoring; NER = net enrollment rate; PISA = Programme for International Student Assessment; STEM = science, technology, engineering, and mathematics; USE = upper secondary education; USS = upper secondary school.
Source: Asian Development Bank.

Appendix 5: Major Development Partners by Subsectors

Development Partners[a]	Project/Program Name	Duration	Amount (million)
Primary Education			
Denmark	Support to Art Primary Schools, 2011–2015	2011–2015	DKr3,900
EU	Support to the Renovation of Education Management	2011–2015	€10.0
UNESCO	The UN Decade of Education of Sustainable Development	2005–2014	$0.1
UNICEF	Education for Children Project	2012–2016	$3.0
World Bank	Quality Deaf Education in Vietnam Project	2017–2019	$3.0
World Bank	Renovation of General Education Project	2016–2021	$77.0
World Bank	Viet Nam Intergenerational Deaf Education Outreach Project	2011–2015	$3.0
World Bank	Viet Nam – Global Partnership for Education Viet Nam Escuela Nueva Project	2013–2016	$84.6
World Bank	Viet Nam School Readiness Promotion Project	2013–2017	$100.0
World Bank, DFID, and BTC	School Education Quality Assurance	2009–2015	$181.4
Secondary Education			
ADB	Lower Secondary Education for Most Disadvantaged Regions Project	2007–2014	$50.0
ADB	Second Lower Secondary Education Development Project	2004–2013	$55.0
ADB	Upper Secondary Education Development Project	2003–2011	$65.4
ADB	Upper Secondary and Professional Teacher Development Project	2006–2014	$34.0
ADB	Second Upper Secondary Education Development Project	2012–2019	$90.0
ADB	Second Lower Secondary Education for the Most Disadvantaged Areas Project	2015–2020	$80.0
UNESCO	Promoting Intercultural Dialogue and a Culture of Peace in South-East Asia through Shared Histories	2016–2017	$0.03
World Bank	Renovation of General Education Project	2016–2021	$77.0
Technical and Vocational Education and Training			
ADB	Skills Enhancement Project	2010–2016	$70.0
Australia	Aus4Skills	2016–2020	AUD146
British Embassy	Building a Vocational Training Model for Vietnam	2016–2017	£0.026
Denmark	Strategic sector cooperation between TVET schools and companies	2016–2019	DKK4.6
GIZ	Programme Reform of TVET in Viet Nam	2008–2014	€16.2
GIZ	Vietnamese–German Vocational Training Center	2011–2015	€2.0
GIZ	Programme Reform of TVET in Viet Nam	2014–2017	€9.0
GIZ	Programme Reform of TVET in Viet Nam	2017–2019	€11.0
GIZ	Regional Leadership and Capacity Building in TVET in Indonesia, Laos, Viet Nam	2011–2014	€3.8
GIZ	Regional Cooperation to Improve the Training of TVET Personnel in ASEAN	2013–2017	€8.0
GIZ	Regional Cooperation to Improve the Training of TVET Personnel in ASEAN	2017–2019	€7.0
ILO	TVET Law revision	2013–2014	$0.1
ILO	Skills for Trade	2013–2016	$0.5
JICA	Project for Human Resource Development of Technicians at Hanoi University of Industry	2010–2013	
JICA	Project for strengthening TOT functions at Hanoi University of Industry	2013–2016	¥260
JICA	Advisor on Vocational Training System	2013–2015	…
JICA	Advisor for National Trade Skill Testing and Certification System	2015–2018	¥27
JICA	Project for Human Resources Development for Heavy-Chemical Industry at Industrial University of Ho Chi Minh City	2013–2018	¥318

Continued on next page

Table continued

Development Partners[a]	Project/Program Name	Duration	Amount (million)
JICA	Advisor for Organizing National Skill Testing System in Vietnam	2010–2013	...
JICA	Project for Strengthening of Tay Bac University for Sustainable Rural Development of the Northwest Region	2010–2014	$3.3
JICA and JST	Development of Crop Genotypes for the Midlands and Mountain Areas of North Vietnam	2010–2015	$3.0
JICA and JST	Establishment of Carbon-Cycle System with Natural Rubber (Hanoi University of Technology)	2011–2016	...
UNIDO	Benchmarking Vietnam's training system for manufacturing skills	2014–2016	€0.341
Tertiary			
ADB	University of Science and Technology of Hanoi Development Project (New Model University)	2012–2018	$190.0
France	Support for Hanoi University	2010–2020	$100.0
JICA	Higher Education Development Support on ICT	2006–2014	¥6,408
JICA	Higher Education Development Support on ICT	2006–2014	¥6,408
JICA	Capacity Building of Ho Chi Minh City University of Technology to Strengthen University-Community Linkage (Phase 2)	2009–2012	¥350
JICA	Can Tho University Improvement Project	2015–2022	¥10,456
JICA	Project for the Establishment of the Master Programs of Vietnam-Japan University	2015–2020	¥3,890
JICA	The Project for Human Resource Development Scholarship	2015–2019	¥353
NUFFIC	The Second Profession-Oriented Higher Education Project	2012–2015	...
UNESCO	Open Educational Resources	2016–2017	$0.02
USAID	Higher Engineering Education Alliance Program	2010–2015	$4.5
World Bank	Viet Nam New Model University Project	2010–2017	$200.6
World Bank	Viet Nam Higher Education Development Policy Program – Third Operation	2013–2014	$50.0
World Bank	Second Higher Education Project	2007–2012	$70.5
World Bank	Viet Nam Enhancing Teacher Effectiveness Program	2016–2021	$100.0
World Bank	Fostering Innovation through Research, Science and Technology Project	2014–2019	$110.0
World Bank	Support for Autonomous Higher Education Project	2017–2022	$155.0
Education Sector Development			
ADB	Secondary Education Sector Development Project	2010–2015	$60.0
ADB	Project Preparatory TA – Second Secondary Education Sector Development Project	2015–2016	$1.0
ADB	Second Secondary Education Sector Development Program	2017–2023	$100.0
DFID	School Education Quality Assurance Program	2008–2016	£12.3
UNESCO	Gender Equality and Girls' Education	2015–2017	$1.1
UNESCO	Education Sector Analysis in support of EDSP mid-term review	2015–2017	$0.2
UNESCO	Strengthening Education for Sustainable Development Policy	2017–2018	$0.2
UNESCO-IBE	Strengthening STEM curricula for girls in Africa and Asia and the Pacific-Phase I	2016–2017	$0.02
Others			
British Embassy	Executive Leadership Training Programme of Vietnam UK University 2013	2013–2014	£0.019

... = data not available; ADB = Asian Development Bank; ASEAN = Association of Southeast Asian Nations; BTC = Belgian Technical Cooperation; DFID = Department for International Development (United Kingdom); ESDP = Education Sector Development Program; EU = European Union; GIZ = Gesellschaft für Internationale Zusammenarbeit; IBE = International Bureau of Education; ICT = information and communication technology; ILO = Intenational Labour Organization; JICA = Japan International Cooperation Agency; JST = Japan Science and Technology Agency; NUFFIC = The Dutch Organisation for Internationalisation in Education; STEM = science, technology, engineering and mathematics; TA = technical assistance; TOT = training of trainers; TVET = technical and vocational education and training; UK = United Kingdom; UN = United Nations; UNESCO = United Nations Educational, Scientific and Cultural Organization; UNICEF = United Nations Children's Fund; UNIDO = United Nations Industrial Development Organization; USAID = United States Agency for International Development.
[a] Sector titles used are from the ADB Project Classification Review (2 April 2014).
Sources: Asian Development Bank; UNESCO; GIZ; JICA; World Bank; and development partner websites.

Appendix 6: Education Policy Framework for Viet Nam

1. Socio-Economic Development Strategy 2011–2020[a]

Overall Direction: Make the country modern oriented and industrial by 2020 by (i) improving the socialist-oriented market economy; (ii) building a united and democratic society with rules, equality, and civilization; and (iii) improving environment quality. By 2020, Viet Nam's education system will have been fundamentally and comprehensively renovated toward standardization, modernization, socialization, and international integration; the overall education quality will have been enhanced; educating of ethics, life skills, creativity capacity, and practical skills will be emphasized. The education system will meet the demand of human resources, especially high-quality staff for the country's industrialization and modernization, and to ensure social equity in education and lifelong learning opportunities for all people. Education and training, and science and technology are to meet the requirements of the country's industrialization and modernization.

Management and Planning	Quality	Access
• Renovate educational management mechanism • Renovate financial mechanism and accredit education and training quality at all levels • Ensure self-control mechanism in association with improving social accountability of training and education institutions	• The rate of trained laborers among total laborers working in the economy will reach 55% by 2015 • Comprehensively implement solutions to increase quality of university education • Renovate teaching and learning content, and program and teaching method in all levels • Improve the quality of foreign languages training • Improve education quality in areas with difficulties, mountainous areas, and those with ethnic groups	• Extend preschool education • Complete the universalization of age 5 preschool education • Universalize primary and secondary education with increasingly higher quality • Review and complete the planning and implement the network planning for universities and colleges across the country

2. Socio-Economic Development Plan 2016–2020[b]

Overall Direction: Ensure macroeconomic stability while striving for high economic growth by implementing breakthrough strategic, economic restructuring associated with the growth model innovation, and improve productivity, efficiency, and competitiveness. To achieve targets and to implement the Socio-Economic Development Strategy's three orientations, the SEDP specifies several tasks, directions, and targets to be achieved by 2020: (i) total gross domestic product (GDP) is to be between 6.5% to 7% per year; (ii) per capita GDP to be $3,200 to $3,500; (iii) labor productivity to increase about 5% per year; and (iv) the proportion of trained workers to be approximately 65%–70% (including diplomas and certificates of 25%). For the rapid development of high-quality human resources, the SEDP emphasizes the enhancement of the quality of education and training and the development of scientific, technological, and intellectual economy. It indicates the need to restructure and reform the education and training system.

Management and Planning	Quality	Access
• Complete the reform of administrative procedures associated with improving the quality of policies and laws toward specific, clear, transparent, accessible, education and training system. • Improve decentralization, ensuring uniform, smooth leadership and management execution from the central to grassroots levels	• Innovate the content and form of inspection, examination, and evaluation of the results of education and training • Research on and issue the mechanism to encourage breakthroughs in scientific research and technical innovation, apply new science and technology into production to increase labor productivity and product value	• By 2020, the net enrollment rate for LSE will be 95% and for USE it will be 65% • Renovate the poor physical condition of school infrastructure to meet the national standards and provide basic materials for improving teaching and learning processes

3. Human Resources Development Strategy 2011–2020

Overall Direction: Identifies Viet Nam's human resources as a foundation and the most advantageous factor for the country's sustainable development, international integration, and social stability and stipulates raising their competitiveness to a level similar to that in advanced countries. The strategy also identifies strategic challenges and bottlenecks and proposes remedial actions along with ambitious qualitative and quantitative targets for education, higher education, TVET, and the health sector.

Management and Planning	Quality	Access
• Develop and improve regulations and basic policies on the appointment, employment, treatment, testing, and evaluation of teachers and education manager. • Improve and finalize salary and allowance policies for teachers and education managers. • Review, evaluate, and amend the system of existing standards and titles of the ranks of teachers and education managers. • Implement management decentralization to provinces/ cities and education units. • Develop and modernize management policies and education systems for pre-service and in-service training units.	• Restructure the curriculum, ensure transferability of grades, deal with relationship between knowledge and learning time of general education and professional education subjects. • Plan for pre-service and in-service training of education managers. • Reform TTC/TTI training methods by (1) instituting new learning methods; (2) promoting self-motivation of the learner; (3) using ICT in teaching and learning activities. • Fully reform TTC/TTI curricula and pre-service and in-service training methods of lecturers and higher education managers. • Plan a network of universities and colleges to build a network of teacher training units. • Organize good planning teacher training universities, pre-service and in-service training units in accordance with requirements and tasks in the coming period.	Amend, supplement, and improve the incentives and public housing policies for teachers and education managers who work in disadvantaged social economic areas and in special schools. • By 2020, meet the following targets: • rate of trained laborers of 70.0%; rate of vocationally trained laborers of 55.0%; • 400 university and college students per 10,000 people; • more than 10 international-standard vocational schools; and • more than 4 international-standard excellent universities.

4. Education Development Strategy 2011–2020[c]

Overall Direction: A comprehensive reform of the education system that will encompass, among others, a reorientation of standards and upgrading of the quality of education to contribute to the industrialization and modernization of the country while ensuring social equity in education and lifelong learning opportunities for each person by 2020.

Management and Planning	Quality	Access
Solutions to strengthen administrative reform: • Implement decentralization in management to provinces and education institutions, particularly vocational training and higher education institutions by increasing their autonomy and accountability.	Improved quality of education at all levels, particularly that of intellectual, moral, life skills, law, foreign language, and information technology education. • Specific objectives by 2020: • 60% of preprimary teachers, 100% of primary teachers, 88% of lower secondary teachers, and 16.6% of upper secondary teachers achieve training standard;	Specific objectives by 2020: • at least 30% of children at crèche age and 80% of children at kindergarten age will be cared for and educated at preschools; • 99% NER for primary education; • 95% NER for LSE; • 80% of youths within the age range for USE obtaining USE or equivalent level; • 70% of students with a disability attend school;

Continued on next page

Table continued

Management and Planning	Quality	Access
• Build a national education qualification framework and classify quality of general education, vocational, and higher education based on the national quality standards. • Manage the education sector based on strategies, master plans, and plans on education development and human resources development. • Build a system of independent accreditation for education quality for all educational levels. • Renovate financial management. • Maintain education budget at 20% share of state expenditures with priority for universalization, disadvantaged regions, ethnic minority areas, gifted students, training of basic science, social science, and humanities. • Implement policies to support higher education institutions, vocational schools, and nonpublic schools. • Enhance linkage among education with utilization, science research, and technology transfer. • Enhance effectiveness in international cooperation.	• 60% of college lecturers and 100% of university lecturers hold a master or higher degree and 8% of college lecturers and 25% of university lecturers hold a doctoral degree (100% of college and university lecturers are fluent in one foreign language); • Solutions: • Consolidate and complete the teacher training system. • Ensure adequate supply of teachers to teach full-day schooling (emphasis on teachers of foreign languages, counseling, special needs, and continuing education). • Standardize training, recruitment, employment, and assessment of teachers and education managers. • Renovate the secondary curriculum and textbooks. • Renovate curriculum and learning materials in vocational and higher education schools based on the needs of employers. • Enhance teaching and assessment methods to promote active learning, creativity, and self-study capability among students. • Improve quality of continuing education programs. • Introduce a national assessment of students' academic performance for quality assurance and improvement. • Increase the association of training with employment, scientific research, and technology transfer. • Prioritize research on educational science.	• 70% of labor force receive vocational and tertiary education; • 98% literacy rate for age 15 or older and 99% for those between ages 15 and 35; • ratio of students per 10,000 population between 350 and 400 at all educational levels; • 90% of primary schools and 50% LSSs implement two-shift schooling; and • increased support for most disadvantaged and ethnic minority areas and for social policy beneficiaries.

5. Resolution No. 29-NQ/TW 8 on Comprehensive Innovations of Education and Training[d]

Overall Direction: Education is the top priority of the Communist Party, the government, and the people. Investment in education means investment in development and is therefore the top priority in socioeconomic development plans. Fundamental and comprehensive changes in education mean changes in viewpoints, content, methods, policies, and conditions of the administration of the government and educational institutions and participation of families, the community, society, and the learners in all levels and disciplines.

Targets: By 2020: **Preschool education** to be (i) exempt from tuition fees, and (ii) be standardized; **General education** to (iii) have new curriculum, (iv) cultivate the gifted, (v) help students determine their careers, (vi) encourage lifelong learning, (vii) make 9-year education compulsory, (viii) require 80% of youngsters over 18 years of age to complete secondary education or equivalent; **Vocational education** to (ix) establish a system of vocational education; **Higher education** to (x) complete the network of higher education institutions to suit the national manpower development plan; (xi) diversify institutions to serve the requirements for developing technology and professions and for national development and international integration; **Continuing education** to (xii) complete the network of continuing education institutions.

Management and Planning	Quality	Access
M1 Decentralization and Accountability	Q1 Preschool	A1 Continuing Education
• Fundamentally change education management and enhance autonomy and responsibility.	• Ensure the quality of preschool education for children under the age of 5, and standardize the system.	• Provide opportunities for everyone, especially those in rural areas, disadvantaged areas, and beneficiaries of incentive policies, to obtain knowledge, receive education, and improve professional skills and life quality; enable workers to change their jobs; and ensure literacy.
• Enhance decentralization, raise the sense of responsibility, and encourage independence and creativity.	Q2 Career Orientation	
• Local education administration agencies participate in making decisions regarding personnel, finance, and administration.	• Ensure that lower secondary graduates have the fundamental knowledge to meet the requirements after lower secondary and upper secondary students undergo vocational guidance in preparation for post-high-school period, and intensify differentiation after junior high school and career guidance in high school.	A2 Private Sector
• Assess education quality of the whole country, each locality, and educational institutions.	Q3 Curriculum	• Encourage the development of nonpublic schools to satisfy demands for high-quality education in urban areas.
• Complete the education quality assessment system, periodically assess the quality of educational institutions and training programs, and disclose the assessment results.	• Simplify and modernize education content to suit the learners' ages, education, and occupations, and increase practice and application of knowledge to real life.	• Intensify private sector involvement, especially in vocational education and higher education.
• Change the mechanism for receiving and processing education-related information.	• Q4 Teaching and Learning	A3 Higher Education
• Grant autonomy to educational institutions and emphasize the role of school councils.	• Keep radically changing methods toward modernism; encourage the learners' independence, creativity, and application of knowledge; avoid imposition of knowledge, passive learning, and rigid memorization.	• Build some universities that provide training in key disciplines and technical education.
M2 Finance	Q5 Textbooks	• Differentiate institutions of higher education toward research, application, and practice.
• Change policies while raising investment effectiveness.	• Compile textbooks and teaching and learning materials that are suitable to learners, paying attention to students of ethnic minorities and those handicapped	• Intensify post-secondary vocational education.
• Achieve at least 20% of the total budget for education.	Q6 Student Assessment	
• Complete policies on tuition fees.	• Fundamentally change the method of examination and assessment of education results.	

Continued on next page

Table continued

Management and Planning	Quality	Access
• Complete policies on supporting beneficiaries of incentive policies, ethnic minorities, and granting credit to financially poor students. • Exempt preschool students from tuition fees. • Encourage employers to support training activities. M3 International Cooperation • Complete policies on bilateral and multilateral cooperation, and adhere to international agreements on education. • Conduct more government-funded overseas training for science and important disciplines. • Develop policies for international participation in training, research, application, and transfer of science and technology.	Q7 Quality of Educators and Administrative Officers • Formulate training plans, standardize educators by level, develop a system of pedagogy schools, provide incentives, and encourage improvement of professional skills. Q8 Science and Technology • Raise the quality and effectiveness of research and application of science and technology, especially the science of education and administration.	A4 Facilities • Keep modernizing the facilities, especially those for information technology.

6. Resolution No. 44/NQ-CP on Radical Changes in Education and Training [e]
Overall Direction: Identifies key tasks and primary solutions for the government to direct ministries and regulatory and local authorities to implement Resolution No. 29 and make action plans, examine, monitor, and evaluate its implementation, making radical changes in education and training and by 2030 raising Viet Nam's educational level in the region.

Management and Planning	Quality	Access
M1 Decentralization and Accountability • Specify the responsibilities of the governing bodies in charge of education and vocational training. • Carry out periodic nationwide and local evaluation of education quality and undergo international education quality assessment. • Inspect the education and vocational training institutes periodically and publish their inspection results; and establish educational testing centers and national vocational skill evaluation centers.	Q2 Career Orientation • Categorize students after secondary education and provide career guidance during compulsory education. Q3 Curriculum • Complete the national education system to meet the requirements of the domestic and international labor market and the need for lifelong study and for international integration. • Change the educational program, developing the abilities and qualities of learners, focusing on tradition, morality, and lifestyles; sharpen the foreign language and information and technology skills to apply the theories to reality and develop creativity and learning autonomy.	A1 Continuing Education • Continue to arrange the continuing education centers and centers of general technical training, and vocational guidance and vocational training centers of districts. A2 Private Sector • Enhance private sector involvement in education, particularly in preschool, vocational, and higher education by adjusting the mechanism for investment and incentives related to land and capital and mechanism for the lease of facilities.

Continued on next page

Table continued

Management and Planning	Quality	Access
• Adjust the legal documents pertaining to the evaluation of governing bodies, institutes, and individuals involved in education and vocational training; and the recruitment, treatment, and appointment according to the assessment of teachers and learners. M3 International Cooperation • Proactively seek and improve international cooperation in education and vocational training.	• Complete the preschool program. • Draw up and approve a new compulsory education program. • Adjust the program of higher education and vocational education. • Increase the application of science, technology, education science, and management science. Q5 Textbooks • Encourage individuals and organizations to participate in producing printed and electronic textbooks. Q6 Student Assessment • Change the form and methods for examining and evaluating the results of learning (combine the overall evaluation with the term and year evaluations). • Change the organization of the GCSE examination by organizing integrated examinations whose results can be used for recognition of the high school graduation and admission to universities and colleges. Q7 Quality of Educators and Administrative Officers • Make radical changes in the aims, content, methods of training and retraining, and evaluation of teachers and management officials. • Develop a force of leading experts and teachers in all educational levels. • Introduce the policies on salary to attract high-quality manpower into education. • Encourage talented craftsmen and artists to teach in the education and vocational training. • Amend regulations pertaining to teacher title systems. • Introduce policies that encourage researchers to take part in teaching and encourage teachers to conduct scientific research. Q8 Science and Technology • Increase the quality and results of research, application of science, technologies, education science, and management science.	A3 Higher Education • Classify universities according to specializations in research, application, and practice • Develop policies that encourage learners to take part in majors that are arduous but needed by society A4 Facilities • Improve the facilities and application of information technology to education • Invest in the facilities of public education and vocational training institutes, especially the information technology infrastructure, sports facilities, and life skills education for students and ensure the facilities of kindergartens and compulsory education establishments meet the minimum requirement for the new educational program. • Invest in education and vocational training in the mountainous and remote areas and localities of ethnic minorities.

7. Decision No. 2653/QD-BGDĐT on the Action Plan of the Education Sector for the Implementation of Resolution No. 29†

Overall Direction: Identifies key tasks and measures to implement the action program for Resolution No. 29. The action plan is MOET's basis for developing implementation plans and directives, and supervising, monitoring, and evaluating the implementation of Resolution No. 44.

Management and Planning	Quality	Access
M1 Decentralization and Accountability • MOET to advise the government to amend some articles of the Education Law. • Complete decentralization of the state management of education, and implementation of autonomy and self-responsibility. • Review and adjust education development plans in conformity with human resources development. • Strengthen the quality of management education. • Coordinate with MOHA and MOF to deploy innovative financial mechanisms and wages tied to the performance of public service units. • Direct the education inspectorate to be innovative in focusing on quality improvement at all levels. • Direct education and training institutions to renovate objectives, content, and form of inspection, examination, and evaluation of the quality of education. • Establish individual education quality inspection centers and develop regulations to organize accreditation of institutions. **M2 Finance** • MOET to coordinate with MOLISA and MOF to mobilize resources from organizations, individuals, and foreign investment. • MOET to coordinate with the MPI and MOLISA to implement innovative investment mechanisms.	**Q1 Preschool** • MOET to adjust network of preschool establishments and general education requirements, and builds childcare centers based in community counseling centers. **Q2 Career Orientation** • MOET with MOLISA implement streaming and career orientation for high school students, agree on the management of professional secondary and vocational secondary schools, and complete Career Education Law. **Q3 Curriculum** • MOET to advise the government on the issuance of a resolution on renewing the general education curriculum. • Build training for unified programs (vocational and higher education), connecting sector, industry, and occupation group, and meet labor market requirements. **Q4 Teaching and Learning** • Direct education and training institutions to promote the renovation of teaching methods. **Q6 Student Assessment** • Establish quality assessment center for national education to innovate examination and recognize high school graduation and college enrollment. • Establish centers for foreign language assessment. **Q7 Quality of Educators and Administrative Officers** • Restructure the teacher training agencies. • MOET in collaboration with ministries and agencies to review, develop, and promulgate legal documents on standard systems of professional titles, job placement, labor norms, working policy, the content and form of examination, and review for promotion of professional titles.	**A1 Continuing Education** • MOLISA, MOCST, and the local government to complete the restructuring of continuing education centers and general technical education and vocational training centers at district level. • Develop continuing education programs to meet the needs of lifelong learning. **A2 Private Sector** • MOET to create conditions for organizations and individuals within and outside the country to invest in construction of preschool education, general education, professional education, and higher education. • MOET to coordinate with the MOF to renovate supporting policies and financial policies for the educational, vocational training, and nonpublic institutions that do not operate for profit. • MOET and the People's Committees develop policies encouraging socialization in investments for infrastructure and construction of a part or the whole project for education or using home funds or existing facilities for nonpublic training institutions to rent. **A3 Higher Education** • MOET shall coordinate with ministries and agencies to develop policies to encourage people to study careers that are difficult and less attractive but needed by society.

Continued on next page

Table continued

Management and Planning	Quality	Access
• MOET to collaborate with provincial People's Committees to adjust school tuition fees. • Continue to implement preferential credit policy for college and university students, priority enrollment policy, and financial support for social policy beneficiaries, particularly in disadvantaged regions. • MOET to collaborate with ministries, branches, and People's Committees of provinces and cities on technical and regulations pertaining to methods and criteria for current budget allocation. M3 International Cooperation • Improve mechanisms of bilateral and multilateral cooperation. • Continue implementing international integration projects on education and vocational training under Decision No. 2448/QD-TTg. • Promote the formation and development of the credit transfer system between the ASEAN countries, expand exchange programs and international student movement, strengthen cooperation agreement and recognized qualifications regionally and globally. • Promulgate policies to encourage organizations, individuals, international organizations, overseas Vietnamese to invest in teaching, scientific research, applied science, and communication technologies. • Develop policies to encourage and attract foreign experts and overseas Vietnamese to be involved in research and teaching in Viet Nam and send experts and lecturers abroad to teach and conduct research. • Develop and issue a program on Vietnamese language for the Vietnamese people living overseas and for foreigners studying in Viet Nam.	• MOET in collaboration with the ministries to propose policies on salary, seniority allowances, and other allowances • MOET to direct and coordinate with local government to build and deploy training, retraining, and regular training for teachers and education managers to meet fundamental and comprehensive education innovations. • Guide local training institutions to develop mechanisms and policies to attract artists. • Coordinate with MOHA to implement recruitment of staff, officials, and employees based on assessment of the capacity of the applicants. Q8 Science and Technology • Educational institutions and scientific research institutes to strengthen scientific research and application of scientific achievements of technology in teaching and education management, build and deploy a national research program on science education and training, and promote scientific research among students. • Develop a mechanism for researchers to participate in teaching activities and scientific research and enhance scientific research capability of higher education. • Strengthen the role of state management over the operation of science and technology and management science and science education.	A4 Facilities • MOET to coordinate with ministries, branches, and People's Committees to increase investment in the technical infrastructure for educational institutions and teacher training establishments. • MOET to coordinate with ministries, branches, and People's Committees of provinces and cities to complete the implementation of quality standards for preschool education, general education, professional education, continuing education, and higher education. • Enhance efficiency of ODA and have policies to attract and mobilize foreign donor investment. • MOET in collaboration with the People's Committees to boost concretization of schools and build housing facilities for teachers in disadvantaged areas. • Coordinate with MOST to implement the project on insurance of infrastructure, capacity building, and innovation in science research and transfer of technology in higher and vocational education. • Direct institutions to strengthen the application of information technology in management and operational support of teaching, learning, and scientific research; develop an open learning material system, electronic library; and purchase the rights to exploit scientific data and international technology for teaching and scientific research. • Implement an education management information system of on a national scale and build a national database.

8. Decision No. 404/QD-TTg Approving the School Textbook and Curriculum Scheme[8]

Overall Direction: Develops and promulgates the innovative general education curricula and general education textbooks in line with general education.

Management and Planning	Quality	Access
M1 One Curricula • Implement the model of one curricula—numerous textbooks. The new curricula being developed, appraised, and promulgated before textbooks, and consistently implemented nationwide, with prerequisite regulations on the student quality and capacity after each educational level, required content, and duration to all students, while at the same time, maintaining an appropriate section for educational facilities to apply depending on local features; encourage publishing houses, organizations, individuals to compose school textbooks and teacher staff to take initiative in textbook selection. **M2 Stages** • School education is divided into two stages: the basic education stage and the stage of occupation-orienting education. **M3 Specificity** • The new curricula shall specify the content and requirements of each subject, class, and educational level, but should not be too specific, so that a significant number of textbooks can be composed based on the curricula. **M4 Approval of Textbooks** • Textbooks compiled by MOET, publishers, organizations, and individuals should be appraised by the National Textbook Appraisal Committee before use to ensure scientific and fair qualities.	**Q1 Basis of New Curricula** • The new curricula combine teaching knowledge with training people, providing practices and allowing development in quality and capacity, with an emphasis on education of patriotism, ethnic pride, morality, personality, lifestyle; discovering and fostering talent and career orientation for each student; strengthening foreign language skills, computer skills, life skills, working skills under international integration condition; promoting the world scientific and technological achievements and application, especially educational technology and information technology. **Q2 Examination and Testing** • Evaluate educational quality based on the requirements of quality and capacity of students, combine the evaluation during the learning process with that at the end of semesters and school years. **Q3 Professional Development of Teachers** • Train teachers to meet with demand of implementing new curriculum and textbooks; effectively promote technical means and new technologies, especially information technology in training provision; put publishers of textbooks in charge of cooperating with the education sector to provide training to teachers on newly approved and issued textbooks.	**A1 Necessary Conditions** • General education facilities should proactively adjust, allocate, and arrange to accelerate efficiency of school facilities and techniques to meet with the demand introduced by the new curriculum and textbooks.

Vocational Training Development Strategy 2011–2020[b]		
Overall Direction: Sets out a list of ambitious objectives and specifies a broad array of respective "solutions" to be implemented under nine systemic reform components.		
Management and Planning	Quality	Access

• Improve the legal system of vocational training by amending the Law on Vocational Training and regulations related to vocational training in the Labor Law.
• Improve mechanisms and policies to (i) attract vocational teachers; (ii) innovate financial policies on vocational training (tuition fees and order mechanism); (iii) make training policies of foreign language consistent with the level of training; and (iv) apply to trained employees.
• Improve the mechanism and capacity of state management on vocational training to clearly define functions, tasks, and competence combined with responsibility and increased inspection and examination activities and assuring supervision by state agencies, sociopolitical organizations, and people.
• Introduce mechanisms for vocational training institutions to operate independently and autonomously.
• Promote IT application in vocational training and vocational management, and set up database for vocational training.
• Implement transferable training qualifications and enhance channeling into vocational training.
• Establish a vocational training assistance fund toward socialization with initial capital from state budget, contributions of enterprises, and other sources to develop vocational training.
	• Standardize qualification of teachers in national, regional, international key occupations in terms of vocational skills and vocational pedagogy: 100% of these teachers shall meet the standards in 2014.
	• Ensure the training and retraining for vocational teachers toward standardization, securing sufficient number of teachers and an appropriate structure by profession and training levels; mobilize scientists, technicians, artisans, skilled workers, and excellent farmers participating in vocational training for rural workers.
	• Arrange and reorganize training and innovative activities, retraining institutes for vocational teachers to train and retrain vocational pedagogy and improve vocational skills for vocational teachers.
	• Establish vocational training institute with the training and retraining function for new technology, training and retraining teachers and vocational management staff, and research vocational training science based on the merger and upgrade of the National Institute for Vocational Training.
	• Develop a framework for training curriculum.
	• By 2020, achieve the following targets (number of VET programs and curricula to be upgraded or newly developed):
	  • International level: 35
	  • Regional level: 70
	  • National level: 150
	  • Elementary level: 200
		• Plan a network of vocational training institutions by region and locality, prioritizing newly established nonpublic vocational training institutions and encouraging cooperation and establishment of vocational training institutions invested by foreign capital, with specialized vocational training institutions for the disabled and the ethnic minorities.
		  • By 2020, establish
		  • 230 VCs (80 nonpublic, 40 high-quality);
		  • 310 VSSs (120 nonpublic); and
		  • 1,050 VTCs (350 nonpublic).
		• Build a national vocational qualification framework compatible with the national education framework. By 2020,
		  • the rate of trained employees will increase by 55%, equivalent to 34.4 million people (23% of collegial and intermediate vocational training);
		  • about 2.9 million people receiving new programs at collegial and intermediate vocational training; and
		  • about 10 million people receiving new programs at elementary level and vocational training under 3 months.
		• Complete the national occupational skills framework. By 2020,
		  • 400 standards of national vocational skills are issued, and
		  • 6 million people are receiving certificates.

Continued on next page

Table continued

Management and Planning	Quality	Access

• Promote socialization and diversification of resources for development of vocational training, including government, enterprises, students, national and international investors, for which the state budget is important (to raise the rate of expenditure on vocational training from the state budget for education to 12%–13%). The government has assistance policies on capital, land, and tax for nonpublic vocational training.
• Standardize the vocational management staff, set up the training and retraining content and program for vocational management staffs, and develop the professional vocational management staff.
	• Quality of VET institutions and programs for focal occupations will be accredited. By 2020,
	  • high-quality schools and model VTC will be accredited;
	  • all key national, regional, and international occupations will be accredited; and
	  • three public (and several nonpublic) quality accreditation centers will be established.
		• Promulgate national occupational skill standards for popular occupations.
		• Receive and transfer sets of occupational skill standards of regionally and internationally prioritized occupations.

ASEAN = Association of Southeast Asian Nations; GCSE = General Certificate of Secondary Education; LSE = lower secondary education; LSS = lower secondary school; MOCST = Ministry of Culture, Sports and Tourism; MOET = Ministry of Education and Training; MOF = Ministry of Finance; MOHA = Ministry of Home Affairs; MOLISA = Ministry of Labour–Invalids and Social Affairs; MPI = Ministry of Planning and Investment; NER = net enrollment rate; ODA = official development assistance; SEDP = Socio-Economic Development Plan; TTC = teacher training college; TTI = teacher training institute; TVET = technical and vocational education and training; US = United States; USE = upper secondary education; VC = vocational college; VSS = vocational secondary schools; VTC = vocational training center.

[a] Approved by the Eleventh Congress of Viet Nam Communist Party. Ha Noi.

[b] Government of Viet Nam. National Assembly Resolution No. 142/2016/QH13 on the Socio-Economic Development Plan (SEDP) 2016–2020. Ha Noi.

[c] Government of Viet Nam. Prime Minister's Decision No. 711/QD-TTg Approving the Education Development Strategy 2011–2020. Ha Noi.

[d] Central Committee of the Communist Party of Viet Nam. Resolution No. 29-NQ/TW 8 on Comprehensive Innovations of Education and Training. Ha Noi.

[e] Government of Viet Nam. Prime Minister's Resolution No. 44/NQ-CP on Radical Changes in Education and Training. Ha Noi.

[f] MOET. 2014. Minister of Education Decision No. 2653/QD-BGDĐT on the Action Plan of the Education Sector for the Implementation of Resolution No. 29. Ha Noi.

[g] Government of Viet Nam. 2015. Prime Minister's Decision No. 404/QD-TTg Approving the School Textbook and Curriculum Scheme. Ha Noi.

[h] Government of Viet Nam. Prime Minister's Decision No. 630/QD-TTg (29 May 2012) Approving the Vocational Training Development Strategy during 2011–2020.

References

Asian Development Bank (ADB). 2007a. *Completion Report: Lower Secondary Education Development Project in Viet Nam.* Manila.

_____. 2007b. *Report and Recommendation of the President to the Board of Directors: Proposed Loan to the Socialist Republic of Viet Nam for the Lower Secondary Education for the Most Disadvantaged Regions.* Manila.

_____. 2008. *Completion Report: Teacher Training Project in Viet Nam.* Manila.

_____. 2011a. *Asia 2050: Realizing the Asian Century.* Manila.

_____. 2013a. *Completion Report: Second Lower Secondary Education Development Project in Viet Nam.* Manila.

_____. 2013b. *Completion Report: Upper Secondary Education Development Project in Viet Nam.* Manila.

_____. 2013c. *Guidelines on Inclusive Economic Growth in the Country Partnership Strategy.* Manila.

_____. 2014. *Technical and Vocational Education and Training in the Socialist Republic of Viet Nam: An Assessment.* Manila.

_____. 2015. *Impact Evaluation Report: The Fourth Year Pilot Conditional Cash Transfer (CCT) Implementation.* Ha Noi.

_____. 2016a. *Country Partnership Strategy: Viet Nam, 2016–2020—Fostering More Inclusive and Environmentally Sustainable Growth.* Ha Noi.

_____. 2016b. *Country Operations Business Plan: Viet Nam, 2017–2019.* Ha Noi.

_____. 2016c. *Report and Recommendation of the President to the Board of Directors: Proposed Loan to the Socialist Republic of Viet Nam for the Second Secondary Education Sector Development Program.* Manila (Loans 3493 and 3495-VIE).

_____. 2016d. *Inclusive and Sustainable Growth Assessment Viet Nam 2016–2020.* Manila.

_____. 2018. *Final Assessment Report: Technical and Vocational Education and Training in Viet Nam.* Manila.

_____. 2019. *Strategy 2030: Achieving a Prosperous, Inclusive, Resilient, and Sustainable Asia and the Pacific.* Manila.

Asian Productivity Organization (APO). 2016. *APO Productivity Databook 2016.* Tokyo: Keio University Press.

Barro, R. and J. Lee. 2010. A New Data Set of Educational Attainment in the World, 1950–2010. *NBER Working Paper 15902.*

Bodewig, C. et al. 2014. *Skilling Up Vietnam: Preparing the Workforce for a Modern Market Economy.* Washington, DC: World Bank. http://documents.worldbank.org/curated/en/283651468321297015/Skilling-up-Vietnam-preparing-the-workforce-for-a-modern-market-economy.

Boocock, S. S. 1995. Early Childhood Programs in Other Nations: Goals and Outcomes. *The Future of Children.* 5 (3). Princeton, NJ: Woodrow Wilson School of Public and International Affairs at Princeton University and the Brookings Institution.

Brauw, A. and J. Giles. 2017. Migrant Opportunity and the Educational Attainment of Youth in Rural China. *The Journal of Human Resources.* 52 (3).

Cohen, D. and M. Soto. 2007. Growth and Human Capital: Good Data, Good Results. *Journal of Economic Growth.* 12. pp. 51–76.

Cameron, S. 2012. Education, Urban Poverty and Migration: Evidence from Bangladesh and Vietnam. *Office of Research Working Paper.* WP-2012-15. Florence: UNICEF Office of Research. http://www.unicef-irc.org/publications/pdf/iwp_2012_15.pdf.

CONFEMEN Programme for the Analysis of Education Systems (PASEC). http://www.confemen.org/wp-content/uploads/2014/01/Plaquette-version-anglaise1.pdf.

Dang, H.-A. 2009. Ch. 8 Viet Nam: A Widening Poverty Gap for Ethnic Minorities. Revised January 2010. http://siteresources.worldbank.org/EXTINDPEOPLE/Resources/407801-1271860301656/Chapter_8_Vietnam.pdf.

Fullan, M. 2001. *The New Meaning of Educational Change.* Third Edition. New York: Teachers College Press.

Garcia, S. and J. Saavedra. 2017. Educational Impacts and Cost-Effectiveness of Conditional Cash Transfer Programs: A Meta-Analysis. *Review of Educational Research.* 87 (5). pp. 921–965.

General Statistics Office of Viet Nam (GSO). www.gso.gov.vn/default_en.aspx?tabid=775.

_____. 2012. *The 1/4/2012 Time-Point Population Change and Family Planning Survey: Major Findings.* Ha Noi: Ministry of Planning and Development.

_____. 2014. *Result of the Viet Nam Household Living Standards Survey 2014.* Ha Noi. http://www.gso.gov.vn/default_en.aspx?tabid=515&idmid=5&ItemID=18411.

_____. 2017. *Report on Labor Force Survey (Quarter 1, 2017).* Ha Noi.

_____. 2018. *Report on Labor Force Survey (Quarter 1, 2018).* Ha Noi.

_____. Various years. Viet Nam Household Living Standards Surveys 2002–2012 and Population and Housing Midterm Survey 2014. Ha Noi.

General Department of Vocational Training (GDVT), National Institute for Vocational Training. 2014. *Vocational Training Report – Viet Nam 2012.* Ha Noi.

Directorate of Vocational Education and Training, National Institute for Vocational Education and Training. 2017. *Viet Nam Vocational Education and Training Report 2015.* Ha Noi.

GDVT. 2012. TVET Quality Breakthrough – Vietnamese TVET. Background Paper for Regional TVET Conference.

Gentilini, U., M. Honorati, and R. Yemtsov. 2014. *The State of Social Safety Nets 2014.* Washington, DC: World Bank.

Government of Viet Nam. 2016a. *Report on the Assessment of the Implementation of SEDP 2011–2015 and Socioeconomic Development Direction for 2016–2020.* Ha Noi.

Government of Viet Nam. 2016b. *The Five-Year Socio-Economic Development Plan 2016-2020*. Ha Noi.

Hargreaves, A. 2007. *Sustainable Leadership and Development in Education: Creating the Future, Conserving the Past. European Journal of Education*. 42 (2).

Ho, T. H. T. and A. Reich. n. d. Historical Influences on Vocational Education and Training in Viet Nam.

Hopkins, D. 2001. *School Improvement for Real*. London: Routledge Falmer.

The International Consultant. 2012. Analysis of Vietnam's Certification Process from an International Perspective. June.

International Foundation for Science (IFS). 2009. Science in Vietnam. Stockholm.

International Labour Organization (ILO). n. d. *Viet Nam Decent Work Country Programme 2012–2016*. http://www.ilo.org/public/english/bureau/program/dwcp/download/vietnam.pdf.

Iyer, P. 2017. Thinking Outside the Box: Do Students in Vietnam Have 21st Century Skills?. *Young Lives*. https://www.younglives.org.uk/content/thinking-outside-box-do-students-vietnam-have-21st-century-skills.

Iyer, P., O. B. Azubuike, and C. Rolleston. 2017. *Young Lives School Survey, 2016–17: Evidence from Vietnam*. Oxford: Young Lives, Oxford Department of International Development, University of Oxford.

Jones, N. et al. 2014. Falling between the Cracks: How Poverty and Migration Are Resulting in Inadequate Care for Children Living in Viet Nam's Mekong Delta. *ODI Report*. London: Overseas Development Institute. http://www.odi.org/sites/odi.org.uk/files/odi-assets/publications-opinion-files/9306.pdf.

Kin, B. W., M. E. Young, and J. Cai. 2012. *Early Child Development in China*. World Bank eLibrary.

LaRocque, N. 2008. *Public–Private Partnerships in Basic Education: An International Review*. Reading: CfBT Education Trust.

Maclean, R., S. Jagannathan, and J. Sarvi, eds. 2013. *Skills Development for Inclusive and Sustainable Growth in Developing Asia-Pacific. Technical and Vocational Education and Training: Issues, Concerns and Prospects*. Volume 19. London: ADB and Springer.

Marsh, C. 1992. *Key Concepts for Understanding Curriculum. Fourth edition*. Norwich: Teacher's Library.

Ministry of Education and Training (MOET). 2012. *Secondary Education Sector Master Plan 2011–2015*. Ha Noi.

_____. 2013. *Upper Secondary and Professional Teachers Development Project Completion Report*. Ha Noi.

_____. 2014. *Education Statistics Yearbook 2013–2014*. Ha Noi.

_____. 2017. *Education Statistics 2015–2016*. Ha Noi.

Ministry of Labour–Invalids and Social Affairs (MOLISA). 2012. TVET Quality Breakthrough. General Technical Background Paper for the Regional TVET Conference in Viet Nam. Ha Noi.

MOLISA. 2017. Project on Renovation and Improvement of the Quality of Technical and Vocational Education and Training – Up to 2020, with Orientation to 2030 (Draft October 2017). Ha Noi.

MOLISA and National Institute of Vocational Training (NIVT). 2015. *Vocational Training Report – Viet Nam 2013–2014*. Ha Noi.

MOLISA and NIVT. 2017. *Key Findings: Viet Nam Vocational Education and Training Report 2015.* Ha Noi.

MOLISA. Report on Vocational Training in the Northern Midland and Mountainous Region. Unpublished.

Ministry of Planning and Investment (MPI). 2011. *Five-Year Socio-Economic Development Plan, 2011–2015.* Ha Noi.

MPI. 2013. *Millennium Development Goals Full Report 2013: Achievements and Challenges in the Progress of Reaching Millennium Development Goals of Vietnam.* Ha Noi.

National Coordinating Council on Disability (NCCD). 2010. *2010 Annual Report on Status of People with Disabilities in Viet Nam.* Ha Noi. http://nccd.molisa.gov.vn/attachments/221_BC%20 thuong%20nien%202010%20tieng%20Anh%20cuoi.pdf.

Nguyen, M. T. 2017. Learner's Quality and Competency-Based Reform of General Education Program. *Vietnam Journal of Education.* Volume I. Ha Noi: MOET.

Organisation for Economic Co-operation and Development (OECD). 2010a. *PISA 2009 Results: What Students Know and Can Do – Student Performance in Reading, Mathematics and Science (Volume I).* Paris.

_____. 2010b. *The High Cost of Low Educational Performance: The Long-Run Economic Impact of Improving Pisa Outcomes.* Paris.

_____. 2013a. *PISA 2012 Results: What Students Know and Can Do – Student Performance in Mathematics, Reading and Science (Volume I).* Paris.

_____. 2013b. *PISA 2012 Results: Excellence Through Equity: Giving Every Student the Chance to Succeed (Volume II).* Paris.

_____. 2016a. *PISA 2015 Results: Excellence and Equity in Education (Volume I).* Paris.

_____. 2016b. *PISA 2015 Results: Policies and Practices for Successful Schools (Volume II).* Paris.

OECD and the World Bank. 2014. *Science, Technology and Innovation in Viet Nam.* Paris: OECD Publishing.

Oswald, L. J. 1995. School-Based Management. *ERIC Digest.* No. 99. http://www.eric.ed.gov/PDFS/ ED384950.pdf.

Phillips, L. 1997. Expectations for School-Based Management. http://clubweb.interbaun.com/~l-pphillips/public_html/website/expect.html.

Psacharopoulos, G. and H. A. Patrinos. 2004. Returns to Investment in Education: A Further Update. *Education Economics.* 12 (2). pp. 111–35.

Robbins, S. P. 1994. *Management.* Fourth Edition. Englewood Cliffs, NJ: Prentice Hall.

Ross, C. 2015. Expansion of Learning Opportunities for Disadvantaged Youth in Secondary Education Sector Development Program (SESDP) 2. SESPD Project Preparatory Technical Assistance. Ha Noi.

Saavedra, J. 2016. The Effects of Conditional Cash Transfer Programs on Poverty Reduction, Human Capital Accumulation and Wellbeing. Paper prepared for the United Nations meeting on Strategies for Eradicating Poverty to Achieve Sustainable Development for All. New York. 1–3 June. http://www.un.org/esa/socdev/egms/docs/2016/Poverty-SDGs/JuanSaavedra-paper.pdf.

Skilbeck, M. 1984. *School-Based Curriculum Development.* London: Harper and Row.

Spohr, C. 2003. Formal Schooling and Workforce Participation in a Rapidly Developing Economy. *Journal of Development Economics.* 70 (2). pp. 291–327.

Thanh, H. X., T. T. Anh, and D. T. T. Phuong. 2013. *Urban Poverty in Vietnam – A View from Complementary Assessments. Human Settlements Working Paper Series: Poverty Reduction in Urban Areas.* 40. London: International Institute for Environment and Development.

Thao, D. P., and W. A. Boyd. 2014. Renovating Early Childhood Education Pedagogy: A Case Study in Viet Nam. *International Journal of Early Years Education.* 22 (2). pp. 184–196.

Tran, L. et al. 2014. *Higher Education in Vietnam: Flexibility, Mobility and Practicality in the Global Knowledge Economy.* London: Palgrave Macmillan.

United Nations (UN). 2015. *Transforming Our World: The 2030 Agenda for Sustainable Development.* New York.

_____. 2015. *Transforming Our World: The 2030 Agenda for Sustainable Development.* New York.

United Nations Development Programme (UNDP) and Viet Nam Academy of Social Sciences (VASS). 2016. *Growth That Works for All: Viet Nam Human Development Report 2015 on Inclusive Growth.* Ha Noi.

_____. 2015. *Country Report: 15 Years Achieving the Viet Nam Millennium Development Goals.* New York.

United Nations Educational, Scientific and Cultural Organization (UNESCO). 2011. *World Data on Education: Seventh Edition 2010–11.* Geneva.

UNESCO Institute for Statistics. 2016. *Laying the Foundation to Measure Sustainable Development Goal 4.* Montreal.

UNESCO Office in Ha Noi. 2016. *Viet Nam Advances the 2016–2020 Action Plan on Gender Equality for the Education Sector.* 23 March. http://www.unesco.org/new/en/hanoi/about-the-ha-noi-office/single-view/news/viet_nam_advances_the_2016_2020_action_plan_on_gender_equali/.

United Nations Population Fund (UNPF). 2011. *The Aging Population in Viet Nam: Current Status, Prognosis, and Possible Policy Responses.* Ha Noi.

_____. 2012. People with Disabilities in Viet Nam: *Key Findings from the 2009 Viet Nam Population and Housing Census.* Ha Noi.

Vietnam Briefing. 2014. Foreign Companies Report Labor and Skills Shortage in Vietnam. 30 July. http://www.vietnam-briefing.com/news/foreign-companies-report-labor-skills-shortage-vietnam.html.

Viet Nam Institute of Educational Sciences (VNIES). 2010. *Assessment of Quality of Upper Secondary Curriculum and Textbooks.* Ha Noi.

Viet Nam News. 2015. President: Viet Nam commits to successfully implementing SDGs. 26 September. Ha Noi. http://vietnamnews.vn/politics-laws/276320/president-viet-nam-commits-to-successfully-implementing-sdgs.html.

World Bank. 2014. *Vietnam Development Report 2014.* Ha Noi.

World Bank and CIEM. 2012. *Skills for Productivity: An Analysis of Employer Skills Survey 2011.* http://microdata.worldbank.org/index.php/catalog/2569/download/37451.

World Bank Group. 2016. *Vietnam Development Report 2016: Transforming Vietnamese Agriculture: Gaining More from Less.* Ha Noi.

World Bank. World Development Indicators. http://data.worldbank.org/country/vietnam.

World Bank and the Ministry of Planning and Investment. 2016. *Vietnam 2035: Toward Prosperity, Creativity, Equity, and Democracy.* Washington, DC.

World Economic Forum. 2016. *The Global Competitiveness Report 2016–2017.* Geneva.

_____. 2018. *The Global Competitiveness Report 2018.* Geneva

World Education News and Reviews (WENR). 2012. Secondary Education in Vietnam. https://wenr. wes.org/2012/04/secondary-education-in-vietnam.

Yu, B. et al. 2010. Impacts of Climate Change on Agriculture and Policy Options for Adaptation: The Case of Vietnam. IFPR Discussion Paper. Washington, DC: International Food Policy Research Institute.

www.ingramcontent.com/pod-product-compliance
Lightning Source LLC
Chambersburg PA
CBHW050043220326
41599CB00045B/7261